About Island Press

Island Press is the only nonprofit organization in the United States whose principal purpose is the publication of books on environmental issues and natural resource management. We provide solutions-oriented information to professionals, public officials, business and community leaders, and concerned citizens who are shaping responses to environmental problems.

Since 1984, Island Press has been the leading provider of timely and practical books that take a multidisciplinary approach to critical environmental concerns. Our growing list of titles reflects our commitment to bringing the best of an expanding body of literature to the environmental community throughout North America and the world.

Support for Island Press is provided by the Agua Fund, The Geraldine R. Dodge Foundation, Doris Duke Charitable Foundation, The Ford Foundation, The William and Flora Hewlett Foundation, The Joyce Foundation, Kendeda Sustainability Fund of the Tides Foundation, The Forrest & Frances Lattner Foundation, The Henry Luce Foundation, The John D. and Catherine T. MacArthur Foundation, The Marisla Foundation, The Andrew W. Mellon Foundation, Gordon and Betty Moore Foundation, The Curtis and Edith Munson Foundation, Oak Foundation, The Overbrook Foundation, The David and Lucile Packard Foundation, Wallace Global Fund, The Winslow Foundation, and other generous donors.

The opinions expressed in this book are those of the author(s) and do not necessarily reflect the views of these foundations.

A Better Way
to Zone

A BETTER WAY
TO ZONE

TEN PRINCIPLES

TO CREATE

MORE LIVEABLE CITIES

Donald L. Elliott, FAICP

ISLANDPRESS

WASHINGTON • COVELO • LONDON

© 2008 Donald Elliott

ISLAND PRESS is a trademark of the Center for Resource Economics.

Elliott, Donald L., 1957–
   A better way to zone : ten principles to create better American cities / Donald L. Elliott.
      p. cm.
Includes bibliographical references and index.
ISBN-13: 978-1-59726-180-7 (cloth : alk. paper)
ISBN-10: 1-59726-180-7 (cloth : alk. paper)
ISBN-13: 978-1-59726-181-4 (pbk. : alk. paper)
ISBN-10: 1-59726-181-5 (pbk. : alk. paper)
   1. Zoning law—United States. 2. Land use—Law and legislation—United States. I. Title.

KF5698.E45 2008
346.7304'5—dc22   2007050910

Printed on recycled, acid-free paper ♲

Manufactured in the United States of America
10 9 8 7 6 5 4 3 2

Keywords: comprehensive plan, density, Denver, development standards, environmental
sustainability, Euclidean zoning, form-based zoning, affordable housing, land use drivers,
mixed-use zoning, New Urbanism, planned unit developments (PUD), Standard Zoning
Enabling Act, transportation, zoning

For Beth, Maya, and Ethan

TABLE OF CONTENTS

ACKNOWLEDGMENTS

MOST OF WHAT I KNOW ABOUT ZONING I learned while working with my exceptional colleagues at Clarion Associates. Although this book does not reflect the opinions of the firm or its partners or associates, it could not have been written without the experiences I gained while working with them. In particular, I would like to acknowledge the contributions of Chris Duerksen, my zoning colleague for the last nineteen years, and of Ben Herman, Craig Richardson, Matt Goebel, Roger Waldon, Tina Axelrad, Darcie White, and Lesli Ellis. The firm's talented associates and staff also contributed, including Bohdy Hedgcock, Molly Mowery, Amy Kacala, Chad Meadows, Heidi Humbeutel, Michele McGlyn, Leigh Anne King, Renae Pick, Jeff Hirt, Erica Heller, and Cara Snyder.

Over the course of complex zoning projects, I also gained insights from those who have to stay and administer zoning ordinances after the consultants leave, including Marsha Bruhn and Rory Bolder in Detroit; Mike Elms and Mike Smith in Arvada; Denise Balkas, Bob Watkins, and Jay Pierce in Aurora; Bob Simpson in Englewood; Jane Tompkins in Cedar Rapids; Harry Finnegan and Valdene Buckley in Winnipeg; Jeff Chamberlain and Rob Bauckham in Kalamazoo; Chad Philips in Routt County; Keith Fife in Mesa County; and Cindy Houben, Ellen Sasano, and Lance Clarke in Pitkin County. Prior to joining Clarion Associates, I worked for the City and County of Denver, where I also learned the ins and outs of zoning from Bill Lamont, Frank Gray, Dick Farley, Dorothy Nepa, and the late Jennifer Moulton. Finally, friends from across the United States listened to the ideas for this book and contributed their own insights, examples, and information, including Stephen Preston from San Gabriel, Bill Anderson from San Diego, Theresa Lucero from Denver, and Rick Bernhardt from Nashville. They may not agree with the thoughts in this book, but their lives are entwined with it.

Finally, I would like to acknowledge Girish Gill, who prepared the illustrations for this book.

INTRODUCTION

ZONING IS NOT A SEXY TOPIC. No one—except people like me—reads zoning ordinances, because they are boring. It's not that the books don't have enough pictures—some modern zoning laws have lots of them. It's because the topic itself is so detailed. To understand zoning, you have to delve through long lists of permitted and prohibited uses, tables (or, worse yet, lists) of maximum building heights and minimum setbacks, landscaping requirements, maximum sign heights and sizes, and myriad other topics. By itself, each topic is a bit of a mental challenge and a struggle against sleep. Put together, they can become mind-numbingly complex. It's a lot like eating sand. Even after reading all the chapters, most readers would be hard-pressed to visualize what can or cannot be built. That's why most cities of any size hire staff whose job it is to understand what is in the zoning law and how it all fits together. That's a good thing—and certainly better than having no one understand how it might fit together. But it would be better if we could all understand it, at least enough to know what we can do with our property.

Public perception of zoning documents was demonstrated vividly in a recent televised public service announcement emphasizing the importance of reading to children. The scene showed a father coming into his daughter's bedroom to read her a bedtime story. After a predictable voice-over about how reading to children helps them learn, the narrator suggests that if parents do not read to their children the kids might not know how interesting books can be. To prove this point, the father asks his daughter what he should read that night and she hands him a copy of a thick book titled *Zoning and Variances*. So not only are zoning laws complex, but they are now the poster child for boring reading. Perhaps only the Internal Revenue Service tax code is more pilloried as an example of turgid, inconsistent, and incomprehensible rules.

That's a shame, because zoning laws (and their half brothers, subdivision regulations) are the filters that determine what gets built on private land—and the vast majority of urban land is private land. In well-run cities, zoning also determines what can be built on public land, but that is another story.

For better or worse, the roots of zoning run deep. Zoning as a legal tool originated about ninety years ago when New York City adopted the first zoning regulation. A lot has changed since then, and zoning has had to adjust many times to keep up with changing market forces and the increasing public demands for control over land. Cities often have wide latitude to update their zoning rules how and when they choose. Some have been pretty good at incorporating new tools, but others have not. As a result, any survey of zoning tools currently used in the United States will find enormous variations. There really is no "standard" approach to zoning—nor should there be. We have not had a standard approach since the Standard Zoning Enabling Act and the Standard City Planning Enabling Act were passed by Congress in the 1920s. Practices have been diverging ever since.

After revising scores of zoning ordinances over the past twenty years, I can confirm that every one is different, but many share common weaknesses. Cities generally don't hire a zoning consultant unless the situation is pretty bad. Many cities start off their first consultant meeting by stating, "We're pretty sure ours is the worst zoning ordinance you've ever seen." But they're wrong in thinking they're unique. Many ineffective zoning ordinances are broken in very similar ways, which led me to write this book.

The fact that local zoning regulations vary from one another is not really a problem—it is just one of the healthy ways in which democracy is "messy." The actual problem is much more serious. The problem is that many current zoning systems

- are more complex than they need to be;
- actually prevent many types of development that cities would like to approve;
- do not provide housing at prices that citizens can afford;
- adjust poorly to changed circumstances; and
- reflect and encourage poor systems of city governance.

Because zoning is so important to the quality of American cities, we really need to make it work better, more efficiently, and more understandably. It is time to take the old zoning machinery apart and ask ourselves, "What is this piece really supposed to do?," "Do we still think that is something we should be doing?," and, if so, "Is this the right piece to do the job?"

This book is an attempt to outline what a better approach to zoning would look like and how we can move in that direction. It explores how zoning was born; looks at how it grew up, including its awkward teenage years; and considers its somewhat dysfunctional adulthood. The story begins with basic Euclidean zoning and wends its way through the major milestones since then, including planned unit developments, performance zoning, and form-based zoning. Of course, there have been other changes as well, but these three illustrate how we have been trying to address some of the problems inherent in the system. Taking into account the various ways different cities have mixed and matched these tools—often just stapling a new chapter on the end of a book we thought was finished—it is not surprising that the results have been mixed at best. Jerry Garcia, was not thinking of zoning when he sang "What a long, strange trip it's been"—but he could have been.

This book asks three key questions that should influence how we design our zoning systems. First, it asks whether the assumptions that underlie traditional zoning tools are still true (or ever were true). Zoning has always been based on assumptions about how to manage the impacts of land use, and if that thinking has been wrong, then we have to wonder whether the tools themselves make sense. Second, this book asks whether zoning really addresses the forces currently driving the development of American cities. If it does not, then it needs to be changed so that it does. Finally, it asks: "Whatever happened to the sometimes-lost art of governance?"—that is, the skill of designing predictable systems of governing that produce good results over the long run without wasting resources. Running a successful city is not just about making the maximum number of people happy on city council night; it's about making decisions that will stand the test of time.

After critiquing the current zoning system from these three perspectives, this book examines the constitutional limits on how zoning can be changed. The technicality and rigidity of zoning lead many to think that "the law" must constrain it to be that way. But states have remarkable freedom in how they can allow their cities to zone land, and many states pass some of that freedom on to the cities. The law of zoning turns out to be anything but a straitjacket. It has a moderate number of fixed rules (mostly constitutional rights and federal laws) and lots of room for innovation. The state of the law is not the problem. In fact, it is part of the solution.

3

Finally, this book depicts a better way to zone. It identifies *how* zoning needs to change but does not offer a model of *what* it should look like at the end. Because of the huge stakes that property owners have in keeping property rights predictable, changes in big city zoning tend to be evolutionary rather than revolutionary. Systemic change in big city zoning almost always happens through a considered process over a period of time—as well it should. Rather than offer another model ordinance, this book identifies ten principles toward which zoning needs to move in order to be simpler, more effective, and able to guide real estate markets to produce better cities. It closes with five pointers about how to get started and make those changes happen.

We all have biases that color our opinions, and here are mine. First, this book is aimed at mature cities—those that include older areas that are ripe for reinvestment and redevelopment, even though they may still be growing with new development on their outer edges. It is not aimed at small towns, rural counties, or brand-new cities. Some of the discussion here may also apply beyond mature cities, and some may not. This is not to imply that other areas are not important, but I find the zoning problems of mature cities particularly interesting and I believe that current zoning ordinances are compounding the problems of mature cities in important ways.

Second, I have a bias for zoning systems that produce faster decisions for applicants. Private landowners are often more aware than city governments that "time is money," but cities should be just as concerned about it. Mature cities need private investors, because they do most of the building and rebuilding in our communities. Private investors—who include not just big companies but also you when you want to add a bedroom to your house—often need clear decisions to approve or deny an application, and they need them fairly promptly. Private landowners with a pending application have sometimes told me in frustration: "I can accept a 'yes' or a 'no,' but I cannot accept a 'wait until next month.'"

Third, I have a bias in favor of simplicity. Unnecessary complexity in any law that the general public has to use is not just unfortunate but also bad governance. Somewhere in the past ninety years, we seem to have accepted the fact that if you are going to get into zoning matters you probably need a lawyer. But that shouldn't be the case. Complex zoning matters may require lawyers, but most should not. Ordinary citizens should be able to understand the zoning ordinance as it relates not just to their property but also to their neighborhood, at the very least. The answer is to

4

make simplicity and understandability not just an aspiration but a guiding principle in zoning. After reviewing and rewriting lots of zoning ordinances, I have concluded that much of the public good comes out of some of the simpler zoning controls, and that some of the details that cause the most vociferous debates have little impact on the future quality of cities. Some readers may accuse me of oversimplifying complex topics in my descriptions of both how zoning works and how I think it should work. Some of that is deliberate. I think it helps to focus on the big picture of "What are we really trying to achieve here" and to regulate from there. So I plead guilty to simplification. Only time will tell whether it is oversimplification.

Fourth, I do not think the fundamental problem with zoning is that it interferes with private property rights. Throughout the ages, most civilizations have qualified the rights of citizens to use their land in order to prevent unwanted impacts. Since 1916, zoning has been the primary tool to condition property rights in the United States, but before that we had the law of nuisance, and if zoning were abolished tomorrow we would have to find another tool to address the same issues. Citizens are always going to care about the quality of their cities and neighborhoods, and in a democracy they are going to continue to support city government in regulating to reduce negative impacts and encourage good ones. However, I do believe that ineffective, inefficient, or unfair regulations are burdens on private property rights and that many cities could improve their performance in these areas. This book is not about *whether* cities should zone but about *how* they should zone.

Fifth, while I support most of the tenets of both New Urbanism and Smart Growth, this book does not advocate those principles and does not assume that readers endorse them. Volumes have been written on both of these planning movements, and I cannot add to that discussion. I believe that cities that support one or both of those movements could implement them through the better way to zone described in this book, with one caveat: very prescriptive use and design regulations often complicate zoning ordinances more than they improve the quality of our cities. It is important to remember that many of the cities we love best do not use detailed design or strict use controls in the areas we love. To be consistent with this book, use controls would have to be flexible, form controls would have to be as simple as possible, and detailed design controls would need to be limited to unique areas. With that one caveat, the approach in this book is consistent with both New Urbanism and Smart Growth, but it is also useful in cities (or parts of cities) that don't endorse those views of the future.

Sixth, although I believe that environmental regulations can and should be integrated into zoning ordinances to achieve sustainable forms of urban development, I have not addressed that topic in this book. Again, this does not imply that environmental standards are unimportant—just that the topic is being addressed by many other authors. The field of environmental regulation is complex, and building sustainability into zoning ordinances is really a topic unto itself. Tomorrow's best zoning ordinances will include controls that reduce resource consumption and pollution through good design and will, in the process, make it easier to comply with state and federal environmental requirements. The approach in this book can incorporate those controls, but in limiting myself to ten directions for the future, I have chosen to leave this topic to the many specialists already wrestling with it.

Finally, although much of my career has been spent as a zoning and land use consultant with Clarion Associates, the opinions in this book are not necessarily those of Clarion Associates or any of its partners or employees. Professionals in any field can disagree, and some of my colleagues at Clarion may disagree with me. Just as importantly, zoning consultants have to tailor their work to respond to unique development patterns, real estate markets, political realities, and personalities in each client city. So I may have given advice to clients that is not consistent with the opinions stated in this book. Sometimes the advice may have differed because the local government was not open to the types of changes discussed in chapters 7 and 8 and we had to search for a second- or third-best alternative. In other cases, the difference occurs because I have learned from experience and changed my opinions over time. After all, that is what this book is all about—learning to think about zoning in different ways than we have in the past.

A BETTER WAY
TO ZONE

CHAPTER 1

A Brief History of Zoning

TO UNDERSTAND HOW ZONING doesn't work, we need to start with how it is supposed to work—or how it was supposed to work when it was shiny and new. We also need to understand how it has already been modified to deal with new problems and pressures. We need not explore the history in detail—several good books already do that[1]—but we do need to understand today's starting point so we can avoid repeating the mistakes of the past. By reviewing how we have already tried to "fix" zoning, we can identify what parts of the fix worked and what parts did not (and why).

"Euclidean" Zoning

Traditional zoning is "Euclidean" zoning, named not after the Greek mathematician Euclid nor because a zoning map looks sort of geometrical, but after the town of Euclid, Ohio, which won the first lawsuit over the legality of zoning. But before Euclid there was New York City, which adopted the first major zoning ordinance, in 1916.[2] If you can imagine the chaos of New York during the early twentieth century, when it was bursting at the seams with more poor immigrants arriving daily, you can understand why the city leaders felt they needed to do something. They had already adopted a partial building code (the Old and New Tenement Laws) requiring that apartment houses be built so that a certain amount of light and air could reach the inner rooms. But now those tenements were sprouting up everywhere, even near factories—and, worse yet, near mansions.

So New York City adopted a "zoning plan" restricting the uses to which land could be put. Basically, they divided the city into "zones" for residential, commercial, and industrial uses. While they were at it, they also established an imaginary box within which buildings had to be built on each site. Some parts of the box— for example, requirements for access and light—were simply concepts carried over from the Tenement Laws of 1867, 1879, and 1901. The sides of the box were defined by distances that the building had to be "set back" from the front, rear, and side lot lines, and the top of the box was a maximum height limit on the overall structure. That was it. There were no parking controls (not many cars back then), no sign controls, no landscaping requirements, and no design controls. This was the backbone of zoning: a division of the city into use zones and boxes into which buildings had to fit in order to avoid crowding their neighbors; to avoid creating public health, safety, or fire hazards; and to prevent land use combinations likely to cause nuisances in the future.

The structure of the zoning document was straightforward. It included one chapter for each zone, with a narrative list of permitted uses and a list of setbacks and height limits. A separate chapter described the procedure for amending the zoning text or the zoning map. Importantly, we could change the text without changing the map (everyone in the affected chapter now had new rules for the future), and we could change the map without changing the text (owners in the recolored area now just followed a different set of rules). This is important, because this book is about changing the text of the zoning ordinance—not the map that applies it to specific parcels of land in the city.

Of course, even back in 1916, people were smart enough to know that no rule will work perfectly. For example, there may be parcels of such a weird shape that they physically cannot meet the setbacks, or instances where the height limits make no sense because the property is in a valley and the surrounding buildings would tower over it. So they allowed for "variances," which required an appearance before a "board of adjustment" to show that yours was a unique situation created by history, or by the land itself, and not by you yourself. You also had to show that, because of that uniqueness, applying the rules rigidly would produce a result that was unnecessarily harsh on you and that flexing the rules for you would not create significant problems for your neighbors. If you created the problem yourself (for example, by selling off some buildable parcels in a way that left you with an unbuildable one, or because you just paid too much for the land and you needed a taller building to break even on the deal), then tough luck. You couldn't create a problem and then ask your neighbors to bear the burden of fixing a problem you could have avoided. This was all very logical and straightforward—a set of simple rules and a way to make exceptions in unique circumstances.

These basic Euclidean zoning tools did not change much until after World War II. The structure of the system was robust. We could do a lot with it. The original New York system had three colors—residential, commercial, and industrial—but there was no reason it could not have six colors, or twelve, or twenty. Instead of a "business" zone, you could have "business 1" and "business 2" zones to cover different types and scales of building. If you wanted a residential zone where the uses and boxes would allow only single-family houses, just create one and recolor a part of the zoning map to the new color. If you wanted a residential zone that makes each box sit far from the others—in effect requiring larger lots and encouraging more expensive houses—just create one. If you wanted to have one zone for heavy (smelly and smoky) industry and another for light (clean and quiet) industry, create them.

So Euclidean zoning remained largely unchanged in concept, but it became more complicated in practice. Denver adopted its first zoning ordinance in 1923 and its second ordinance in 1957. Table 1.1 shows how the menu of districts within the city changed over time. Not only were the basic categories (residential, commercial) being sliced into more varieties, but entirely new types of zones appeared.

Zones typically are shown on maps in different colors—lots of them. Residential zones are often shown in yellow, so as residential zones multiplied, we could use dark yellow and then light yellow and then lemon yellow. Anyone with a computer monitor knows that there is no shortage of different colors out there—but there *is* a limit to how many variations of yellow the human eye can distinguish when they appear next to one another on a map. Multifamily residential is often shown as somewhere between yellow and brown, but not all of us can spot the difference between dark orange, rust, and burnt sienna without constantly referring back to the map legend. So even though each new zone could have its own color, both the public and the planners sometimes had trouble keeping track of

Table 1.1: Denver Zoning Districts

1923	1957	1994
5 residential	5 residential	16 residential
3 business	6 business	12 business
3 commercial	1 office/institutional	7 mixed-use
2 industrial	1 park	2 office
	3 special	1 park
	3 industrial	3 industrial
		1 planned unit development (PUD)
Total = 13	Total = 19	Total = 42

what the different colors meant. This foreshadows one structural problem in think-ing of each zone district as a world unto itself.

As the number of Denver's zone districts expanded, the number of topics cov-ered also expanded. The 1957 ordinance covered new topics like parking; loading; the emission of heat, glare, radiation, fumes, and vibration; zone lots (for cases where zoning was applied to something other than a single platted parcel); and special zone lot plans.[3] By 1994, the list of topics was too long and complicated to summarize. To its credit, Denver is now engaged in an ambitious effort to simplify the ordinance. Similar changes were taking place in many other cities over the same time period.

Perhaps the most important addition to Euclidean zoning between 1920 and 1960 concerned the automobile. Particularly after World War II, it became clear that even if the building uses and boxes were compatible with those around them, some of those uses attracted lots of cars that clogged the streets and annoyed the neighbors. Addressing this issue did not require the creation of a new zone but instead required the addition of a chapter that was stapled to each zone through cross-references. Now you had to provide a certain number of park-ing spaces that varied depending on your land use, and those provisions applied in nearly every zone district. This was an important change. Now zoning regu-lations did not vary just by zone district; some regulations varied by specific use rather than by the zone in which it was located. When sign controls came along, they were handled the same way.

Something similar happened with floodplains. Planners and engineers have always known that some places flood and they worry about it. Engineers try to keep it from happening and planners try not to have lots of people where it happens. But every type of zone district may have some parcels of land that are located in floodplains and others that are not. One solution might be to create more new zone districts—for example, for every "business 3" zone, there would also be a "business 3 floodplain" zone with fewer allowed uses and more prohibited types of buildings to protect public safety. But that would double the number of zone districts (and colors). To avoid that result, some planners decided to create a single new zone called *floodplain* and then "lay it over" all of the mapped flood areas. This was like drawing the floodplain boundaries on a clear sheet of plastic and taping it over the zoning map: you could see right through the plastic to determine the color of the zone where your land was located, and you could see whether the additional restrictions for the floodplain applied. There was no need to double the number of districts, but the practical effect of an "overlay zone" was the same. Again, this was an important change. These regulations varied based not on the underlying zone or the specific use but on geography or some other factor.

So now we had lots of zone district chapters describing uses and boxes, some overlay zone districts that might apply to all or none or some of the underlying districts, and some freestanding chapters (like parking and signs) that applied pretty much everywhere. The document was becoming more complex. There was a lot of overlap between chapters—you had to look in more than one place in the ordinance to find out what you could do on your property. But that was better than repeating identical parking and floodplain text in every zone district chapter, which would really have made the book an exercise in heavy lifting.

Along the way, planners and lawyers were discovering one of the wonderful loopholes of zoning law. Although state enabling laws often required that every property within a zone be treated the same, there was nothing to prevent you from creating as many zones as you wanted. You could create a new zone even if you suspected that it would be used only once, and you didn't have to admit to that when you adopted the text of the new zone; you just mapped one piece of land, and in the future you could color other parts of the city into the new zone if you wanted. But if tomorrow never came, so what? As far as the law was concerned, everyone whose land was in that zone (all one of them) was being treated the same. A legal doctrine on "spot zoning" emerged to stop unfair use of this loophole if the rules that were applied to one parcel differed too dramatically from the rules applied to the neighboring parcels (see chapters 4 and 5), but it was used rarely and it did not address the proliferation of almost-but-not-quite-identical zone districts.

Although zoning was now in common use, not everyone was happy with it. In addition to generalized angst by those who thought there should be no land use controls, criticism of Euclidean zoning came from two other quarters. First, there were those who wondered whether the system was getting too complex. In theory, there was no limit to the number of zone districts that could be created. Didn't that start to erode the idea of uniformity behind the use of zoning districts? How much time and effort did the city want to put into operating this zoning system, and how hard would it be for the public to understand the regulations that applied to their property?

Second, some folks—lawyers mostly—wondered whether the move from a few general districts affecting large classes of people to many smaller and more specialized zones opened up possibilities for unfairness and abuse. Changing a widely used zone district, such as "business 3," could not be done in the dark. Text changes usually required newspaper notice—not individual notice to every property owner—but that works well only for large districts with many owners. Many "B-3" landowners would see the newspaper notice, and some inevitably would object. A debate would follow and city council would at least be informed about the objections when it decided whether to approve the amendment.

But as zoning districts proliferate, the more specialized zones often apply to smaller groups of landowners. A general "B-3" zone district might be refined so that a new variation called, for example, "B-3.2" applies only to properties along collector streets, and then further refined so that a variation called "B-3.2.5" applied to properties along minor collectors with significant industrial traffic. Amending the text of the "B-3.2.5" district would affect only a small number of properties and might not get much attention from the media or industry groups. It might be harder for the landowners to learn about the proposed change, and if they objected to the amendment their few voices might sound like only minimal opposition.

The expansion of zoning to cover new topics also had consequences. One predictable outcome was that variances were needed more often. A site that was buildable before the adoption of parking or landscaping standards might not be once those requirements were added. Over time, boards of adjustment found that they had a steady, if not daunting, workload. In some cities, the board's hearing calendar was backed up for months, even for property owners who were requesting something minor. The basic idea that land could be regulated through a few simple zones addressing a few topics, and that exceptions would be rare, was on shaky ground. But in spite of its weaknesses, Euclidean zoning was still the bedrock of most American cities' land use controls. So many people rely on the predictability of the Euclidean zoning approach that increasing complexity and concerns about fairness and due process have still not discredited this most basic tool.

Standard Zoning and Planning Enabling Acts

When New York adopted its zoning plan in 1916, it acted alone. There was no national model that it "tweaked." But the same problems were occurring in other American cities, and the idea caught on. Edward Bassett, chairman of the New York committee that drafted the 1916 zoning ordinance, was a true believer who visited every state in the United States between 1917 and 1927 to spread the gospel of zoning.[4] By the 1920s, America was in the midst of the municipal reform movement, and talk about better ways to run cities was on many lips. This was the era that gave us the city manager form of government, merit-based municipal civil service systems (as opposed to patronage), and requirements for competitive bidding for city contracts. Zoning became associated with the reform package, and it spread in part because of the broader wave of urban reforms washing over America's cities.

During his years as Secretary of Commerce and then President, Herbert Hoover helped lead the movement toward progressive urban government and took a great interest in planning as a solution to urban problems. By 1922, some states had already adopted enabling acts for zoning and some cities had adopted zoning laws without waiting for state authority. Hoover appointed an Advisory Committee on City Planning and Zoning, which produced the Standard Zoning Enabling Act in 1924 and then a revised version in 1926.

Three things about the Standard Zoning Act are notable. First, it was just a publication. This "Act" was not an "Act of Congress." The federal government published it as an example of progressive legislation that individual states might want to adopt. No one was forcing cities to zone, but some in the federal government thought it was a good idea. If your city wanted to zone, this was a good place to start. Second, the Standard Zoning Act required that zoning be "in accordance with a comprehensive plan," but it did not recommend what specific controls zoning should contain. It focused primarily on procedures: how to adopt and amend a zoning ordinance and how to allow variances. Third, one of the most strongly debated sections of the Zoning Act was the one authorizing variances—the rules on how much latitude the board of adjustment should have to vary the zoning rules and when they could do it. This debate foreshadowed ninety years of continuing discussions about how zoning should reconcile the need for both predictability and flexibility.[5]

In 1928, the Advisory Committee went on to publish the Standard City Planning Enabling Act, which outlined the establishment of a planning commission to draft a "master plan," street plans, controls for the subdivision of land, and even the need for regional planning.[6] Again, this was a publication of the Commerce Department, not an "Act of Congress." These two publications very effectively promoted both city planning and zoning. By 1930, the U.S. Commerce Department reported that thirty-five states had adopted legislation based on the Zoning Act and that ten states had adopted statutes based on the Planning Act. These were ideas whose times had apparently come.

The sequence of these events, though, has created lots of trouble for planning and city management ever since. Most importantly, creating legal authority to regulate land before creating the authority to plan for future land uses puts the cart before the horse, at least in the minds of planners. It reflected a "ready-fire-aim" approach to land use and suggested that it was OK to set the rules for what could be done with land based on current conditions—and without thinking about the future. In publishing the two Standard Acts separately, Congress was only suggesting that states might want to do both, or one, or neither. Although most well-run cities now support both planning and zoning, the connection between the two is often weak, and the legal structures underneath them are very different. And we still have large cities that zone without planning first as well as those that plan without zoning (well, actually, just Houston, which does it just to prove that it can).

Less important, but still frustrating to planners, the Standard Zoning Act used the term *zoning plan*—but the Planning Act four years later used the term *master plan*. So was the zoning plan different from a master plan? Evidently so, and more troubling (again for planners), the term *zoning plan* really meant "the map that shows you where the different zones are located in the city"—which is really a "map," not a "plan." To planners, a plan involves some amount of thinking ahead and deciding what to do about the anticipated future. Of course, by stating that the zoning had to be "in accordance with a comprehensive plan," the Zoning Act did imply (maybe) that thinking about the future was necessary.

But if that was what the Advisory Committee meant, why did they use the term *comprehensive plan* in the Zoning Act and *master plan* in the Planning Act? That difference suggested that the document guiding zoning was something different from the master plan envisioned in the Planning Act, which really did have to think about the future. Even today, state zoning enabling acts modeled on the Standard Zoning Act (a surprisingly large number, given that the model is ninety years old) still use this term, and state legislators are still confused as to what a zoning plan is. Debates about what these various terms mean still occur regularly when amendments to state acts are proposed.

The Standard Zoning Act showed merely the outlines of this powerful new tool to shape cities. Essentially, it allowed the "police power" of the cities to be used not just retroactively (by removing nuisances that were threatening citizens' health and safety) but proactively (to prevent bad things before they occurred). This was a watershed in legal thinking about property rights. Although the use of Standard Acts was a very effective way to "broadcast" the use of these powers across the nation, it had its downside. All of the flaws inherent in the zoning-then-planning sequence of publication and the confusion over the different names of the required plans were also broadcast nationally.

It is interesting to think about what might have happened without the Standard Acts. On one hand, it is unlikely that the use of zoning would have spread nearly as fast as it did, because each state that wanted to use the powers would have had to find models from other states (without the Internet) and then choose among them or create its own, and that would have taken time. On the other hand, it is unlikely that so many states would have confused zoning with planning so thoroughly. Somewhere along the way, some smart state legislature would have gotten the sequence and terminology right, and the logic of that approach might have made it the preferred model for later adopters.

Nevertheless, by 1928, the United States had Standard Acts for both planning and zoning. In the following years, state after state climbed on the zoning bandwagon, and the nations' citizens and city planners never looked back. Zoning appealed to planners' innate sense that the world would be better if there was "a place for everything and everything in its place." More importantly, it appealed to citizens who wanted to protect their homes from factories and industrialists who wanted just the opposite. And it appealed to city councils, which now had a new tool with which to respond to their constituents' complaints about conditions in their neighborhoods. In fact, zoning has come to be one of the most zealously guarded city council powers because it's so "real." It touches the land and people's lives in ways that they care about, and it's so much more interesting than just approving municipal contracts and settling lawsuits.

Planned Unit Developments

It was only a short jump from the idea of creating new zones that looked like normal zones but would probably be used by only one landowner to the idea of a *planned unit development* (or PUD) custom-designed for one parcel of land. PUDs differed from specialized Euclidean zones because no one pretended that they would ever be used on any land other than the parcel for which they were written. Probably the first PUD ordinance adopted was in Prince George's County, Maryland, in 1949.[7] State PUD enabling acts soon proliferated across the country. This time, the federal government did not have to publish a Standard Act. PUDs were a tool that invited negotiation between cities and property owners to create something that met both their needs. And they were needed.

By the 1950s and 1960s, planners and the elected officials who hired them had moved beyond concern for uses and boxes; they also wanted quality. Landscaping was becoming a standard development practice, and ever-increasing parking requirements led planners to start asking that at least the big parking lots have some trees and bushes. A few cities were talking about requiring quality in other areas as well, including walkways for pedestrians, bicycle parking, lighting controls, erosion controls, and even architectural controls addressing the design of build-ings. Raising the bar to require that all new developments include these types of "quality" often provoked opposition from landowners and developers who felt the added costs would come from their pockets, so change was slow and sporadic. But the trend was clear: more zoning topics and more complexity.

The situation was different, however, when a property owner asked for a zon-ing change. Here was someone who needed something from the city, something discretionary and usually within the power of the city council to grant or not. In theory, thought the planners, someone who wants a discretionary approval from city council should be a little more willing to increase the quality of development—and that was sometimes true. In fact, because developers often found that they needed variances for some of their proposed uses or boxes and because planners wanted the bells and whistles of quality, negotiated zoning districts looked like a classic win-win situation.

State legislation authorizing PUDs simply legalized this practice. Instead of adopting more and more specialized residential districts with shades of yellow indis-tinguishable to the human eye, the city could adopt one PUD ordinance authoriz-ing the creation of individualized PUDs. Each PUD had to be adopted publicly—with due process, as an ordinance—but it didn't have to be published as a new chapter in the zoning book because each one was so tailored that it would not be used again. PUDs were sort-of-zoning and sort-of-a-contract situations, and not every city contract has to be published in full. Officially, PUD ordinances gave permission for developers and cities to reach acceptable compromises that balanced innovation, quality, and flexibility, and that compromise would become the zoning. Large, mature cities generally added PUD regulations as an option to be used on a case-by-case basis to replace individual pieces in the Euclidean zoning map.

Cities began encouraging their developers to apply for PUDs so that they could negotiate for more quality. Developers used PUDs not only to authorize new layouts and combinations of uses not allowed by standard zone districts but also to buy time. They sometimes used PUDs to "lock in" the right to build certain amounts of development while leaving the details vague.

But this created some challenges. If a PUD were approved today but the landowner did not have to really decide the final land uses and layout until later, how was the city to plan for adequate roads and infrastructure? It was well and good to say that the land use would be residential and the overall density would be X dwelling units per acre, but different types of housing generate different amounts of traffic, and it could make a big difference whether that traffic would exit the site onto Main Street or Cedar Drive.

Many PUD systems solve this problem by requiring two or more approvals before the new zoning is final. The ordinance allows the applicant to file a general plan laying out basic land use "bubbles," transportation and open space systems, and total amounts of development, and that general plan has to be approved when the land is rezoned as a PUD. Once the general plan has been approved, the applicant can talk to builders and tenants and banks about a much more specific project, with much less risk that it will not happen. But she still cannot build because the ordinance requires that once the developer knows what she really wants to do within those bubbles, she needs to come back and get a "site plan" approval showing that the detailed layout works, that the connecting roads and pipes are big enough, and that the whole thing is consistent with the approved PUD general plan. Sometimes the site plan can be approved administratively, but many cities require that it go back to city council for approval. While landowners would generally prefer not to go back for a second approval, the added flexibility still makes the deal worthwhile—it just makes the administration of PUDs more complex than other zones.

Still, some landowners and developers began to get a little skittish. What had started out as a way to vary standards for flexibility could now become a no-holds-barred negotiation in which the government held the upper hand. When an old Euclidean zone was being modified for the developer, the city had to at least pretend that the terms of the new district would be applicable to other landowners who might want the same type of zoning. They had to sound like good policy for the city in general. But PUDs were a one-on-one customized negotiation, so the city could tailor its negotiating strategy to the strengths and weaknesses of particular landowners and could even (unofficially) take into account what they knew of the developer's financial position and time constraints.

On the other hand, sometimes it was the landowner who was more sophisticated and had the stronger bargaining position. When an applicant was offering development to a city that had little, or if an applicant had more experienced planners than the city had reviewing the plans, the negotiation could be one-sided in the other direction. At the extreme, developers used PUDs as a way to get large-scale "variances" without offering any innovation or better quality. Instead of having to prove that every lot had a physical problem that the landowner had not caused, the owner could now ask that the standards be lowered for all of the lots and not have to show any hardship at all. If the city council was not smart or strong enough to extract some quality in return for the flexibility, what of it? A deal was a deal.

As PUDs moved from being the exception for innovative development to a form of zoning used regularly and for not-so-innovative projects, cities woke up to a problem. PUDs took a lot of time to negotiate, to draft, to get adopted, and to administer. One source of time delay was the two-approval system discussed above; many of the steps involved in rezoning had to be done twice, once for the initial PUD zoning and general plan and then again for approval of the site plan.

But that was not the only source of complexity and delay. In the old days, the city's planners all knew what uses were and were not allowed in the "business 3" zone, how tall the building could be, and how far back from the property lines it had to be. They could keep the basics of all the zones in their heads, plus general information about how much parking was required. But no one could memorize every PUD—there was too much detail, and there were too many of them. Questions that used to have a short answer now evoked responses like "Please wait while I go and pull the file (and read it for the first time)" or "We'll have to call you back on that."

In addition, some PUDs were overly detailed. High levels of detail may have seemed good to both the city and the developer at the end of a long, drawn-out negotiation, but they could seem like overkill to their successors. At their worst, PUDs locked in a very specific idea and allowed nothing else: the applicant showed a pretty picture, the city negotiated over the picture, difficult issues were resolved by hashing out the details, and when they reached agreement they locked in those details. That was bound to cause problems down the road, because life rarely comes out like the picture on the box.

A PUD was a snapshot of what was acceptable to one developer and one city council on a given date, but that snapshot now became the law. The developer often wanted to sell parcels of the newly zoned PUD land, and the buyers sometimes shook their heads when they reviewed the detailed provisions regulating those lands. The more detailed the PUD was, the greater the likelihood that the new owner would need to change it when conditions changed and market assumptions proved wrong. The same was true for the city council, who found that outdated ideas of quality were hard to change ten years down the road.

Because PUDs basically treated all of the land in their boundaries as a "unit" within which the development must achieve its goals (hence the "U" in "PUD"), they often contained provisions allowing individual lots to be smaller, in return for larger parcels of contiguous open space somewhere else on the site. Often, that is good planning. But it also means that if you need to amend a PUD in the future, you will probably need to get consent from every property owner in the "unit." The owners of the small lots were intended to benefit from that open space, so the PUD could not be changed without consulting them. This was hard to do after parts of the land had been sold off. Technically, a property owner on one side of the development parcel could object to the redesign of an open space corridor on the other side, even if the owners of the parcels along the open space did not object. So not only did PUDs seem to require a lot of amendments as conditions changed, but the process of amending them was cumbersome.

Finally, PUDs proved vulnerable to misuse. If you are not careful, PUDs could become a zoning narcotic. I have worked with several cities that became addicted to negotiated zoning and begged for the cure. The problem is that once you start using PUDs, you have trouble drawing the line between what should and should not be negotiated. Recall that PUD zoning was originally created to address innovative developments where the applicant would give increased quality in return for flexibility. It was not intended to be a back door way to package variance requests without showing hardship. And it was not supposed to be used to legitimize zoning problems by "shrink-wrapping" their current operations into personalized zone districts. Shrink-wrap zoning happens when a use or structure is clearly illegal but wants to remain in business and the neighbors will accept that as long as the illegality does not increase and the operations maintain their current levels of impact. The neighbors say: "This can stay, but it must be limited to the current square footage and the three trucks a week that currently visit the site. Expanding your operations from within your current facility is not OK," and the owner agrees. Although shrink-wrap zoning is often legal, it is not what PUDs were created for and it shows an unhealthy addiction to the tool itself.

But in spite of these problems, PUDs survive and in most cities they are thriving. At their best, they are used for truly innovative developments by thoughtful builders who offer quality in return for flexibility. In a fair percentage of cases, they fall prey to strong-arm tactics by either the city or the developer and result in one-sided deals. At their worst—and this really happens—they are used because it is easier to negotiate case-by-case deals than to fix the problems with the underlying

Euclidean zoning ordinance. Planners may know that the setbacks are wrong or that the parking standards are too low or too high, but there is no political will to fix the problems in the zoning ordinance. Worse, some cities' basic ordinances have been amended so often that they contain serious inconsistencies, and planners may be reluctant to approve Euclidean rezonings that may have unpredictable outcomes. It's much safer to do a series of one-off deals, even knowing that they will be more labor intensive to administer and modify over time.

Importantly, though, PUDs did not and really cannot replace zoning, except perhaps in very small towns. PUDs address new development—but most of every mature city is old development that is not coming forward for redevelopment approval. Even if all significant new development were forced into PUDs—which is not wise, but it has happened in some cities—there would be a need for preexisting, underlying zoning. Property owners who want to add a room to their house or commercial property owners who want to change from a shoe store to a lawyer's office, for example, should not be made to go through a negotiation. There have to be basic rules with a defined amount of "breathing room" so that the vast majority of property owners with smaller projects can simply get a building permit or a nondiscretionary approval without having to negotiate or obtain city council approvals.

Performance Zoning

Because of the rigidity of Euclidean zoning and the complexity that seems to accompany both Euclidean zoning and PUDs (after they are approved), a second alternative to Euclidean zoning also gained adherents. Performance zoning is listed third in this history not because of chronology (some cities moved in this direction long before PUDs came on the scene) but because it can apply to both standard Euclidean zoning and PUDs.

Performance zoning says: "Many zoning provisions are really trying to avoid a bad impact on neighbors by creating distance between them or setting a numerical limit on some dimension of development. Why don't we just prohibit the bad impact and let the developer figure out how to do it? Maybe we don't need that

23

much distance or rigid size controls. We'll regulate land to require the performance we want and not try to guess what physical shape that has to take."

Performance zoning makes a lot of sense, particularly for commercial and industrial land uses. Early Euclidean zoning addressed "heavy" (i.e., possibly smoky, noisy) industry primarily through separation. While a "light" industrial use could have setbacks of 50 feet, a "heavy" factory might require setbacks of 200 feet so that the smells and noise and maybe glare and heat from the operations could dissipate before they reached a nearby shopping area. Obviously, that was a pretty blunt instrument. What if the operations were completely enclosed? What if they used a technology that produced no smells or noise? Why 200 feet?

Performance zoners tried to quantify what levels of noise, smoke, emissions, glare, radiation, and other bad impacts were tolerable at the property lines and then wrote zoning provisions to prohibit anything higher. Then they reduced or removed setbacks and other physical spacing and dimension requirements. Where there was a requirement for a wall or hedge or buffer to keep out unwanted impacts, they took it out. It was up to the developer to decide which, if any, barrier would be installed if and when it turned out that the facility violated tolerable impacts. Performance zoning was designed to improve flexibility, and it did.

Strong adherents of this approach felt that many physical standards throughout zoning ordinances could be replaced by performance standards. Moderate followers tended to limit performance standards to commercial and industrial development and to the operation of those facilities after they were built. Most large cities did not replace Euclidean zoning with performance zoning, but they did adopt some performance measures over time. It is rare to find a large city without some kind of performance standards (usually related to noise impacts). Unlike PUDs, which are so different from uniform districts that everyone remembers when the tool came into being, performance zoning snuck in under the radar. Although there was a period in the 1970s and 1980s when performance zoning was a hot planning topic, many cities had already adopted performance-oriented industrial standards before they became trendy.

Also unlike PUDs, performance zoning generally did not require enabling legislation from the state government. If the standards were uniform, then the fact that they were not physical standards was a point too subtle to attract many lawsuits. Those who did challenge performance zoning generally lost, because the idea was so logical (or it looked so "scientific") that the courts concluded it must be OK.

So why didn't performance zoning sweep the board? After all, it solves all those problems with rigid boxes and setbacks that need to be varied or negotiated? There are two reasons. First, writing and administering performance standards was complicated. Developing the standards themselves took time (What is a tolerable level of vibration? How do we know that?). Consultants and engineers had to research the issue and come up with a standard that not only would pass judicial muster under the "rational relationship" test (there must be a rational relationship between what city council does and the outcome it is trying to achieve) but also would pass political muster when opposed by those whose facilities would not meet the standards. But once technical standards were established, some of them could be shared between cities—at least between cities with similar soils and climate and geography.

But the bigger problem was administering the standards once they were adopted. A builder could show up and say, "I've used the best architects and engineers for this job. It meets the performance standards. They all say it will not create vibration beyond X or smells beyond Y." While a capable planner could review a drawing to see that it included a 200-foot setback, the same planner could not look at a drawing and tell that the building's foundation engineering and ventilation system would in fact take care of the vibration, noise, and glare impacts.

The planners could take the builder's word for it, but if it turned out to be wrong, there would be some angry neighbors at city council meetings and a builder complaining that he had just invested a fortune in the facility and could not change it. That was an unhappy prospect, so the city council had to either require the builder to indemnify the city for mistakes (which builders are very reluctant to do) or develop the internal staff capacity to check the work before it was built (in effect becoming quasi-engineers in specialized fields themselves) or hire consultants to do it for them. All of these cost money and took time. Training departmental staff was also subject to the "skilled public employee" problem. If the city trained a planner in the technical skills to confirm that development plans really met the performance standards, there was nothing to prevent another city government or a developer from simply hiring her away. Easier to hire away a skilled planner for a small raise than to risk training one yourself and losing that one. So, as a practical matter, it proved difficult to create an efficient, sustainable system to enforce broad-ranging technical performance standards.

The second problem was that many zoning regulations are not really designed to avoid measurable negative impacts; rather, they are designed to make development more predictable. Some neighbors—particularly residential neighbors—do not just want to know that your house will have no adverse impacts on their property. They also want to know that your house will not look weird compared to theirs and others in the neighborhood. Many neighbors want the area to look and feel pretty much like it does now, at least for a while. Planners know that you can have nice residential communities with 30-foot front setbacks, 20-foot setbacks, 15-foot setbacks (provided that any cars in the driveway don't overhang the sidewalk), 10-foot setbacks (if there are alley garages), or even zero-foot front setbacks (for urban townhouses). There is no magic number that produces "health" in the community. Residents in all of these neighborhoods are happy because they choose to live there, but they generally want others to follow the same pattern. Try putting a house with a 10-foot front setback in a neighborhood where everyone else has 30 feet and see what happens. That's because one of the impacts that neighbors care about it is consistency with what they already have.

Even where there is a desire for consistency, however, there may be room for performance standards. Increasingly, cities are treating front setbacks in residential areas as a performance zoning item for which you have to show that you addressed the impact not of noise or glare but of "inconsistency"—that is, you pretty well match your neighbors. This is an evolution of the original, technical idea of performance standards, but one that has worked because it leads to a different kind of predictability. So performance zoning does not necessarily lead to unpredictability, but it sometimes results in creative (read "unexpected") solutions, and that sometimes leads to opposition, particularly within residential neighborhoods. The desire for predictability is one of the main reasons why performance zoning did not replace Euclidean zoning as the bedrock of American land use control.

Form-based Zoning

A third departure from Euclidean zoning has emerged only in the past twenty years. Proponents of form-based zoning are trying to rebalance the elements of Euclidean zoning to focus more on the form of development (hence the title of their movement) and less on permitted uses. The trouble, they say, is that standard zoning was never right in the first place, because it is based on a crude assumption that commercial, residential, and industrial uses have to be separated for their mutual good whereas most people can see with their own eyes that this is not true. Americans spend their vacation money to visit places where the uses are all mixed together—if not Europe then at least older American cities like Boston and San Francisco. Saying that residential and commercial uses cannot exist side by side or in the same building does not even pass the straight-face test. People seem to prefer mixed-use environments at least some of the time. So why not allow—or even require—mixed use more often?

Although form-based zoning is not the same as mixed-use zoning—cities can and do sometimes endorse one without the other—the two topics often get confused. To keep the issues straight, let's take a short detour to look at why mixed use might be a good idea regardless of whether a city adopts form-based zoning. Three basic arguments support mixed-use zoning. The first is that it leads to more interesting, less sterile development. Anyone who has driven through endless suburban streets trying to find an address, or who has walked through an old-style urban downtown trying to find an open restaurant after 6:00 p.m., gets the point. Too much of any one land use in one place gets boring.

The second argument is that mixed-use development is safer. Jane Jacobs made this argument famous in her book *The Death and Life of Great American Cities* with her plea that planners design for "eyes on the street."[8] Her point was that people tend to pay attention and informally monitor public spaces (streets and parks and plazas) near where they live, and that vigilance makes places where people live safer than places where they don't. That is not always true, of course, but it appeals to our gut instincts—many people don't feel safe walking at night where nobody (except possibly those who are waiting to cause them trouble) can see them. William Whyte's research in *The Social Life of Small Urban Spaces* tends to confirm that the liveliest spaces are those where people can see and be seen.

The third argument is that mixed-use zoning is more efficient, in terms of both land consumed and transportation and infrastructure dollars required to serve the development. It is more efficient in terms of land because the same parking areas can be shared between commercial uses (which need spaces during the day) and residential uses (which need them mostly at night). In addition, many stores need to be on the ground floor to attract walk-in traffic, but apartment dwellers and condo owners often prefer not to be on the ground floor, because the upper floors offer better views and feel safer. There can be a natural sharing of land by allowing residential-over-commercial uses.

Something similar happens for roads and pipes. Streets used only for office development have to be designed for peak loads during morning and evening rush hours but are often underused during the rest of the day. Shopping centers have their own peak-hour traffic demands: they open later than offices and close later. Residential traffic is more evenly distributed over the day as drivers do nonwork errands and make incidental trips. If the land uses can be combined, then a given road may be better used more of the time and we might have to construct fewer big-but-often-empty roads. Water and sewer pipes are similar; the same mains could carry water to different uses at different times of the day if they were located close together. Offices need water during work hours, but people cook and shower in their homes before and after those hours. For these reasons, mixed-use zoning has understandably become a discussion topic in its own right—even apart from form-based zoning.

In all fairness, many Euclidean zoning ordinances already allowed mixed uses through "pyramid zoning." Each less-restrictive zone allowed all the uses from the more-restrictive zones. Industrial zones often allowed the uses permitted in commercial zones, but not vice versa. If you had a shop and you wanted to locate it in an industrial zone, you could. That was your choice, and best of luck to you. But a factory could not be located in a commercial zone. The same was true for residential zones. It was OK to put apartments in a commercial area, but not OK to put shops in a residential area. This was also a fairly crude instrument, but it did allow some degree of mixed use.

Along the way, however, pyramid zoning got a bad name, partly because it implied that some uses are inherently more favored than others. It used the language of "higher" and "lower" uses and zones; residential was often considered "higher" and industrial "lower" (although in land use intensity and impacts, it could be the other way around—even planners got confused). Some planners thought that the one-way ratchet of allowing "higher" uses in "lower" zones but not the other way around was a little simplistic. There could also be residential areas where corner shops were appropriate—that is, a "lower" use in a "higher" zone might be OK. And some light industrial buildings fit just fine into commercial areas—the line between heavy commercial and light industrial uses has always been blurry, after all. Instead of a one-way ratchet, a better approach to mixing uses was needed.

But form-based zoning goes well beyond the idea of mixed use. It also suggests that zoning should pay far more attention to the form of development. Defining an imaginary box within which buildings had to fit was only a lazy man's tool to reduce the impacts of neighboring uses—separate them from each other and they won't complain as much. But many of the great places we like to visit don't fit into site-specific boxes at all. Some have continuous frontage along the streets with no spaces between buildings; some have occasional buildings much taller than the rest. Many allow public and religious buildings and monuments to violate the boxes, and having a big town hall or church or synagogue at the end of a boulevard makes the area visually exciting. That can't easily be done with standardized boxes unless you handpick the box for each site.

But the problem is not just with generalized, uniform patterns of boxes; the problem is that the buildings inside the boxes can be beautiful or ugly. We can all point to some modern buildings that are about as visually nourishing as eating sand and to others that fit into the same box but manage to feed the soul. We gaze at the latter and avoid the former. And no, it is not just a matter of taste. To some degree, we can also tell the difference between good and bad buildings through objective standards.

Early proponents of a form-based approach included Peter Katz, Peter Calthorpe, Douglas Kelbaugh, Andres Duany, and Elizabeth Plater-Zyberk. Peter Katz's book *The New Urbanism* brought together examples of developments that deliberately created a more human, less auto-oriented scale of development and helped "reconstruct the urban fabric," while Doug Kelbaugh and Peter Calthorpe's *Pedestrian Pocket Book* helped popularize the idea of compact designs based on walkable streets focused on transit access nodes. Those works, together with the writings of the husband-and-wife team of Andres Duany and Elizabeth Plater-Zyberk, emphasized the need for zoning to go far beyond the idea of "boxes" for each building, to focus on the relationship of the building to the street, to surrounding buildings, and to people as well as cars, and to recognize that the location and design of each building should better reflect its function in the community.

Each of these authors is now identified as a New Urbanist, and planners have had more than a decade to enjoy the debate about whether New Urbanism is right or wrong. Instead of joining that discussion, however, this book will focus not on the planning vision behind New Urbanism but on the tool that is often used to implement it: form-based zoning. For purposes of this book, we need to recognize that form-based zoning is a fourth approach to land use regulation that is not the same as the vision of New Urbanism. Form-based zoning does not have to be linked to New Urbanism (or to mixed use, for that matter); one of the most ambitious uses of form-based zoning even links it to rural development patterns. To avoid perpetuating this confusion, we will not pursue the discussion of New Urbanism here.[9]

The early form-based zoners were building on two important works that preceded them. The first was Christopher Alexander's monumental work, *A Pattern Language*.[10] Professor Alexander upset some of his fellow architects with claims that, by examining how different architectural elements "feel" to a broad spectrum of users, he could develop a series of principles of what was good and bad, which could be applied to everything from a window detail or a sitting area to a building, a block, a city, or a region. According to Alexander, style was not just a matter of taste; there could also be a somewhat rational method behind it.

The second work was *Visions of a New American Dream*, by Anthony Nelessen.[11] Mr. Nelessen (and others) developed a system of "visual preference surveys" by presenting a series of pictures of buildings and places and then asking groups of people which pictures they preferred. By analyzing the results of a wide variety of pictures and responses, Nelessen could identify what elements people liked— be it porches, or open spaces with a sense of enclosure, or continuous sidewalks unbroken by driveways, or distinctive public buildings on corners. He didn't claim that it was completely objective or scientific, but it was at least documented and (through statistics) could be shown to reflect public opinion fairly accurately. Under most state statutes governing zoning, city councils have to base their decisions not on science but on a "rational relationship" between the action they are taking and the outcome they hope to achieve. The visual preference surveys clearly passed the rational relationship test: if you required these types of plans and buildings, it was very likely that your voters would think the city was a better place. And it was better than guessing whether architect A was more right than architect B.

Standing on the foundation laid by Christopher Alexander and Anthony Nelessen, form-based zoners said that good urban form requires regulating much more than imaginary boxes within which buildings could be built; it requires some level of control over the architecture of the buildings themselves—not only individually but in relation to their neighbors. After all, if we know what makes "the people" happy, we should require builders to do some of that. A few free-spirited architects might complain, but city councils aren't there to make the architects happy. So form-based zoning tends to be somewhat prescriptive about what buildings should look like, sometimes including such things as height relative to the width of the street, degree of detail on the facade, placement of parking in relation to the building, placement of public buildings within a block, and, in some cases, even the architectural style of the buildings. In general, the controls are intended to create a more pedestrian-oriented layout and scale and to focus on "place making" rather than a uniform set of rights for each lot.

The poster children for form-based zoning are the Traditional Neighborhood District (TND) ordinance (intended to be applied to a residential neighborhood) and the SmartCode (intended, on its face, to be used for an entire city). The model TND ordinance was developed by Brian Ohm, James LaVro Jr., and Chuck Strawser at the University of Wisconsin and by Duany Plater-Zyberk & Company (DPZ) with the help of affiliated firms and professionals. The SmartCode was drafted by DPZ.

A fair number of cities have adopted the TND ordinance in its "as published" form, but many more have consulted the model and adopted parts of it or variations on it. Basically, cities that find the idea attractive start with the canned TND ordinance and then send it through both staff and public filters to eliminate regulations that are considered excessive or inappropriate and then produce a version (often watered down) that is politically acceptable. The degree of detail in the TND is so high that lots of compromises can be made and a city can still wind up with something very different from standard Euclidean box controls.

The SmartCode is much more ambitious than the TND ordinance and has been adopted by far fewer cities.[12] Essentially, the SmartCode attempts to apply TND principles (and others) to an entire city. It takes some of the principles articulated for walkable, urban, residential/mixed-use areas; does similar analyses for higher- and lower-density areas; and proposes design-based templates to cover all of them. The authors identified six "transects," or idealized models of good design, that start with the most dense neighborhoods and taper off to the least dense at the edge of a prototypical city. SmartCode advocates say that most built-up areas fit into one defined transect or another and that, if you choose the one that is right for the density and function of the area, its regulations will produce a better development than standard Euclidean controls. The tool is not intended to be concentric—you might apply a denser transect model to an area farther from the core than some lower-density transect controls. Go with what is on the ground or the type of place you are trying to create, but apply the controls for that type of transect. SmartCode also allows for special zones (such as airports) that do not fit one of those six transects. Many of the SmartCode controls can be summarized into a single chart, although, like Euclidean zoning, the chart sometimes has cross-references to regulations that are not on the chart.

Because it is so ambitious, it is not surprising that few cities have decided to replace their current zoning ordinances with the SmartCode. Among the twelve cities reported as having adopted the SmartCode by summer 2007, about half have adopted it as an option to be used at the request of the landowner. Some larger cities—including Fort Myers and Sarasota, Florida; Gulfport, Mississippi; and Petaluma, California—have adopted forms of the SmartCode but have made its use mandatory in only specific areas of each city. The small number of adoptions to date is not intended as a criticism, however; at least fifty-eight additional cities had SmartCode discussions in process by early summer 2007, and that is a pretty high number for a fairly radical reform program.

In contrast, many more cities have adopted TND zoning ordinances or some hybrid form of TND. In some cities, the tools have been adopted only as "floating zones"—chapters of the ordinance that are not yet applied to specific lands but are available if and when the city needs them or a property owner wants them. In other cases, they are optional or required for some but not all of the land in the city. In yet other cities, they are adopted as an optional alternative alongside the Euclidean zones. Usually, they implicitly assume that some Euclidean procedures (like standard provisions for permits and variances) will remain in place. Like PUDs, both TND and the SmartCode have been applied where they seem to be most appropriate or where the property owner requests or consents to it. Most commonly, a downtown area, a key "main street" area, a prime mixed-use node, or the land around a transit stop gets form-based zoning but the rest of the city does not.[13]

While it is still maturing, form-based zoning is clearly having a positive impact on how we think about zoning. Even if many cities start from the TND and Smart-Code models and then create homegrown hybrids between those models and standard Euclidean/PUD/performance tools, new paths are being charted.

Unlike PUDs and performance zoning, which were created to make Euclidean zoning more flexible, form-based zoning was aimed at a different failing: that earlier tools were not producing the types of neighborhoods people wanted. Because the goal of form-based zoning was not really administrative simplification, it is not surprising that the result is not simple. In fact, the result is a mixed bag. It makes regulation of uses easier and regulation of building design more complex.

Form-based tools substitute drawings of preferred or required building types for zoning text where possible, and the trade-off is illustrated by the amount of computer memory involved. Graphics require lots of memory. In the old days, a zoning ordinance text might require two or three megabytes of computer memory. As more graphics were inserted to illustrate the text concepts, we started seeing zoning ordinances requiring ten or fifteen megabytes. The most recent version of the SmartCode uses fifty-six megabytes.

As with most good ideas, the strengths of form-based zoning are also its weaknesses. Its advantages in communicating intended patterns of development also make form-based zoning a relatively static tool. Unlike PUDs, which can always be negotiated to reflect the latest trend in development and architecture, or performance zoning, which might be satisfied in different ways as new technologies emerge in the future, form-based zoning is more of a snapshot tied to the present. Although proponents make a fairly strong case that there is a semiobjective difference between "good" and "bad" design forms, only time will tell whether they are right. After all, in the 1970s we all had orange carpets and olive green appliances. If all the neighborhoods met the requirements of the TND ordinance—theoretically resulting in a residentially perfect city—would it become a cliché? Would we see buyers start to demand something else just to be different? Is some of the attraction of form-based places the fact that they contrast with what is around them? The jury is still out as to whether form-based zoning is more or less time bound than other forms of zoning.

In addition, the benefits of lightening up on use control are offset in part by the fact that some uses really do matter. Bookstores are different than bars. Mainstream cinemas have different impacts than adult film arcades. What the form-basers really mean (I think) is that many forms of retail, commercial, and (at least) light industrial uses can be substituted for one another with few, if any, adverse land use impacts on surrounding areas. And there is no inherent reason why most commercial, institutional, and residential uses *need* to be separated, as long as the scale of the uses is compatible. Some may want them to be separated and others may want them together, but there is no reason why the government *has* to separate them. At a minimum, the mixing of those uses should be allowed in some places, and perhaps even be required in others, because of some secondary public benefits (e.g., less traffic).

Finally, the strength of focusing on building forms may be offset in part by overfocusing on details. The standard text of the TND ordinance is very prescriptive—it includes much more detailed design requirements than we are used to imposing on private development. Certainly, PUDs have been negotiated to include very detailed standards, but those are "deals" that apply only to the parties that negotiated them. Sometimes we also impose very strict design standards in historic areas, but most people agree that those are special cases; the historical architectural character can be identified in minute detail, and we want new buildings to fit in with that character. But to impose very detailed design standards—minimum as well as maximum heights, requirements for porches, balconies, consistent cornices, consistent window dimensions, and even mandatory locations for public or institutional uses—as general requirements for nonhistoric areas is not common.

In fairness, the TND ordinance is a voluntary tool. It was intended to be used primarily when a landowner buys into the vision of a traditional neighborhood and is willing to subject herself to very strict regulations in order to achieve that vision. It is sort of like a pre-packaged PUD: "If you like the picture, then here are the regulations to make it happen." In contrast, the SmartCode was intended to be adopted either in pieces or for a city as a whole. Its six transects all relate to one another. They use a common vocabulary and similar types of tools. But adopting a new zoning ordinance for a large city is not a consensual act on the part of the landowners. It is done by a city council when they believe that the new tools will promote the public good better than the old tools, even though a significant number of landowners may disagree. In this case, the relatively strict form regulations would be applied not voluntarily but over the objections of at least some of the landowners.

The Result: Euclidean Hybrid Zoning

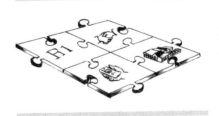

In most cities, the result of these four streams of zoning thought—Euclidean, PUD, performance, and form-based—is a hybrid zoning approach: its roots are clearly in Euclidean zoning, but its branches have grown pretty far from the original idea. The resulting mélange of tools differs by city, but that does not prevent us from sketching the basic outlines of a typical mix. The term *Euclidean* still deserves to be in the name because few, if any, big cities have actually replaced the fundamental idea of coterminous zone districts that collectively cover the developable land area in the city. "Euclidean-ish" zone districts cover the land area the way counties cover all the land in a state. There is no part of Nebraska that is not located within a defined county, and there is generally no land in a city that is not located in a defined zone district.

Most variations suggested by PUDs, performance zoning, and form-based zoning build on this Euclidean foundation, but they do not replace it. PUDs are generally an owner-initiated alternative to standard zones, and they appear on the zoning map the way cities appear on a state map; they cover discrete areas of land but not all of the land. The areas between PUDs are still generally subject to Euclidean zoning. To be sure, a few cities (generally small ones) have said: "Everyone has to do a PUD—we negotiate everything." But those are few and far between. Usually, the city allows some uses and densities without negotiation, and that is good practice.

Although performance zoning could in theory replace Euclidean zoning, that is rarely seen. More often, performance measures are "injected" into the text of the zoning ordinance rather than seen on a map. The map may still say this is a light industrial or mixed-use zone, but if you read the text of that chapter you find that some topics that could have been addressed by physical parameters (heights, set-backs, or even parking) are now governed by performance measures.

There are exceptions, but they are notable in part because of their instability. Fort Collins, Colorado, developed a Land Development Guidance System (LDGS) that won both national and state awards for implementing a "do (almost) anything (almost) anywhere as long as you mitigate the impacts" approach. But the LDGS was eventually repealed because the pendulum of city politics swung away from flexibility toward predictability. Some neighbors did not want to know only that the new development next door would have no adverse impacts; they also wanted to know that it would be houses instead of shops. The demise of the LDGS experiment helps prove the point that Euclidean zoning is hard to replace. There may be parts of the city where performance zoning is appropriate, but in and around stable middle- and high-income neighborhoods, there will still be a demand for zones that produce more predictable development.

Form-based tools are still in their adolescence, but I believe that in the end they are likely to supplement rather than replace Euclidean zoning. Although form-based ordinances are often being used as optional alternatives to Euclidean zoning or as mandatory replacements in only limited areas of the city, they leave much of the Euclidean framework in place around them. This is not to diminish the accomplishments of form-based zoners, because their influence on zoning has been very positive. It has encouraged us to avoid overfocusing on specific land uses, reinforced the importance of good design in general, and led planners and citizens to rethink what makes a great city. But form-based zoning will not completely replace Euclidean zoning for two reasons.

First, most form-based tools do not address the full range of issues that need to be addressed in zoning. Form-based zones focus on building form, streetscape, and land uses. But they often ignore matters like minor or accessory structures (fences, swimming pools, satellite dishes, telecommunications antennae), procedures (how to get an approval), nonconformities (how properties that don't meet the rules are treated), variances (what happens when you want to build something new that doesn't meet the form rules), enforcement, or definitions. If you are yawning now, you are in good company. Those topics represent the unsexy side of zoning, but they need to be addressed. In addition, some form-based tools don't address more significant issues like environmental protection (at least storm drainage and runoff), sustainability, and parking. Despite claims that form-based zoning can replace Euclidean zoning, I believe it is really designed to replace the building design and land use aspects of particular zones and not the whole structure. That is why, to date, form-based zones generally show up as islands surrounded by non-form-based zones.

The second reason is that not every "place" (with a lowercase *p*) is a "Place" (with a capital *P*). More specifically, not every "place" in the city is so important to the public health, safety, and welfare that the city wants to spend taxpayer money to create detailed form-based controls that will make the area a memorable "Place." The fun part of physical planning is helping to design a memorable, notable, beautiful "Place"—a neighborhood, a park, a transit-oriented development, or a mixed-use building—that may actually get built. Maybe you'll even win an award for it! "Place" makers tend to focus on some of the major elements of urban design highlighted by Kevin Lynch in his landmark book, *The Image of the City*: paths, edges, districts, nodes, and landmarks. Those are the kinds of areas that citizens see or visit often and that they can see in their mind's eye when they are somewhere else—locations where good urban design is particularly important because it contributes to the image of the city and to citizens' ability to understand and enjoy it. When these important locations are attractive, the public fights to preserve them; when they are rundown, the public wants them restored.

But in between those important "Places" are lots of other "places" that don't leave images in the public mind—back streets, middle-of-the-block locations in stable neighborhoods, warehouse zones, bus parking lots, heavier commercial areas, and areas in transition from one use to another. These are places that most citizens don't see or visit very often or where the neighborhood's primary goal is just to have everything "fit in" with its neighbors. They are important to those who live and work there, but not to the image of the city as a whole. Could a good urban designer make these "places" into "Places"? Absolutely, and it happens regularly. But does the government require that all the "places" become "Places"? Not usually. Or, rather, it assumes that compliance with basic heights, setbacks, parking, and landscaping requirements will create an acceptable public image, given the importance of the location.

In addition, carefully designed "Places" happen only when a private or public landowner spends the money to build them. At any one time, only a small fraction of the property owners in a mature city are actively planning for redevelopment or willing to spend money on it. The rest of the property owners are happy with what they have or are only vaguely thinking of change sometime in the future.

Another way to state this is that many landowners do not want to create a "Place" on their property, and I don't think that city councils are going to force them to. Some form-based zoners have complained that existing zoning uses difficult-to-understand text rather than easy-to-understand drawings to show what types of development the city wants to see, and that if more drawings were used most landowners would understand the form preferred by the city and would be happy to develop their property that way. I think that argument is logically flawed. While zoning ordinances clearly need drawings to illustrate building controls and incentives better than words alone, not all landowners wake up wanting to make the city government happy. Many property owners wake up wanting to build what *they* want to build. They don't walk in to the planning department asking, "What does the city want me to build?" Rather, they walk in asking, "What am I legally permitted to build?" I think that is unlikely to change. In light of this reality, city councils will continue to limit strict form and design controls to more visible and important locations.

This is heresy to some urban designers, I know, but I think it is true. Cities will continue to have to draft and administer zoning ordinances that treat most aspects of land regulation as urban management tools rather than design tools, simply because there is not enough time, money, or political support to treat every

part of the city as a separate "Place" worthy of more detailed form and design controls. So, while I would like to see form-based tools flourish and I welcome their
integration into the zoning toolbox, I don't think they will replace other forms of
zoning throughout our cities.

Now that we have reviewed how Euclidean hybrid zoning got to be the way it
is, let's look at how well it is doing its job. The next three chapters review how zoning matches some basic assumptions about how it should work, how it responds
to new forces driving land development, and how well it promotes sensible governance of our cities.

CHAPTER 2

Failed Assumptions

A Few General Rules Will Do It

EUCLIDEAN HYBRID ZONING is grounded in assumptions about how cities ought to be and how land use regulation should work. These assumptions are the foundation underneath the zoning structure we have cobbled together over the years. If the foundation was laid in the wrong place, then it is not surprising that the building does not look like we thought it would. And if the foundation was right for its time but has now become obsolete, then the building itself may be obsolete. I think that many of the assumptions behind zoning do not stand up to scrutiny.

The need to question assumptions was graphically illustrated in David Sobel's book *Longitude*, which describes the search for a way for sailors to tell where they were east-to-west on the face of the earth. Mariners had long known to determine latitude by looking at the stars—they looked different at night depending on how far north or south you were. So the great minds of the day were fairly sure that longitude could also be determined by looking at the stars. Their search took them deeper and deeper into a morass of calculations. But each apparent solution had exceptions that required a different calculation. And then some of the special calculations themselves had internal problems that required special-special

39

calculations. This pattern of solutions-upon-solutions reminds me a little of the evolution of zoning through Euclid, PUD, performance, and form-based approaches. In the end, the problem of longitude was solved not by the stars but by time. In an era when clocks were rudimentary and watches were unknown, the solution was to find a way that sailors could always know what time it was in London, check the local time from the sun, and calculate the difference. Only by questioning the assumptions could a better solution be found.

So let's look at some of the assumptions underlying early zoning. This chapter and the two that follow it contain three different critiques of the current zoning system, but they do not provide answers. The answers come later, in chapters 7 and 8. But just to keep you interested, these chapters provide a few hints about what the critiques mean to the future of zoning and the general directions where we might look for solutions.

The first mistaken assumption of early Euclidean zoning was that it would be easy—that only a few simple rules would be needed. This assumption turned out to be wrong for both technical and political reasons. Technically, the Euclidean model was overly simplistic. Dividing future city development into just residential, commercial, and industrial areas did not match existing development patterns in even the most livable cities and turned out to be a poor model for future development. Ironically, the very simplicity that made the model flawed may have helped build public support for the adoption of early zoning ordinances, because they didn't seem that complicated. At the time, the mixed-up pattern of urban land use was seen as a historical mistake that needed to be solved. Now, with the benefit of hindsight, we can see that some mixed use is natural and healthy. Seeing land use "messiness" as the basic problem led to the assumption that it could be solved through simple tools.

Evidence that urban land could not be regulated by a few simple rules also came from the political arena. Both citizens and real estate interests started asking for "a zone like X, but a little different," which led to large numbers of zone districts and overlay zones (see chapter 1). Following World War II, these were supplemented by an increasing number of development standards, including design controls, historic preservation standards, and environmental requirements, each of which could be combined with zones and overlay zones in different combinations. The primary color palette of residential, commercial, and industrial zone districts gave way to a virtual Rubik's Cube of regulation. In 2003, the Denver zoning staff created a poster illustrating the vast number of combinations of land uses, districts, standards, and conditions in the zoning ordinance—all 24,000 of them. The resulting chart was 32 feet long.[1]

It turns out that regulating land development, particularly in cities, requires either a detailed set of rules or a very flexible set of rules. We tried both. Basic Euclidean zoning became more detailed, while performance zoning and PUDs tried to insert flexibility. Form-based zoning had elements of both, with its more detailed approaches to building form and its simpler approaches to uses. But in spite of these attempts, most citizens do not find zoning easy to understand.

The bad news is that zoning probably cannot be very simple in a medium or large city. Real estate development and redevelopment create many impacts on neighboring properties, the city as a whole, and the environment, and many of them really do need to be addressed. But the good news is that some parts of zoning can be simplified. It doesn't have to be as complicated as it has become in many cities. The major point for now is that we have been trying to rebuild a fairly complex structure on top of a very simple foundation ever since zoning was young. Regulating land in mature cities sometimes requires simpler rules in places where the foundation is strong enough to support more, and sometimes requires more detailed regulations where the authors of the Standard Acts did not bother to lay much of a foundation at all. That mismatch needs to be fixed.

Hint for the future: Hoping that zoning can be simple gains us nothing and flies in the face of ninety years of experience. But we do need to separate those tools that are necessary to manage cities from those that have accreted over the years to solve one-off problems or satisfy narrow constituencies. We need to be diligent about removing complexity in areas where it doesn't clearly result in better cities.

Separate the Uses

Because the sins that zoning was originally designed to cure related to uses—that is, industry located near homes—the Standard Zoning Enabling Act focused on designating and separating land uses 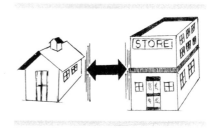 as the crux of zoning. The maximum heights and minimum setbacks were concepts carried over from the Old and New Tenement Laws. What was new about zoning was the separation of uses.

The same forces that led to a proliferation of zone districts also led us to continual refinement of the lists of permitted uses into ever-more-detailed categories. This happened for several reasons, more than one of which may have operated at different times within a single city. First, the zoning administrator may have wanted a system with "zero discretion," that is, a system where one name exists for every possible use of land and there are no gaps between the defined edges of those named uses. This creates sort of a "cubbyhole system," where staff mentally place each use in one and only one imaginary zoning cubbyhole. Sometimes the desire for a cubbyhole system is driven by the personality of the administrator—he or she is an order freak. Other times, it is driven by the quality of zoning staff or the personnel rules of the city. Zoning administrators sometimes tell me that they need a zero discretion system because they have no way to rate the performance of their staff unless each question has only one right answer. When that happens, the zoning ordinance is being asked to make up for the sins of the city's personnel system, and the quality of the city will suffer.

While you might think that the creation of more and more narrowly defined cubbyholes would make zoning easier to administer, that is not true for at least three reasons. First, zoning is intended to control the land use impacts of each property on surrounding properties and on the city as a whole. If two or more listed land uses have the same or very similar land use impacts, then there may be no reason for zoning to treat them differently. Cubbyhole systems are prone to this—treating similar land uses as if they were different, while treating uses with very different impacts as if they were the same.

In many cases, it is the scale of the use, rather than its name, that determines its external impacts. There is all the difference in the world between a 15,000-square-foot neighborhood hardware store and a 150,000-square-foot True Value Home Center, but many zoning ordinances still list them both as "hardware store" or "home supply store." To treat them differently, you can either come up with two different names, or you can regulate the scale of the use within a single name. This is one area where form-based zoning is clearly right. The scale of the activity matters—it *really* matters—and Euclidean hybrid zoning sometimes doesn't address scale very well. Focusing on scale also allows planners to better match land uses to available transportation capacity, since smaller-scale stores generally do not become major retail destinations that can quickly overwhelm available road capacity.

The second reason that cubbyhole systems fail is that the world changes too fast for them. Zoning administrators who think they can create new land use names as fast as the real estate market can think up new products are fooling themselves. I worked in one large city where the zoning ordinance was amended almost monthly to add new permitted uses, most of which had land use impacts very similar to existing listed uses. Is this really how staff should be spending their time? Constantly amending the use list to wring all the need for judgments out of the system? I think not. The goal should be for a system with limited discretion guided by clear criteria, so that mistakes can be corrected on appeal. We expect police officers, judges, teachers, and even utility workers to use their judgment, and we should expect the same from planners.

The third strike against cubbyhole systems is a technical one. (Readers who do not live and breathe zoning might want to skip this or else risk falling asleep.) In Euclidean hybrid zoning, each property has a primary use, but it may also have accessory uses that are "secondary and incidental" to the primary use. For example, a hotel may have a restaurant, but the restaurant is accessory to the hotel. If the zone district does not allow restaurants as primary uses, then the restaurant is legal only if it is part of the hotel. The same goes for a Ford dealership that sells auto parts and services cars. In some zone districts, neither a freestanding repair shop nor an auto parts store would be allowed, but parts can be sold and cars serviced if those activities are incidental to the selling of cars.

As the number of cubbyhole uses multiplies, questions about which is the primary use also multiply. What about a building that contains several offices, some jewelry craftsmen, some jewelry sellers, a restaurant on the ground floor, and a for-profit parking garage not restricted to building tenants? What is the primary use? Are all but one of the uses accessory to that one? If the area devoted to for-profit parking has the biggest square footage, does that make it the primary use? Can you have multiple accessory uses to a single primary use? Can you have an accessory use to another accessory use? How many layers deep can that go? Who cares? The more narrowly you define each use, the more these arguably unimportant questions proliferate—and the more time planning staff members spend sorting them out, even though it makes little difference in terms of land use impacts or the quality of the city. We can solve the problem by allowing multiple primary uses, but most cities limit that solution to the downtown core even though the problems created by "cubbyhole" uses occur throughout the city.

A second reason why the list of land uses proliferates is political deal making.

For example, a veterinarian wants to open up a clinic in a small-scale neighborhood business zone but that is not a permitted use. The question has not come up before, and the city decides that it did not really intend to keep veterinarians out of neighborhood commercial areas. They are, after all, a neighborhood service. The city proposes an amendment to add "veterinarian" as a permitted use. The neighbors object and will support the zoning text change only if it is limited to a 5,000-square-foot facility. "Done," says the city. Now the ordinance has "veterinarian" and "veterinarian, under 5,000 sq. ft." in the list of permitted uses. But the following year, when the scenario plays out again across town, a different set of neighbors insists that there not be any animals on the premises at night. That eliminates the risk of barking for the houses across the alley. "Done," says the city. Now we have "veterinarian, under 5,000 sq. ft., no overnight boarding" in the list. Next, someone wants a big facility and the neighbors are afraid of the noise and smell of the outdoor dog run, so "veterinarian, no outdoor enclosures" is added.

This may seem humorous, but it really happens this way. Council members have an incentive to find deals that keep as many voters as possible as happy as possible. The planning director and city attorney may know that the zoning ordinance is getting gummed up, but on any given city council night the need to find a deal outweighs the long-term interest in simplicity and good governance.

Note that this example of land use proliferation came from neighbors' attempts to control perceived impacts of proposed uses. Impacts are what zoning should be about, but controlling them doesn't necessarily require more listed uses. Instead, zoning should incorporate clear standards on how uses can be operated (not just how they are built) and then enforce them. This is a much better solution than proliferating uses to indirectly address possible impacts that may not happen. In this case, it is the performance zoners who were right. Operating standards should apply not only to industrial areas but also to mixed-use and residential areas, and using them gives property owners an incentive to find better ways to operate activities so that they do not produce impacts on their neighbors.

History shows that although separation of some uses is necessary, separation of others is not. In fact, it is sometimes harmful. Many politically inspired use definitions do not stand the test of time; they soon create more land use problems than they solve, because the zoning ordinance starts treating very similar uses as if they are really different. The logic seems to go something like this: Zoning distinguishes uses so that we can separate them to avoid unwanted impacts. We're having some unwanted impacts, so we must have gotten the use list wrong. Let's go back and slice it thinner and then separate those new uses.

There is some irony in the current efforts to design and refine "mixed-use" districts, because it was only zoning that separated them in the first place. Performance zoning advocates came near to identifying this weakness when they questioned whether we should be focusing on lot sizes and setbacks to separate uses instead of focusing on the actual impacts themselves. But only the most aggressive proponents of performance zoning extended the logic to the uses themselves. Few performance zoners went so far as to ask, "What's in a use name as long as the impacts are the same?"

More recently, form-based zoners have made the critique of use distinctions a centerpiece of their argument, and they are more than partially right. We really have gone too far down the road of use- and separation-based zoning. And once uses are separated, they tend to stay that way—Euclidean zoning has a tendency to become a one-way ratchet in which new uses are added but old uses are seldom removed or combined. Just because some land uses once needed to be separated does not mean they need to be separated today.

Hint for the future: Although use does matter and the future of zoning will include significant use controls, the assumption that zoning is fundamentally about uses needs to be reexamined and rebalanced against actual impacts. Many of the fine-grained distinctions currently found in our ordinances really don't matter to those around them. We need to be diligent about eliminating those kinds of distinctions.

Greenfield Standards Are Better

One of the most flawed assumptions inherent in many zoning ordinances is that a single set of development standards can apply in both old and new areas of the city. Of course, the zone districts themselves could be different; we may apply a residential district allowing 5,000-square-foot lots in older areas and a different residential district requiring 12,000-square-foot lots on the suburban edge. But aside from basic lot and building dimensions, most zoning ordinances still require that both homes provide at least two off-street parking spaces. Landscaping, lighting, fencing, buffering, and sign standards also often fail to differentiate between newer and older areas.

Recall that these types of development standards were later additions on top of the district-based foundation of Euclidean zoning. They were different because they varied by land use (parking, for example) or based on some other factor (signs often varied based on the amount of lot frontage), and they were assumed *not* to vary by district. But in many cases, they *should* vary by district, or at least between older and newer areas of the city. To simplify this discussion, I use the term *greenfield* to refer to undeveloped sites and the term *mature* to refer to previously developed sites (even if they are currently vacant). I use the term *development standards* to refer to most zoning requirements other than those addressing permitted land uses, the density or intensity of development, and the procedures for getting approvals or variances.

Where development standards are allowed to differ between mature areas and greenfield sites, those for mature areas are usually couched in terms of exceptions to the greenfield standards. For example, Nashville's zoning ordinance requires two off-street parking spaces for each single-family home and then provides that the standard can be adjusted downward if the lot is within a quarter mile of a bus line, or if there is a public parking lot nearby, or if on-street parking is allowed in that part of the city.[2] San Diego's zoning ordinance states that where two off-street parking spaces are required, they cannot be designed in a "tandem" layout (i.e., one behind the other, so that one car has to be moved before the other can get out) but then adopts an overlay zone within which an exception is made and tandem parking is allowed under certain conditions. Implicitly, the basic standards have become the greenfield standards, with mature areas treated as exceptions to the way the world should be.

This is not too surprising, because planners often spend a lot of time working with raw land subdividers and developers laying out new residential areas on the edges of the city. Those new neighborhoods require lots of up-front planning to design systems of drainage, infrastructure, traffic circulation, and open space networks—systems that have already been established in mature areas. But then the process goes awry. After all that hard work developing standards for edge development, a proud city council says, "These are great! Why don't we just apply them in the other neighborhoods, too? Level playing field and all that." I've seen it happen. This is usually a very poor idea because the vast majority of any city's buildings have already been built and are subject (for better or worse) to the existing patterns of lots, streets, infrastructure, drainage, and open space. Standards that work well when the land is a blank slate often do not work well when it is already colored in—and the existing pattern of building may reflect exactly the character that the city and the neighbors want to encourage in older areas.

The same problem comes up in the world of building codes. For years, building officials have known that very old structures often cannot be made to meet building codes designed for new buildings. Those who insist on a single building code for old and new buildings claim that the new building standards are the minimum necessary to protect human life and property, but in fact the standard is set somewhere above those minimums. When judgment calls are made—especially when "human life is at stake"—professionals tend to get cautious, and the combined effect of several conservative judgments can be a standard that significantly exceeds what is really required. Demanding that old buildings meet new building codes is in effect saying that people are safe only in new buildings, when we know that is not the case. Unfortunately, this was the position of many cities for many years, and it led to the destruction of some old buildings and to delays of the very reinvestment that could keep others functional.

As a result, building officials have developed both an International Building Code (IBC) and an International Existing Building Code (IEBC). The IEBC has been developed so that existing buildings are required to be safe but are not required to be built to the same standards as new buildings. One IEBC guiding principle is that the effort required to meet the standards should not be disproportionate to the level of reinvestment being made. Minor investment in the building will not trigger the need for expensive, unrelated improvements to meet new building standards. If the building is undergoing a total renovation "down to the studs," then the building standards may be much closer to those required for new buildings.

In recent years, thanks in part to the efforts of historic preservationists and those who promote the IEBC, more and more states and cities have adopted separate building codes for older buildings. The states of California, Wisconsin, Rhode Island, New Jersey, and Maryland, and the cities of Wichita and Denver, among many others, have adopted legislation allowing different rules to apply. The rationale for this change is that meeting those standards that can reasonably be met in older structures is better for the city than insisting that the old building be replaced with a new one or delaying building investments due to the high costs of meeting the new building code. This is an eminently sensible trade-off, and a similar approach is needed in zoning.

Assuming that greenfield standards are the right ones implies that failing to meet those standards is a problem that needs solving. This creates a built-in disadvantage to the very redevelopment of older areas that most planners and citizens want to see. Instead of going by a standard that reflects the (often attractive) scale and pattern of the older area, the redeveloper often needs to find an exception—or many exceptions—to the greenfield standards.

Hint for the future: Zoning development standards need to pay more attention to what actually works in existing developed areas. When large areas of mature neighborhoods are redeveloped, it may be reasonable to impose some of the greenfield standards. But for small-scale redevelopment and individual building replacement, the benchmark should be the built fabric of the surrounding neighborhood. More importantly, land use regulation in mature areas should be treated as primarily a land management issue instead of a land design issue.

Variances Will Be Rare

VARIANCES

In addition to thinking that zoning could be based on a few general rules, zoning drafters assumed that exceptions to the rules would be infrequent. The traditional procedure for getting an exception—a hearing before a board of adjustment—is fairly labor-intensive for minor variances, but it was assumed that the effort would not have to be made very often. Tell that to a member of the board of adjustment in any medium or large city, and she will laugh.

In practice, most large cities see a constant stream of requests to vary the rules. Between 1984 and 1987, the City of Boston received requests for variances at the rate of almost six hundred annually—an average of almost two each day.[3] Until recently, the City of Winnipeg, Manitoba, was receiving more than one thousand requests for variances each year—an average of three a day. To its credit, the city is now revising the zoning bylaw to reduce the number of variances. In many cities, each request for a variance requires submitting an application form, sometimes posting a sign on the property or mailing a notice to the neighbors, and preparing a staff report, all in addition to the board of adjustment hearing itself. Advocates of both performance zoning and PUDs thought those tools would help reduce the need for variances, and they probably have, but the volume remains high in many cities.

The number of variance requests is also related to mistaken assumption number three. If a city's development standards implicitly reflect greenfield ideals, then it should come as no surprise that redevelopment and reinvestment in mature areas may require exceptions. The two are closely related.

Two of the most common variance requests are for exceptions to minimum setbacks and minimum parking requirements. Most economically healthy cities are blessed with families that want to invest in their homes, and growing families are often faced with a decision as to whether to expand their existing home or buy a different one. Many families' first choice is to expand their existing home, which regularly leads to requests to build a few feet closer to a boundary line or a few feet taller than the ordinance allows. In addition, stable older neighborhoods often have storefronts and other commercial buildings originally designed without off-street parking—buildings that could be redeveloped into small stores. If the zoning ordinance requires that all commercial uses provide off-street parking at greenfield rates, then a request for a variance is almost guaranteed. The alternative to parking exceptions is destroying neighboring buildings to provide more parking, which the neighborhood often finds more offensive than a parking variance.

Hint for the future: Requests for variances from zoning rules represent a big part of zoning life and are one of the most prominent threads running through zoning history. They reflect the continued search for "flexibility" that Euclidean zoning has not satisfied. Future zoning should either allow for a minor degree of variation by right or adjust those regulations that are giving rise to the most variances (or both).

Nonconformities Will Go Away

A fifth assumption behind Euclidean hybrid zoning is that nonconformities will go away over time. By "nonconformities," I mean lots, buildings, uses, parking areas, and signs that do not meet the requirements of the ordinance. Euclidean hybrid zoning assumes that redevelopment will replace obsolete places and structures with ones that meet the zoning requirements within some reasonable period of time. To help "push" them out, nonconforming uses and structures are not allowed to expand and substandard lots are sometimes not allowed to be developed at all. Cities differ in how strictly they enforce these requirements, which can get very technical. If a wall is already too close to the lot line, is it an "expansion" of the structure to extend it horizontally? How about vertically? Can a nonconforming use expand within a conforming building? What if no one can tell from outside? What if it doesn't generate any more traffic or parking needs? There are almost as many different answers as there are cities.

The assumption that nonconformities will disappear is not completely mistaken, because it does sometimes happen. Sometimes property values justify the redevelopment of nonconforming commercial areas for the housing uses that are supposed to be there, or vice versa. Sometimes an urban renewal agency steps in and replaces the old with the new. But each time a greenfield development standard is adopted for general use throughout the city, the number of nonconformities tends to increase, unless the drafters are very careful. So it is not clear that the overall number of nonconformities is decreasing over time or that the most serious ones are going away.

When Hurricane Katrina devastated the Gulf Coast in August 2005, it left behind tens of thousands of houses that needed to be rebuilt or replaced. Obviously, houses in areas now known to be flood prone involved public health and safety issues, but there were also many older houses on smaller lots that were outside of floodplains. Many of those older houses did not meet the required setbacks in their zoning districts. Gulfport, Mississippi, had a clause in its zoning ordinance that explicitly allowed the rebuilding of structures following a natural disaster, so although homeowners had a myriad of financial and insurance problems to sort through, getting a zoning variance to rebuild was not one of them. Down the road in Biloxi, the ordinance did not have a natural disaster clause, and the mayor and city council members debated whether to adopt one.[4] In New Orleans itself, Mayor Tom Nagin used his posthurricane emergency powers to suspend parts of the zoning ordinance. The point is that cities sometimes decide that zoning nonconformities do not have to go away. When eliminating nonconformities will inconvenience large numbers of people, cities can get pretty creative to avoid that result.

Why do we care about nonconformities in the first place? The first, and less important, reason is that Euclidean hybrid zoning ordinances say that if a property is damaged to the point where repairs will cost more than 50 percent (or 67 or 75 percent) of its value, then it cannot be rebuilt without bringing it into compliance with the new standards. But what if the entire value of the structure is tied up with the feature that makes it nonconforming? What if the popular restaurant was developed before parking standards were adopted, and it is then damaged by fire, but requiring it to be rebuilt in compliance with standard with greenfield parking standards would reduce the restaurant itself to a size that is not viable? Banks might hesitate to make the loan required to rebuild it.

Obviously, when public health and safety are concerned, replacement structures should not be allowed to re-create those problems. A popular riverfront restaurant originally built in the floodplain should not be allowed to rebuild there. But there are many cases where damaged structures are not allowed to rebuild even though it would not endanger the health or safety of the occupants or the public. Remember the example of nonconforming buildings in Gulfport and Biloxi? Sometimes, rebuilding nonconforming structures is exactly what the city wants to do. But serious damage and destruction of properties is pretty rare, so this nonconformity issue does not arise very often.

The second, and more important, reason we care about nonconformities is that the current rules create barriers to reinvestment. When property owners go to their banks to get loans to update, expand, or redevelop their buildings, the bank application often asks, "Is the property in compliance with the zoning ordinance?" Loan officers use this as a basic screening device to reduce lending risk. If the property is in compliance with zoning, then there is less risk that it will be shut down for a violation, which might interrupt the stream of loan repayments. This has been a particular problem with residential uses in industrial areas.

Even now—ninety years after zoning began—we have areas where industry and homes were developed in an odd mishmash before cities were incorporated or zoning was adopted. When a city now determines that the predominant character of an area is industrial, it zones the area for industrial uses. Existing homes are allowed to continue, but new homes cannot be built and old ones cannot be expanded in the now-zoned-industrial area. When homeowners go to the bank to get a housing loan to remodel the basement or to install a new furnace, the bank checks with the city and learns that residential is a nonconforming use in an industrial zone. The lending officer then thinks: "This could be a problem. Maybe the city might decide to make them leave some day, or maybe they will have trouble finding a buyer if they decide to sell before the loan is repaid. Safer to deny the loan." In fact, under the law of nonconformity, the owner could sell the property and the new buyer could use the property the same way. Legal nonconformities are not personal; they run with the property. But the bank is right on one point: a potential buyer who wanted to expand the property or change its use to another nonconforming use might be scared off, which could increase the lending risk.

The rules against expansion and reinvestment for nonconformities create several quirky situations that provide good cocktail conversation for planners. (Again, nonplanners may want to sleep through this discussion.) The first situation is when the building on a lot is perfectly legal (not too tall, not too close to the boundaries) but part of the building is occupied by a use that is no longer permitted in that zone and the rest is either vacant or occupied by a legal use. This is the "legal structure/nonconforming use" problem. Under the one-size-fits-all nonconformity theory of Euclidean hybrid zoning, even if the nonconforming use is successful, it cannot expand within the envelope of the legal building even if the rest of the building is vacant or the other legal uses leave the building. Why? Because that would be "expansion of a nonconforming use," and the law has a bias against that. Nonconforming uses are on a sort of zoning parole, and this would violate the terms of their parole.

The second situation is where the use is perfectly legal (say, a residential use in a residential zone) but the structure violates the zoning ordinance (it's too tall or too wide for the site; maybe it's a prezoning carriage house apartment). Under Euclidean hybrid zoning, the owner of the conforming house next door has a right to go to the board of adjustment and say: "I need to add a mud room at the back of my house, but it will violate my rear setback. My neighbors don't care, and here's why it would be a hardship to deny me." The board of adjustment can then decide to approve or deny the request. But if the owner of the nonconforming house next door has the same request, he cannot go to the board of adjustment for the same mudroom variance because his building is already nonconforming. Worse, he cannot even add the mudroom if it *would not* violate the rear setback (i.e., he has more setback than he needs and he wants to use some of it for a mudroom). Why? Because it would be "expanding a nonconforming structure," and that is a no-no.

Situation three is where the use and structure are perfectly legal but the sign outside is not. The sign was built before zoning required signs to be shorter or smaller or farther from the road. Does the rule against expansion of a nonconforming use or structure mean that the building cannot be expanded (even within the applicable setbacks) because of the sign? Or that the use cannot expand to vacant areas of the building because of the sign?

Some cities have addressed this issue through exceptions. Some ordinances say: "Thou shalt not expand a nonconforming structure in a way that increases its specific nonconformity." That way, if it is the side setback that violates the ordinance, an addition to the rear might be all right, because it does not make the illegal part of the building *more* illegal (it does not make the illegal side setback worse). This type of fix also addresses situation three—an illegal sign on an otherwise conforming property would not prevent an expansion unrelated to the sign.

But the nuances continue. What if the house has a wall 30 feet long located 4 feet from the property line and the ordinance requires a setback of 5 feet? This is clearly a nonconforming wall. The owner comes forward and says: "In order to put in a mudroom, I want to extend that wall 10 feet farther." Most ordinances say "no go," since a 40-foot-long wall 4 feet off the property line is "more nonconforming" than a 30-foot-long wall 4 feet off the property line. It would increase the nonconforming aspect of the building. Some cities would allow the owner to go to the board of adjustment and ask for a break, but others would not.

Somewhat ironically, adopting new development standards sometimes means that nonconformities stay in place longer, because the owner knows that a replacement structure will cost more or that the new sign will have to be shorter than the existing sign. Rather than come into compliance, it makes more financial sense for the owner to keep the old structure and sign in place. The money that would otherwise have gone to build a new building is then spent on making the existing (nonconforming) building last longer, which undermines the assumption that nonconformities will go away. When Denver adopted a 400-foot height limit on the edge of its downtown area, there was already a 500-foot building in place. Because of the enormous revenue generated by the top floors of a skyscraper, the building's owners and lenders vowed to oppose the height limit unless that particular building was allowed to rebuild regardless of how badly it might be damaged in the future. So an exception was made, and that is one very large and visible nonconformity that will not go away in the foreseeable future.

Those who drafted early zoning ordinances probably realized that these tensions existed and that some forces would tend to keep nonconformities in place. But they probably did not foresee that ninety years later some of the original nonconforming structures not only would remain but would now be valued. History shows that many nonconformities do not disappear quickly, and the creation of additional nonconformities through new zoning amendments means that a fair part of the urban fabric may be nonconforming at any one time.

Why is there such a mismatch between the assumption (nonconformities should and will go away) and the reality (actually, we don't mind if they stay)? One reason is that nonconformities tend to be concentrated in older areas of the city. By definition, they were developed before the ordinances that made them illegal. Variance laws usually require that the owner demonstrate a hardship that is unique to the property and not caused by the owner, and older properties are often able to meet these standards. Having uses and structures that are older than some of their competitors in outlying areas, they may be able to show economic hardship. In addition, older areas often have platted lots that are "unique" because they were laid out before modern subdivision ordinances regulated the shapes, sizes, and grades of each parcel. City council members are often sympathetic to property owners in older areas and may make it clear to their appointees on the board of adjustment that they do not really want to force nonconformities to shut down. Like Nashville and Denver, some cities have formally changed some of their rules to acknowledge the legality of substandard lots and the ability to rebuild damaged structures.

I believe that the mismatch between the assumption and the reality of nonconformities is a fundamental indicator that Euclidean hybrid zoning is broken. Many politicians, planners, and citizens do not want nonconforming structures and uses to be forced out, and they are willing to be flexible to allow them to remain and even expand as long as the impacts to their immediate neighbors are not too serious. This is particularly true when jobs are involved. What planners and politicians really intend is that new standards apply to new greenfield development, and maybe to large-scale redevelopment of older areas, but not to zoning decisions involving individual older properties, especially when compliance with the standard would put them out of step with their neighbors or result in loss of jobs. By accepting the fact that many nonconformities are minor and that nonconformities often remain in place for decades, and by finding a legal status for these situations that does not discourage lending for reinvestment, cities could help support the sustainability of mature neighborhoods.

Hint for the future: Zoning should lighten up on nonconformities in older areas. Most investments in mature areas involve piecemeal, not wholesale, redevelopment, and regulations need to address the predominance of incremental changes in an established pattern of urban development. Where impacts are small, the rules should be flexible. Zoning may want to encourage some types of non-conformities to leave, while ignoring others.

Zoning Rules Need to Be Static

A sixth assumption was that zoning could be "static"—that once the city had adopted its picture of the future (i.e., its plan), zoning could be made to match that picture and would guide future development to achieve it. But the time and effort needed to update zoning to match each new plan are substantial. Even a neighborhood plan can take two years to draft and adopt, and comprehensive plans can take longer. After the plans are adopted, it often takes another two or three years to complete the serious negotiations required to make zoning reflect the plan picture. The significant effort needed to prepare plans and zoning amendments means that many cities revise them infrequently—and in the case of zoning, *very* infrequently. If you think debating the plan stirred up controversy, watch what happens when you try to change the zoning. In those states where there is no legal requirement to do so, the theory that zoning should match the plan is honored more in the breach than in the observance.

More importantly, the bigger the plan and the bigger the city, the harder it is to make a picture of the future. Although it may be practical to create a plan that lays out the land uses, densities, building types, street networks, and open spaces for a neighborhood, most larger cities find that it is impossible to do that on a city-wide basis. There is just too much land to cover, too many unknowns, too many details, and too many existing knots in the urban fabric. So the city decides that the plan will be simply the citywide strategic plan (and maybe the transportation plan) plus any approved neighborhood-specific physical plans. But most large cities have neighborhoods for which physical plans are either missing or obsolete. Medium or large cities whose comprehensive plans paint a complete picture of future physical development are rare indeed.

In addition, cities sometimes need to be opportunistic about economic development. Over the past decades, scores of large U.S. cities have built new professional sports stadiums or expanded existing ones. Although keeping sports franchises and tourists downtown is a high priority for many cities, the size and scale of these new facilities create problems. They often disrupt the downtown fabric, require the closing of streets, and involve complex negotiations with many small, longtime downtown property owners. The site that is eventually chosen is often not the city's first choice but the one that turned out to be politically least painful or that the owner of the sports franchise wanted. Planners can complain that this is poor planning, but for big facilities (stadiums, regional malls, convention centers, and transit centers), plans are often interpreted flexibly, or changed, or just ignored.

The need to remain flexible and respond to big economic generators makes some elected officials reluctant to draw detailed planning pictures of their cities. And if detailed physical plans are adopted, they stand a fair chance of becoming obsolete if economic forces operate in unforeseen ways. What happens if the plan strives to protect residents from the traffic impacts of a large manufacturing complex but the plant then goes bankrupt and shuts down? Or what if an area is zoned for small neighborhood shops rather than a shopping mall, but after eight years of waiting the owner can only get financing for a single big electronics store on the site?

Because competition for both jobs and tax base drives many city governments (see chapter 3), some cities have moved away from physical plans. Many major cities now adopt "policy plans," "strategic plans," "framework plans," or "vision plans" that deliberately avoid painting a physical picture of the future. They do this not only because they want to avoid the difficult political decisions required for detailed physical planning but because they do not want to hear citizens complain, for example, that the location of the proposed stadium is inconsistent with the physical plan. By way of example, the Blueprint Denver citywide land use and transportation plan identifies "areas of stability" and "areas of change" as a way of sending a basic message to the market regarding where reinvestment will be particularly welcome and where neighborhood residents may be willing to accept a greater degree of change. Rather than getting specific about what physical changes are needed, it leaves that to a small area planning process that supplements the citywide plan.

But the more fundamental problem is that even if you manage to get a good snapshot of the future, that picture is static. In contrast, real estate markets are dynamic—very dynamic. For a real estate developer, the view of possible future uses of a parcel of lands is constantly changing. As one property is redeveloped, the possible viable uses of nearby properties can change, sometimes dramatically. The adoption of a mixed-use PUD on the corner of an otherwise residential area makes nearby landowners rethink their options in light of those mixed-use facilities and services. Any system that tries to govern an ever-changing real estate market with fixed rules is going to create tension, which in part explains the high volumes of variance requests in many cities. Implicit in almost all of zoning is the assumption that things should change slowly, but in fact we know that they change remarkably fast. I am not suggesting that zoning should allow whatever the market wants to build—that would destroy the predictability of zoning for the surrounding area—but we need to question whether the rules themselves need to be static in order to be predictable.

For all of these reasons, in many cities, the comprehensive plan no longer paints a physical picture of the city's future. In addition, the mosaic of neighborhood physical plans that is supposed to constitute the physical picture of future development is incomplete or nonexistent. And we know that even if we could draw a picture of the desired future, that picture is likely to change regularly. So how can zoning be designed to achieve the theoretical picture of the future portrayed by all those plans (and missing plans)? The same factors that are leading away from detailed citywide physical planning call for a type of zoning that is equally flexible—or at least functional—in the absence of a detailed physical plan.

This is an important point of this book, so I want to recap it clearly. The theory of planning and zoning assumes that there will be a clear picture of the city's desired future; but in many places that does not exist. The theory says that zoning rules can and should be brought into alignment with some picture of the future, but in fact this happens only partially and sporadically. The theory assumes a level of clarity and an ability to keep zoning current that is simply not there in many large cities.

Hint for the future: Because market forces will continue to push cities to be more flexible in their planning, and because updating zoning ordinances will continue to be technically and politically difficult, we need to think in terms of zoning standards that change automatically, in predictable ways, as plans change and as the real estate market evolves.

Zoning Is a Technical Matter

A seventh assumption was that zoning could be made into a technical exercise. Planning has a technical approach, after all. To make a plan, you start with an inventory of existing conditions, generate projections of population growth and economic activity, identify physical constraints that limit where you can put what, calculate how many acres of residential/commercial/industrial land you will need to meet the projected population and economy, locate those areas to minimize impacts to surrounding areas (or where streets exist or can be built to serve them), figure out where to fit in the public facilities (parks, fire stations, water plants) to serve those people and buildings, and color the map. If zoning were to be equally technical, it would just "freeze" that picture into zoning rules and we would be done. Zoning was originally imagined as a fairly technical process run by professionals.

In part, this technical paradigm of planning and zoning arose out of the municipal reform movement that was in full swing when zoning was young. As an antidote to the inept cronyism of many nineteenth-century city governments, the twentieth-century reformers wanted to pursue "scientific" approaches to urban government that involved the hiring of qualified staff and a system of legal checks and balances. Both planning and zoning looked as if they could be made technical enough to avoid or at least restrain the excesses of politicians. In fact, the authors of the Standard Zoning Enabling Act (see chapter 1) clearly wanted elected officials kept out of planning, so the act called for a planning commission of nonpartisan appointed officials.[5] Those who believed that zoning was to be based on nonpartisan, apolitical plans thought that zoning decisions should be that way too.

In many ways, the technical approach to planning still applies, although it is often watered down. Other countries use models that are even more technical than the U.S. approach. In India and Japan, for example, the required ratios among land uses, public facilities, and transportation facilities are more narrowly defined than the guidelines used by American planners. At international conferences, planners from other countries want to know how many square feet of neighborhood shops American planners require per single-family home, and they can quote me the ratios they are required to use. The same is true for the ratio of homes to small clinics, medium-sized clinics, and hospitals (which makes some sense) and veterinarians (which makes less sense).[6] They are generally surprised and disappointed to find that while we have lots of studies and guidelines, American planners seldom have required ratios for different land uses. One Canadian planner responded to my vague answers about U.S. "norms" for urban land uses by concluding, "So basically, anything goes?"

But the differences between the planning theories used in the United States and in other countries are generally only differences of degree. Our process is less rigid than those in many other developed countries, but more structured than those found in some less developed countries. The bigger difference is between the theory and reality. In the United States, zoning is not a technical exercise; it's a political act. Creating the plan may remain a somewhat technical activity with a fair dose of politics, but zoning is much more closely related to property rights and property values and is very often dominated by politics. Richard Babcock made this point eloquently in his landmark book *The Zoning Game*, and Roger Waldon makes the same point in his book *Planners and Politics*.[7]

In the future, zoning should acknowledge this reality and address it directly. At its best, the politics of zoning makes land use regulation better able to respond to new opportunities—for example, by allowing quick adoption of regulations to keep the city competitive or to prevent environmental damage. But the political dimension of zoning often leads cities to make short-sighted decisions merely to satisfy a narrow constituency—for example, by rezoning poorly located land for commercial uses in a long-shot attempt to lure tax base from neighboring cities.

At its worst, the politics of zoning feeds the "Not in My Back Yard" (NIMBY) syndrome; it allows elected officials to deny a proposed development that substantially meets all applicable standards because of the opposition of immediate neighbors. Sure, they have to find some sort of technical failure to meet the city's standards, and they can usually find one if they look hard enough, but they sometimes deny even without a good reason. When a technical failing is found during political hearings, it is sometimes used as a reason to deny the application; but in the same situation, an administrative reviewer would have allowed the applicant to fix the problem and then allowed the application to move forward.

Hint for the future: Zoning should be designed to address the inherently

political nature of zoning and to include safeguards to limit inappropriately political decision making. Boundaries for political decision making need to be established based on long-term analysis of the results of past practices. We need to better
separate those aspects of zoning that can and should be politically responsive from
those that should be apolitical and administrative.

CHAPTER 3

Evolving Land
Use Drivers

AS SHOWN IN CHAPTER 1, THE HISTORY of U.S. zoning can be described almost without mentioning the forces that drive land use. We have been able to discuss zoning without bringing in how land is bought and sold, how loans for land development are structured, or the different motivations driving landowners, land developers, and builders. That may be part of the problem.

Applications for rezoning or development approval may be filed by owners interested in selling the land, in which case the owner's primary concern may be to obtain zoning that maximizes the value of the land. Or the application may be filed by a land developer who installs utilities and roads in order to resell the land to builders, in which case the applicant's concern may be to minimize restrictions that might discourage potential buyers (which may not be the same as maximizing value). Finally, an application may be filed by a builder whose only concern is that the zoning permit the building she has in mind for the site (which is not the same as maximizing land value or minimizing restrictions on other types of buildings). Failing to recognize the different needs of various actors in the land development process can make zoning unnecessarily rigid at some points in the process and ineffective at others.

The evolution of zoning since 1916 has been largely the story of how we modified a simple model so that it could better respond to some of the forces it was regulating. When the "pure" idea of zoning ran into the realities of how land is transferred, financed, and developed, and the political pressure that accompanies those forces, the pure model had to adjust. But it seems that zoning is always playing "catch up" with those forces. The following paragraphs describe some important forces driving land use today and how they have changed over time. Rather than reacting to each of these forces by constantly inventing new tools to staple onto the existing Euclidean zoning structure, it may be wiser to rethink zoning based on a more honest appraisal of how these forces will affect zoning decisions.

I should clarify, however, that I am not criticizing zoning for "morphing" over the years to reflect and respond to changing land use drivers. In fact, I think it is good that zoning has been able to do that. Changes in zoning reflect the public's strong and continuing desire to use police power to proactively guide development patterns. The only thing worse than having zoning stretched and bent to accommodate the economic and political reality of real estate development would be if it had *not* been flexible enough to change. In fact, many countries have more rigid forms of zoning than the United States, and their experience shows that overly rigid systems can make zoning almost irrelevant to urban governance. During the last few years, I have worked in Winnipeg and lived in New Delhi, both of which have less flexible systems than do many U.S. cities, and both of which are now trying to insert more flexibility into their regulations.

Many Canadian zoning bylaws have evolved from the older British tradition of top-down land use controls. Unlike the Standard Zoning and Planning Acts, which presume that Congress does not have a significant role in regulating land, the British system assumes that the central government figures significantly in both planning and zoning. Under Canada's system, some large cities have only those powers set forth in their charters, and those charters are sometimes subject to adoption or approval by the provincial government.

Until recently, Winnipeg's zoning system required that most significant land use changes be approved through a rezoning by city council. Because rezonings are inherently political (they require a public hearing and a majority vote of council) and rezoning fees were charged to offset the impacts of the new land use, applicants tried hard to avoid them. The city, on the other hand, liked the ability to collect rezoning fees and to consider and condition each individual development, so zoning did not evolve to allow more flexibility in land use. PUDs were not used, and even conditional uses required approval by a subcommittee of city council. Responding to that rigidity, landowners filed almost 1,400 applications for variances and conditional uses each year—that is, they used the only avenues to flexibility open to them if they wanted to avoid rezonings and related fees. The result was a system sometimes referred to as "zoning by variance." A tool originally designed to handle exceptional situations had in fact become the norm.

As a dramatic contrast, New Delhi's land use controls are incorporated into its master plan and subsidiary documents. Instead of separating planning and zoning tools, the master plan includes both the desired land development patterns and the regulations that govern what can be done on different types of property. Grounded in India's quasi-socialist economic model (now abandoned), those regulations took a very detailed, top-down approach. Numerical standards determined the amount of commercial area, open space, and government facilities that had to be provided in conjunction with different types and amounts of housing; it was all very formulaic. The Delhi Development Authority was charged with buying land and doing most of the developing for India's premier planned city. The private sector had almost no role except to bid on construction projects issued by the Authority. Although that may have been feasible in the 1950s, when the city had a population of about 1.4 million, it worked poorly as the city grew to its current population of almost 14 million.[1]

In addition, when India liberalized its economy in 1991, it set free the forces of the private market, which immediately started generating more demand for retail and commercial space than was included in the approved top-down plans. A freer economy resulted in more investment, which created demand for more office space, while the rising incomes of the middle class created demand for more and better places to shop. This happened on a scale that Delhi's planners had never dreamed of and for which their existing plans were unprepared.

As with many local governments around the world, the Delhi government was less sensitive to the time value of money than were private landowners and builders. When the government owns land, it is generally not making monthly payments on a land loan just to hold on to the property and it can afford to take more time refining its plans for development. As the city took its time moving through the mechanics of drafting a new master plan, the private sector responded to the lack of land for commercial and retail uses by illegally converting existing buildings to those uses. In the face of these powerful market forces, enforcement was poor if it happened at all. By 2005, it was estimated that somewhere between 40 and 80 percent of properties in the city either were illegal structures or contained illegal uses.

In this case, the city's assumption that its rigid land use regulations would still control development created a situation where zoning became almost irrelevant to land use. By 2005, the major planning issue had moved from "How should Delhi develop in the future?" to "How can the planning system catch up to what the city has already become?"

Compared with the experience of both Winnipeg and Delhi, the evolution of American zoning over time has strengthened it and kept it relevant. But looking at some of the powerful land use drivers now at work may enable us to reform zoning so that it responds to these forces more effectively and efficiently than it does now.

The Enormous Market

More than $1.3 trillion each year—that's the estimated value of the U.S. construction industry. One primary determinant of land use—some would say the *only* significant determinant—is the market for various types of real estate. In the United States, real estate development and construction has always been big business, but the scale of the industry and the force that it wields on local economies has moved from big to staggering. When zoning emerged in 1916, the self-amortizing real estate mortgage had not been invented. Most real estate development was a cash business, and mortgages (if they were used at all) were of the "short-term balloon" type, which meant that a fairly narrow segment of U.S. society could borrow money to buy real estate. In 1910, only 46 percent of Americans owned their own homes.[2] Most commercial real estate construction was for identified users, rather than in speculative anticipation of future users.

All that changed in 1937 (with the Federal Housing Administration's program to ensure self-amortizing long-term mortgages), in 1945 (with the end of World War II), and in 1957 (with the approval of the federal Interstate Highway System). By the 1960s, a full 66 percent of U.S. families owned a home.[3] At the same time, the federal government was subsidizing highways to allow those homes to occur farther from city centers, and commercial and industrial development was commonly being built and financed on a speculative basis (i.e., without a specific final user in mind).

Which brings us to the enormous size of the real estate industry today. By the end of 2001, more than 1.5 million Americans were employed in real estate.[4] Founded in 1913, the National Association of Realtors by the early 1970s had become the largest trade organization in the United States; it now has a membership of more than 850,000.[5] Membership in the National Association of Home Builders stands at more than 235,000.[6] Between 1910 and 2000, the share of U.S. gross domestic product coming from real estate activities stayed relatively constant at around 11 percent, but its role in U.S. debt markets increased dramatically. About 35 percent of all debt outstanding in 1985 was attributable to real estate, but by 1999 that figure had risen to 44 percent—and the real estate share of non-mortgage debt rose from 8 percent to 19 percent.[7]

Although the share of Americans employed in construction declined during the twentieth century, the share employed in other types of jobs related to real estate development, lending, and sales increased. Reflecting the importance of consumer spending, the amount of gross leasable retail space rose from 14.7 to 20.2 square feet per capita between 1986 and 2003. That represents a total increase of 2.4 billion square feet of selling area in the past twenty years alone.[8] In April 2006, the *Washington Post* reported that the share of U.S. goods and services created by the real estate industry was at its highest level since 1950, that the share of the population employed in real estate fields was at its highest level since the 1970s, and that "the U.S. economy is more dependent on housing than it has been in a half-century, as the sector fuels consumer spending and has accounted for nearly three-quarters of the nation's job growth in the past five years."[9] Unfortunately, all that activity has not resulted in housing being more attainable to average Americans (a trend that we will discuss in more detail below).

Both speculative building construction and speculative land development were important factors in the dramatic growth of the real estate economy. Landowners began making sure that zoning was in place and installing utilities to the edge of their property before the market for developed land arrived. But if zoning was not being put in place to match the surrounding neighborhood (which was often farm fields), and the city did not yet have a plan for what would happen on those fields, then why not ask for zoning that would make the land as valuable as possible? That usually meant zoning for denser housing development or for commercial development. Thanks to the loose (and logically backward) connection between the Standard Zoning Act and the Standard Planning Act, zoning was often put in place prior to serious planning for new development areas on the urban fringe. In short, zoning began to be driven by efforts to increase land values on the expanding edges of cities well in advance of actual need in a way that was probably not foreseen by the Euclidean zoning model.

Along with the land development industry, the real estate lending industry grew up in the mid-twentieth century and began to influence zoning as well. As car ownership skyrocketed after World War II, it quickly became apparent that commercial parcels were valuable only if they had adequate space to park cars. As Joel Garreau eloquently describes in his book *Edge City*, the power of the market quickly reduced this fact into a set of formulas. Stores need X parking spaces per 1,000 square feet of sales area, offices need Y parking spaces per 1,000 square feet, and industry needs Z. Because commercial businesses with inadequate parking could fail, banks became very focused on the adequacy of parking; when it came to judgment calls, lenders required that parcels provide more rather than less parking, just to hedge their bets. By the end of the twentieth century, zoning requirements for minimum off-street parking had become much less important than the ratios builders thought they needed to lease the space, which were often higher than the city's figures. And those were in turn less important than the ratios the banks used for loan approval criteria. Because a developer without a construction loan cannot build, the developer's ratios tended to converge with those of the lenders.

All of this undermined the box approach to zoning, at least for commercial development. Instead of having buildings located in boxes defined by city setbacks, building locations were defined as the land left over after you provided the parking that the lender thought was necessary for the development to succeed. The city's zoning-determined building envelopes sometimes became almost irrelevant, and where they conflicted with lending requirements, they were often forced to change.

By the 1980s, the strength of the real estate market was shown in yet another way. Real estate became more corporatized. The proliferation of franchising and chain stores increased competition to capture market share from other similar stores, and one response was to "brand" your store in an unforgettable way to attract to the public. Every Midas store had to have a mustard yellow oval sign, every McDonalds sign had to have golden arches, and both had to be as tall and visible as possible. The corporatization of real estate is symbolized most dramatically by fast food drive-throughs; the relevant box was not one that made the building set back from its neighbors to mitigate its impacts but one that would allow cars to circle the building as they picked up their orders. Franchise chains had their own standards for stores, signs, and parking (and sometimes landscaping—or lack of it). When the city's standards were in conflict, the chain might not sell a franchise, which meant that the buyer could not buy it, the builder could not build the store, and the landowner could not sell the land. Over time, some corporations decided to be more flexible (in effect, being flexible about the appearance of the store became a more sophisticated form of "branding"), but others did not. So pressure was sometimes applied to get zoning standards changed to allow corporate models of preferred development, and they often were. This, too, was not foreseen by the early Euclidean zoners.

In short, in the ninety years since New York City began the grand zoning experiment, the real estate industry that zoning sought to regulate has grown and diversified in myriad ways. It has become a more important and lucrative part of the U.S. economy, and one that touches many more citizens' lives much more directly. The real estate development industry has generally supported zoning ever since its inception, because it increases the predictability of what will happen on nearby properties and thereby reduces the risks of real estate investment. But it has also been very effective at changing zoning to serve the needs of the various development industries. Those who believe that zoning can stand in the way of an unwanted market trend often find themselves engaged in a slow step-by-step retreat over the long run. Zoning can "bend" some aspects of real estate development (e.g., require shorter or smaller buildings or better landscaping, or parking, or building design), but it often cannot withstand a frontal onslaught by the market forces behind a new and profitable use of land. Put another way, the predictability of Euclidean zoning has been supported by the real estate markets in part because there are ways to change the zoning rules and insert flexibility.

Another example of market influence comes from the push for more flexible zoning districts. Let's start with the distinction between residential and commercial zones. In the old days, business was done in commercial or industrial zones. Exceptions to that rule were so few that we could list the types of limited businesses homeowners could do in residential zones. Winnipeg listed artist, sculptor, author, composer, dressmaker, seamstress, tailor, small-scale arts and crafts (ceramics, model building, rug weaving, lapidary work), instructional classes for no more than four people, and office (but only for physician, dentist, medical professional, photographer, precision instrument repairer, accountant, architect, art dealer, engineer, insurance agent, land surveyor, or lawyer). In addition, the bylaw permitted "any office limited to paperwork and taking orders," which significantly broad-ened the previous list and showed the direction things were headed.

As of 2005, Delhi took a similar approach to dealing with office uses in resi-dential areas. In response to widespread complaints that entire single-family homes were being converted to much more intensive rental offices, the city government proposed a list of four permitted residential office uses: doctors, lawyers, account-ants, and surveyors only. This approach was immediately criticized. Some pointed out that doctors' offices can have some of the highest traffic and parking demands, while others started listing other paperwork-based offices with potentially fewer impacts than the four on the list. Two months later the list was expanded to seven—chartered engineers, management consultants, and media professionals were added (with a suggestion that perhaps astrologers might be added later).[10] Complaints about the list continued, and one month later it was expanded again to include cost-work accountants, company secretaries, and . . . town planners! See the trend? Each revised list was not much closer to identifying potential office uses with minor impacts than the list before it.

The point is that the list approach to defining what you can do in your home without annoying the neighbors or hurting property values doesn't work. We should have seen the writing on the wall around 1995, when Internet use started proliferat-ing. Any remaining doubts should have been eliminated when we read Thomas Friedman's description of the changing world economy in *The World Is Flat*.[11] If JetBlue Airlines could run its reservation system through home-based workers in Utah, the list of services that can be provided without any inherent traffic or deliv-ery impacts is almost unlimited. And regardless of the fate of JetBlue, that home-based strategy will no doubt be used by other companies. Early in 2007, a home-based business in England successfully promoted a punk band's song to debut in the top forty list, because under recently revised rules songs were eligible for that list even if the band had never produced or sold a compact disc that you could hold in your hand. Under a list approach, "music production" would almost certainly have been a commercial use with assumed impacts (i.e., noise), but no longer.[12]

Not only does the Internet allow for more of us to work at home (this book was written in a home office), but it also allows office buildings to coexist with multifamily buildings without nearly the volume of couriers and delivery vehicles that used to be required. Whenever office uses were proposed in or near residen-tial uses, the first complaint used to be: "Think of all those clients and couriers and delivery trucks coming and going by our homes." But widespread use of broadband Internet allows many of those deliveries to be made electronically. The remaining physical delivery traffic can be controlled through neighborhood-enforced traffic limits or more formal transportation demand management systems. The reasons behind separating at least multifamily residential and office zones are less persuasive than they used to be.

A second distinction is between commercial office zones and public/institutional use zones. This one is a little trickier, because there are legitimate reasons for treating some public/institutional uses differently. In some cities, institutional use zones are used to control the expansion or impacts of hospitals, universities, schools, public health facilities, or other uses that either predated zoning or would otherwise be lumped together with commercial uses. In Denver, the hospital zone districts were created because neighborhoods wanted protection from the creeping growth of medical complexes; they wanted to know when the expansion would stop and the demolition of houses for new medical buildings would end. In other cities, the opposite occurs. A hospital announces that it is closing or moving, and the neighbors demand that the site not be opened up to commercial uses. They wouldn't mind something like a hospital or a research center, but no shopping centers please.

Although there are legitimate reasons for having a zone district designed for large, unique, multibuilding institutions, some cities don't use the institutional zone district that way. Rather, they use it to allow nonprofit organizations to operate in areas where for-profit businesses are not allowed. But this distinction no longer holds up. Nonprofit, quasi-governmental services are outsourced to the private sector on an almost daily basis, and the land use impacts of the activity seldom depend on whether the organization providing the service is in business to make a profit.

A third distinction under attack is that between commercial and light industrial zone districts. Many North American cities have struggled with this issue in recent years, and the debates are almost always caused by newly emerging types of businesses or market-driven development patterns. The "industrial" and "manufacturing" labels used to conjure up visions of smokestacks, railcars, and outdoor storage yards, plus a general impression of something you would not choose to live beside. But most industrial uses have not fit that mold for a long time. The Clean Air Act, the Clean Water Act, and other federal and state environmental regulations have made almost all forms of commerce and industry cleaner and therefore better neighbors than they used to be. Not only does industry pollute less than it used to, but other impacts, such as noise, vibration, glare, odor, and radiation, can be addressed directly rather than by targeting uses by name.

The breakdown of the commercial/light industrial distinction is nowhere more obvious than in the marketplace. During the 1960s, 1970s, and 1980s, many cities took advantage of federal and state incentives to create new industrial parks. Some cities had a legitimate shortage of industrial land served by utilities, but in other cities the parks were constructed on the speculative "build it and they will come" theory. Then a funny thing happened. In many communities, it took a long time to sell all those lots in the new industrial parks. That was not the funny part—just a reflection of supply and demand. Lots of new parks were in competition for users, so there was a buyer's market. The funny part was that other uses found the park sites attractive. Unsold industrial sites were occupied by commercial repair shops, wholesale distribution centers, film production studios, recording studios, plant and garden supply facilities, roller-blading arenas, greenhouses, and a host of other uses that the cities classified as "commercial" uses. More recently, the list of uses bidding for space in industrial zones spaces has expanded to include call centers, back-office data processing, and even large churches. Expansion of other uses into industrial zones has reached a point where some large cities, including Chicago, Winnipeg, and New York, have enacted restrictions to protect the supply of industrial land for industrial uses.

The blurring of this line continues. The past two decades have seen a proliferation of "business parks" that would seem almost unimaginable to the early authors of zoning. Midquality office buildings are routinely mixed in with light industrial and production facilities, some of which have ancillary sales of the products they assemble and produce. Large-format retailers like Sam's Club and Office Warehouse have joined the mix, as have multiscreen theaters, back-office call centers, Internet sales operations, auditoriums and performance spaces, large churches, and medical clinics. Edges and corners of the site may even contain retail shopping malls or multifamily apartments whose users know their street address but don't know they may be shopping or living in an industrial zone.

Internet sales facilities are one of my favorite examples. How do you categorize an attractive but undistinguished building in which some people sit in cubicles and work on their computers retrieving Internet orders for a product and where others take the product off the shelves and ship it to the buyers? It isn't really office, because there is shipping going on. It isn't really wholesale, because the buyers are individuals; they just don't show up in person to get their goods. It may be retailing, but without all the cars that the zoning ordinance thought would come with a retail use. Is the retailing accessory to the shipping and office uses? Or maybe the office uses are accessory to the shipping? If the product is tiny PCMCIA cards for computers, then the office space might be larger than the shipping space, but if the product is bean bag chairs it would be the other way around. What if they start by selling bean bag chairs and then shift to PCMCIA cards? Does the use change? Does it matter? The only things the neighbors notice is what the building looks like, how many cars and trucks come and go, and at what time of day they pass by.

Obviously, many of the commercial uses described above find light industrial uses to be good neighbors (and vice versa) or they would not be in the business parks together. The key to most users is the look, feel, and quality of the development, not the details of what goes on inside the buildings. Good planning can create the desired look, feel, and quality without limiting most of the desired uses. Both the performance zoners and the form-based zoners got that part right.

Hint for the future: Future zoning will do a better job of working with market forces to achieve city planning goals. That does not mean that zoning should allow whatever speculative developers want, but that cities need to be even more sensitive to market trends and economics than they are now. Cities should use zoning to send clear messages about the types of development they are looking for and then remove barriers to market activity in those areas. In addition, zoning should better recognize the fact that time is money and that every dollar spent by a landowner in getting development approvals is a dollar that cannot be spent for higher levels of quality, walkability, or design.

Tax Limits

Almost no one enjoys paying taxes, but all taxpayers expect their cities to provide high-quality services and infrastructure. As a result, city governments spend a lot of time finding the revenue to pay for all those services the voters say they want. In the eastern United States, real estate taxes historically have been a large source of municipal revenue. As you move west across the country, the role of sales taxes generally increases and the importance of real estate taxes declines. In the old days, city councils simply set property and sales tax rates to cover the costs of the services they provided. But rising tax rates led to charges of inefficiency and then to voter backlash. Citizens used voter initiatives to limit both the tax rates that cities can charge and the amounts of revenue that cities can collect.

Residents of California were among the first to experience the dramatic effects of tax ceilings following the approval of Proposition 13 (the People's Initiative to Limit Property Taxation) in 1978. My home state of Colorado followed with Amendment 1 (the Taxpayers' Bill of Rights), which imposed even stricter taxing and spending limits, in 1992. When combined with other provisions of the Colorado Constitution, Amendment 1 limits the amounts by which real estate tax rates could increase each year *and* the amounts that local revenues can increase each year, *and* requires that residential taxes be kept low even if the value of residential real estate grows faster than the value of commercial and industrial properties. Forty-three states now have some type of property tax cap in place.[13]

At the same time, there is little evidence that voters have reduced the types of services or facilities that they expect local government to provide. So the increasing variety of tax restrictions has made it more difficult for cities to please their voters. The existing revenues need to be spread ever thinner, and the search for ways out of the financial box has become high-stakes political business—so big, in fact, that in some states the quest is actually driving land use decisions and resulting in "fiscal zoning."

It happens like this. If residential real estate taxes are restricted, then city councils start looking more favorably on commercial development because it will produce more revenue and demand fewer services from the government. If both residential and commercial property taxes are limited, then councils move toward sales tax generators. But because those are generally commercial uses, the result is the same: a bias for commercial development. Throughout the western United States, this focus has led to overzoning land for commercial uses in the hope of generating more city revenues, even where commercial development isn't likely to occur in amounts even remotely approaching the amount of zoned land. While it is wise policy to zone more land for development than what will probably be needed (in order to avoid creating commercial land monopolies and to allow the market freedom to operate), it is *not* wise policy to zone for a large multiple of the commercial development that is expected to occur, because that can restrict the amount of land available for residential uses and drive residential land prices up.

This is a key point. Under Euclidean hybrid zoning and traditional approaches to use separation, zoning land for A means it is not available for B. Creating an artificially inflated supply of commercially zoned land means you are creating an artificially restricted supply of housing land. The recent move toward mixed uses makes the situation somewhat better, but not a lot. Mixed-use zoning means that land that is available for commercial use is not unavailable for housing use, but as a practical matter commercial land prices are often higher, so the landowners often do not offer the land for residential development until it becomes clear that commercial buyers are not going to knock on their doors.

The general priority for zoning land in tax-limited cities seems to be (from most to least popular)

- •retail (creates some jobs and both property and sales taxes)
- •commercial (creates jobs and property taxes)
- •clean industrial (creates fewer jobs and some property taxes)
- •expensive houses (for image, less traffic, and fewer school kids, plus some property taxes)
- •less expensive, more attainable housing (creates less image, more cars and kids, and few taxes).

In many western states, the dream of commercial property and sales tax generation is leading city councils to zone even poorly located land for commercial development. It also leads them to zone too little land for attainable and workforce housing. Every council hopes that it will win this gamble (i.e., that their commercially zoned land will actually get developed instead of land in the neighboring city), while knowing from past experience that they could well lose the gamble to their neighbors or just break even (i.e., that overzoning will just lead to relocation of commercial development from one site to another within their own city, with little increase in tax revenue to show for it). A surprising number of American elected officials seem to confuse commercial zoning with commercial development. They seem to think, "If the map is red, then we can plan for commercial taxes from that area." But zoning can no more create commercial or retail demand than it can create housing demand in areas where people don't want to buy houses. Real estate demand should be reflected in healthy zoning decisions, but zoning does not create demand.

Something similar was happening in Russian industrial zoning when the Iron Curtain fell. During the Communist era, Russia's top-down system emphasized industrial development, because it produced goods and jobs for the people. The system ignored lots of commercial activities because they were not producing anything you could hold in your hand. As a result, cities dramatically overdesignated land for industrial development. If an industry wanted more land around its factory, that land was duly designated for industrial expansion. Planners operated under the delusion that more industrial land meant more industrial production, but it turned out to mean mostly more vacant industrial land. It may be true that growing industries will need more land, but giving more land to industry will not automatically make them grow. At the time I worked in St. Petersburg in 1995, six years after the fall of the Iron Curtain, some Russian planners who knew that the city had too much industrial land were still loathe to redesignate it because that went against their biases about what was a "good" and a "bad" land use.

With the benefit of hindsight, it's easy for us to see that Russia was overzoning land for industry and constraining land for residential and commercial uses based on assumptions that were not true. But many U.S. cities are engaging in the same self-deception with respect to commercial land as a response to tax caps. This is another failed assumption behind the Euclidean zoning model—it did not anticipate that zoning decisions would be driven by tax limitations and the biases they introduce in municipal decision making, and it has no way to counteract that bias.

Hint for the future: Future zoning should acknowledge that municipal tax limits will remain an important determinant of land use policy. But it should also include tools to discourage zoning significantly more land than will be needed for commercial and industrial uses. Greater use of mixed-use zoning may create better opportunities for cities to capture their share of commercial and retail sales taxes without overzoning for commercial and underzoning for residential land uses, but it may be necessary to require—rather than simply allow—a mix of uses that achieves that result.

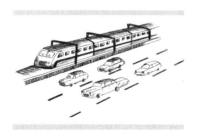

Transportation Systems

Over the past forty years, Americans' love affair with cars—as well as rising real incomes to support that love affair—have dramatically affected the shape and structure of U.S. cities.[14] The most obvious effects have been

74

well documented: bigger residential lots and houses, outward suburban growth, and very high spending on highway construction and maintenance. All of these changes have required zoning to create new zone districts and standards to ensure compatibility among new types of development. In addition to impacts between land uses, zoning has also had to address increasing impacts from the transportation system itself, particularly adjacent to freeways, rail lines, and airports. One unintended consequence has already been mentioned—many development standards created for suburban development greenfields were then mistakenly assumed to be wise policy for older areas of the city.

But planning has been affected even more profoundly. Transportation access and traffic counts virtually drive the commercial real estate market (certainly the retail market) and strongly influence residential land markets. Paradoxically, without good access for lots of cars, you do not have a viable commercial development site; among those sites with access, higher traffic counts generally mean more potential shoppers and a better commercial site. But beyond a certain point, high traffic counts lead to unacceptable congestion and erode the commercial value of sites that have to use those roads. Everyone wants to be on College Avenue—until it gets so crowded that drivers avoid College Avenue. But by that time, the size and cost of investments in College Avenue may mean there are few other viable routes to move significant traffic through the area.

On a greenfield site on the edge of the city, this just means that the transportation system, building sizes, and parking areas have to be in balance. Any competent site planner can balance the building size, parking, and access points, but that is not enough. The problem is that capacity of the road adjacent to the property is affected by land uses, road networks, and intersections far away from the site—parcels that the site planner has no control over. As a result, transportation planners have had to develop ever more sophisticated modeling systems to do their transportation planning. And constructing, maintaining, and replacing roads is so expensive—by far the most expensive public works system run by any city—that it has become increasingly necessary to find ways to squeeze more "mobility" out of each system without building lots of new roads.

Although researchers have been studying the relationship between transportation mobility and land markets for several decades, it is still not clear exactly how the cause and effect works on a complex road network, and even less clear how to apply land use policies to create the most efficient use of transportation infrastructure.[15] Put another way, we know what policies we can apply to individual sites and small areas to reduce traffic generation, but sometimes we do those things and the overall traffic congestion still does not improve, so other harder-to-model forces are also at work.

Nevertheless, there is a strong commonsense argument that land use and transportation planning need to be more closely coordinated, and that is happening. Several states have started reflecting this reality in their own planning. Several groups in Oregon developed an analytical tool called "LUTRAQ: Making the Land Use, Transportation, and Air Quality Connection" in order to improve the quality of both land use and transportation planning in constrained situations. Because of the increasing pressure to better coordinate land use and transportation planning, in the mid-1990s the Federal Highway Administration, the Federal Transit Administration, and the Environmental Protection Agency created the Transit Model Improvement Project (TMIP).[16] This effort did not result in a single improved model, but it did spur several state, local, and university efforts to improve modeling, including Oregon's Transportation and Land Use Model Integration Project (TMUIP) and an evolving UrbanSim model. Work in this very complex area continues, but progress has been slow because so many factors are involved in human decisions about where to live, work, shop, play, and educate children as well as when and how to get between these places.

Italian carmaker Etore Bugatti is famous for having said: "If you want more power, build a bigger engine." Prior to 1991, U.S. transportation policy was sort of similar to that approach. In effect, it said: "If you want to move more people, build more roads." But the history of cars shows that building a bigger engine may in fact be the worst way to get more power. By using better technology, we now get the same power from engines one third or one quarter as big as the ones Bugatti built. And optimizing the efficiency and integration of road systems, bus systems, bikeways, and rail networks has turned out to be a much more efficient way to move more people through cities than just building more roads.

In 1991, the federal government reflected this reality in the first of the "new generation" of transportation funding bills: the Intermodal Surface Transportation Efficiency Act (ISTEA). ISTEA offered carrots and sticks to encourage transportation engineers to think of all other solutions before they built new lane miles of roads with federal dollars. This approach was followed to a somewhat lesser degree by its successors, the 1998 Transportation Equity Act for the 21st Century

(TEA-21) and the 2005 Safe, Accountable, Flexible, Efficient Transportation Equity Act: A Legacy for Users (SAFETEA-LU). Each succeeding bill kept most of the ISTEA principles in place, but the expanding pie of federal transportation dollars watered down the bias against new lane miles that was at the heart of the 1991 act.

Although some environmentalists would like to take credit for this healthy change in planning, I think it was about one part environmental concerns, one part reality check, and two parts cost. Yes, there is a bigger-than-expected bloc of citizens who are prepared to lobby and vote against new roads, but that was not usually decisive. In spite of the enormous costs, voters still regularly approve bond issues to support major road improvements. The reality check was that it is often impossible to expand roads in mature urban areas, because doing so would rip the heart out of adjacent neighborhoods. Elected officials from urban areas started to see that the build-new-roads bias reflected in federal transportation funding for the previous forty years was putting mature cities at a serious disadvantage.

But the real killer was cost. Roads are just really, really expensive over the long haul. Even if a private developer constructs the roads in the first place, the real costs come later in maintenance and reconstruction, which almost always fall on the tax-payers. State government payments to maintain and repair the Interstate Highway System dwarf the federal government's cost to build the original system, even if you compare them in constant dollars. City council members facing tax caps and budget cuts could not help seeing that building and maintaining roads generated massive budget costs. Elected officials were faced with planners who didn't want to gut old neighborhoods, a fairly big bloc of "greens" and other voters who would lobby against the new highways, a realization that more road maintenance would push taxes higher, and a few builders who liked the build-new-roads bias. They chose the voters.

In short, land use planning and transportation planning got married. We now know that land use patterns and transportation systems don't just have to work hand-in-hand; they have to be joined at the hip. In the old days, land use plans were created, the public works people told you how big the road had to be to serve those uses, and it was built. Many planners now believe this approach has been turned on its head. In recent years, the transportation engineer looks at the proposed land uses, looks at existing traffic flows, and tells you how many more cars or people the road can move without huge new investments, and then the planners go back and adjust the land uses to fit within the available traffic capacity. In practice, it is much messier than that, but when road capacity and preferred land uses come into conflict, the realities of transportation costs and constraints win a lot more battles than they used to. We have learned that land use planning without a good understanding of transportation constraints is a waste of time and money.

Of course, some of these impacts can be addressed through investments in light rail or heavy rail or bus lanes as opposed to cars, and that is happening. But those options are much more constrained in terms of where they can realistically be retrofitted into the landscape—and they also cost big money. I fully support the New Urbanist and Smart Growth emphasis on non-auto transportation networks, but even if those movements are very successful, we will have inherited a huge inventory of roads and related facilities that will influence land use economics for generations to come.

The tension can also be addressed through more mixed-use zoning, and that is happening. Individually, each mixed-use project solves only a small fraction of the transportation problem. Only a tiny percentage of Americans really live and work within the same mixed-use development, and they can decide to change jobs or move houses at any time for a variety of factors (e.g., getting closer to Mom in her old age, getting closer to the kids' school, getting closer to the open space system). But collectively, the mixed-use trend can have a significant impact, because as mixed-use developments proliferate, Joe Commuter may decide to live in Mixed-use Glen and work in Mixed-use Plaza a mile away. Or, Joe could decide to live in Residential Acres and work in Mixed-use Plaza rather than Downtown Plaza. As long as the uses are closer together than where Joe used to live and work, or as long as he can get there on public transit, we may have relieved pressure on the transportation system.

Most Euclidean zoning ordinances were not drafted with transportation-driven land use systems in mind. They still talk almost exclusively about land uses, density, and development standards. Traffic generation is mentioned, if at all, only for large and complex projects like regional malls, office buildings, and large subdivisions. In addition, Euclidean hybrid zoning standards are generally static; they do not adjust the permitted intensity of development or its allowable traffic generation to match the capacity of the surrounding systems. Just as the vision of the city can change quickly as new opportunities arise, the ability of transportation systems to handle traffic can change as new development (even development located a fair distance away) occurs, as old traffic generators shut down or move, or as new transportation facilities open up.

Hint for the future: Future zoning will need to acknowledge the increased importance of aligning land uses and densities with transportation systems. Greater use of mixed-use zoning is one way to do that, because it allows greater market flexibility for responding to changes in transportation capacity. It would be even better if zoning standards could change automatically in response to increases in available transportation capacity.

Housing Affordability

Throughout most of the United States, the last two decades have been "good times." Between 1990 and 2006, the U.S. GDP grew at an average annual rate of 3 percent.[17] Sure, there was a short recession from March through November 2001, and there have been areas (such as New Orleans) where natural disasters have devastated the local economy, but the economic path of the past sixteen years has clearly been upward. The economy has been creating jobs, and the unemployment rate has trended generally downward from about 7.5 percent to near 4.0 percent.[18]

During most of this period, mortgage interest rates have also remained low, allowing hundreds of thousands of citizens to become first-time home buyers when they otherwise could not have afforded to do so. If there was a time when housing affordability should have improved, this has been it.

But that has not happened. Instead, housing affordability is declining. In December 2004, the *Wall Street Journal* and the National Association of Home Builders measured housing affordability at its lowest point since 1991.[19] The median percentage of household income spent to rent a home rose from 19 percent in 1960 to 29 percent in 2005, and the percentage of rental households who spent more than 30 percent of their income on housing rose from 23 percent to 49 percent.[20] Real estate markets are nothing if not cyclical, so we can always look at short-term changes with a dash of skepticism, but these are very long trends—figures of growing unaffordability that increase every decade without fail.

Between 2001 and 2005, the median housing rental costs for those categorized as "not low income" rose at 14 percent while their median annual incomes rose at 8 percent. During the same period, for homeowners categorized as "not low income," median housing costs rose at 18 percent while median incomes rose at 11 percent. In the case of both renters and owners, the situation was even more serious for those categorized as "low income," "very low income," or "extremely low income."[21] Housing cost increases outstripped their incomes by an even wider margin. That tells the story.

Low mortgage rates have been hiding a difficult truth that should have been keeping planners awake at night. The cost of building houses and apartments has been rising faster than the ability of many Americans to afford them. Although affordability generally will rise and fall with the national economy, it has been rising when it should have been falling, which suggests that it will get worse if the economy slows or if mortgage rates continue to rise. This issue will become more serious over time because, in very simple terms, the housing affordability problem has become a part of the structure of the U.S. economy: the types of jobs we are creating (on average) cannot afford the housing we are building (on average) by a little more each year. This is true for many reasons, but for the purposes of this book, two key reasons deserve discussion.

First, building traditional "stick-built" homes is fairly labor-intensive, and labor-intensive goods tend to get more expensive relative to non-labor-intensive goods over time. In many knowledge industries, we have been actively replacing labor with technology, and the overall productivity of U.S. workers is a marvel of the world economy. But the productivity of on-site house building is not rising as fast as other sectors of the U.S. economy. You can't get the Internet to drive a loader or drive nails. Although we can count on the housing industries to find any labor-saving solutions out there, it is hard to see how the productivity curve in housing will ever catch up with changes in other sectors that do not require people to be present and to perform physical work on the land. I mention this reason not because planners can do something about it but because we cannot. This is one reason why we need to look at other solutions.

The second reason is land cost. As the price of land rises over time, it tends to drive up development costs. The cost of the finished housing unit will rise unless some other change offsets the increase. We used to think that land made up about one third of the cost of housing—or at least that was a good basic guess given the wide variations in land markets across the country. However, recent studies suggest that between 1984 and 2004 the share of housing costs explained by land prices rose from about 35 percent to almost 50 percent in many large U.S. cities.[22]

Unfortunately, many Euclidean hybrid zoning ordinances tend to compound this pressure. Although the price of land is largely outside the control of planners, changes in the price of housing are less so. To use a common example, if the zoning ordinance is amended to require more land per house, that is something within the city's control and it tends to make housing more expensive.

Cities usually increase lot sizes for one of two reasons. First, it may be an attempt to deliberately drive up the value of the homes in order to collect more property taxes. Many city council members now know that routine residential development—meaning nonluxury homes—rarely pays as much in property and incidental taxes as it costs to serve. Property tax caps have made this worse. As the importance of land prices to housing affordability rises, the importance of permitted lot sizes and development density also rises. Requiring larger lots will affect housing prices differently in different markets, but it often requires the developer to reevaluate the market and to build larger or nicer houses (or more houses) to cover the increased land cost per home. These efforts rarely result in growth paying for itself because the point at which single-family homes cover their costs is often far above the average house value in the city. But elected officials who follow this approach believe that closing the gap—that is, losing less money serving each house—is worthwhile in itself.

Cities also push for larger minimum lot sizes at the request of neighboring property owners. Neighbors sometimes believe that having more expensive homes nearby will increase the overall value of the neighborhood (as well as the value of their own home) and that larger lots mean fewer cars on the roads and fewer additional children in local schools. This is entirely predictable, because the residents of any given neighborhood don't really have an interest in overall housing affordability in the city. Efforts to allow smaller lots and higher residential densities will always require the leadership of elected officials or organizations with a citywide, as opposed to a neighborhood-specific, perspective.

Hint for the future: The housing attainability problem is now part of the structure of the U.S. economy, and future zoning should include better tools to address it. One approach will be to look for greater land efficiency, so that more units can be built per acre of land, and to better integrate those units into the urban fabric. A second key will be to remove restrictions that limit creativity in the types of housing that are built. A third path will be to create development approval systems that better integrate citywide needs for attainable housing into review of individual projects.

NIMBYism

The fifth new land use driver is the "Not in My Back Yard" syndrome, or NIMBYism. No matter how hybrid our current zoning systems, they all assume that city council will use its legislative judgment to zone the land properly, rezone it when circumstances require, and then allow landowners to build buildings and operate the uses that meet zoning requirements.

PUDs brought in the reasonable concept that landowners might not know in detail what they want to build at the time flexible PUD zoning is approved and that someone in city government might need to take a "second look" at the actual plan for the property once the details are known, just to make sure it does not create unacceptable impacts on the surrounding properties at that time. After all, PUD general plans often have vague land use "bubbles" and allow buildings to be moved around on the site. Years might pass before anything is actually built, and by then some combinations of uses and densities might be unacceptable. This became a self-fulfilling prophecy. Because the city was going to require a second approval of a "final site plan" before you could build, the city could make the initial PUD approval pretty conceptual. This also met the needs of the land use developer, who often did not know who would buy the property or what they would want to build.

As cities got used to a "second, detailed look" at PUD developments, some city council members began to wonder why they should not also get a second look at development under Euclidean zoning. The same arguments applied, especially when large properties were involved. On larger lots the owner had the freedom to put the buildings on the north, south, east, or west side of the parcel as long as setbacks were met, and the same was true of the parking areas and open spaces. Again, development might not occur for years, by which time some locations for the buildings, parking lots, and traffic access points could create unacceptable impacts that some future city council might want to prevent.

So some cities started requiring "site plans" for non-PUD zoning. They were often limited to commercial, industrial, and multifamily development and/or other large development parcels. They were almost never applied to individual house sites, because subdivision controls were supposed to control the impacts of single houses on individual lots. Non-PUD site plan requirements were often simpler than those required for PUDs, because Euclidean zoning allowed less flexibility in the first place.

Some cities had site planning requirements in place long before PUDs arrived, and some allowed planning staff (rather than city council) to review and approve the site plans. But some city council members *like* to have the final say about new development, and many of their voters *want* them to have the final say, so there was always a temptation to have site plans come back to city council for approval. Again, the analogy to PUD site plans helped fuel the argument that all site plans should come back to city council. Some cities succumbed to that temptation.

Site plans for non-PUD zoning made sense from a planners' point of view because they address the impacts of proposed development when the development is really going to be built. But they did not make as much sense to the speculative real estate market, because many landowners counted on selling the property to buyers who would buy only if they were reasonably sure about what they could build, and "second look" requirements decreased that certainty. Although no one said so at the time, one should-have-been-anticipated result of having site plans reviewed by city council was that zoning decisions got a lot more political.

The family home is often the largest single investment made by an American family, and housing appreciation is the single most common way in which Americans generate wealth. As noted above, single-family housing prices continue to rise faster than average incomes, and many Americans have to borrow more money than ever before to become homeowners or to move up to a nicer home. So they are more concerned than ever that their largest single investment does not lose value. To ensure that this doesn't happen, many suburban homes now come with private restrictive covenants ensuring that no one makes, adds to, alters, or even paints his house in a way that will diminish the value of his neighbors' houses. Mandatory membership in homeowners' associations helps ensure that restrictive covenants are enforced, but it also makes it easier to communicate about possible threats to neighborhood property values from outside the development.

Concern with protecting the value of homes, protecting perceived areas of open space, and reducing neighborhood traffic has made homeowners much more interested in nearby development proposals, and mandatory homeowners' associations make it easier for the owners to organize their positions for or against proposed development. Some homeowners believe that any additional development in the area will hurt home values or make their lives more complex. Other residents would make an exception for single-family homes that are larger and more expensive than their own homes, which they think will raise the value of homes in the neighborhood. But many proposals for commercial, multifamily, and less-expensive single-family development are faced with the "Not in My Back Yard" reaction. NIMBYism is a significant force resisting the market demand for more attainable housing throughout the United States. Requiring site plans to come back to city council for final site plan approval has made NIMBYism much more powerful than it would be otherwise—and more than a little of that power is aimed against attainable housing.

Of course, the reality is that cities change. They will continue to change in the future, and zoning ordinances should anticipate that change. Effective zoning ordinances acknowledge the forces of change and guide those forces toward investments that are consistent with the comprehensive plan. NIMBYism is fundamentally anti-change and puts city council in a position where it must agree with an anti-change position or risk alienating at least some voters.

Now the really bad news. Not only should mature cities expect change to be the norm, but in economically healthy cities that change will commonly be toward greater development density, intensity, height, or variety of uses—at least in some areas. Cities that grow without densifying at least some of their neighborhoods are going to sprawl. In fact, most growing cities do both—they densify *and* they sprawl—but the more they discourage reinvestment to densify existing areas, the farther and faster they sprawl.

There is just no other option. Growth means that people (and hopefully businesses) are moving in. To accommodate them, developers can do one of three things. They can (1) fill in the gaps in the urban fabric, of course—undeveloped holes in the urban doughnut, brownfield lands that need some cleanup before they are reused, and grayfields (i.e., already used but unpolluted sites that require demolition before reuse), or (2) redevelop existing neighborhoods to accommodate more people, or (3) move to raw land at the edge of the city. NIMBYism tends to push growth toward the edge because there may be fewer neighbors (or no neighbors) to object and less traffic on the roads.

Because landowners and developers now expect NIMBY responses from even far-flung neighbors, their response is often to ask for more development density, intensity, and flexibility as part of the initial zoning. That way, when opposition arises, they have more room to negotiate reductions that can still allow profitable development. And if the opposition succeeds in reducing or defeating development along one edge of the property, other areas are still available for building. Again, this was not anticipated when Euclidean zoning began. The exercise of assigning zoning to land was originally envisioned as a technical process, perhaps subject to some pressure from business interests. But the strength of NIMBY pressures goes far beyond those original expectations. Just as the framers of early zoning did not expect that pressure from property owners would result in a need for individualized PUDs outside the Euclidean system, they did not anticipate that pressure from neighborhoods would result in political review of projects that met substantive zoning requirements.

Hint for the future: Zoning will continue to be heavily influenced by local politics, but the system should be designed to direct those political pressures toward long-term plans and objective zoning standards. More importantly, zoning should be designed to avoid political pressure during the application of objective zoning standards to specific applications in the site planning process. Discretionary review and public hearings should generally not be held late in the development approval process.

CHAPTER 4

Governing
Well

DISCUSSIONS ABOUT WHAT IS RIGHT AND wrong about zoning often describe issues in terms of a zero-sum game between government and property owners. Articles on the subject sometimes describe every win for the government as a loss for property owners, and vice versa. Not only is this misleading, but it misconstrues the fundamental nature of the government's interest in zoning. Most large, mature cities have professional planning staff who may have their own strong opinions about what makes a good city, but they take their marching orders from elected leaders. And those elected officials generally take their orders from the voters. As a result, local government usually has several distinct interests in zoning: an interest in carrying out the "will of the people," an interest in achieving its planning goals for a "good city," and a generalized interest in "good governance."

At a minimum, discussions of zoning should recognize three major groups of players: (1) the applicant for a development approval, sometimes with staff planners in support of their request; (2) other property owners (usually neighbors), sometimes with staff planners in support of their position; and (3) the local government, which should be trying to achieve its goals for good planning and governance but is sometimes relegated to finding a compromise between other competing interests regardless of those goals. All three perspectives are usually in play when zoning ordinances are drafted and applied. For every story about an applicant who thinks the city has sided with NIMBYs against her property rights, there is a story about a resident who thinks the city has sided with property developers over the interests of her neighborhood—and *also* a story about a planning director who feels the council has sacrificed the long-term health of the city on the altar of short-term political expediency. It all depends on your perspective.

When the applicant for a zoning change is the government itself, of course, roles 1 and 3 get combined. But the law still requires that the city council treat the application as it would any other—that is, that it try to remain objective regardless of the fact that city staff prepared the application.

The point of this chapter is that—in the press of political concerns, limited budgets, and the "tyranny of the immediate"—property owners and local governments sometimes lose sight of the need for good governance over the long term. The "government-versus-property-rights" rhetoric or the "developer-versus-the-neighborhood" sound bites drown out the voices calling for systems that produce better decisions over time. That third perspective gets lost in the shuffle, which is dangerous. America owes part of its stability and prosperity to systems of local government that are perceived as relatively fair, prompt, and efficient over the long run—regardless of whether voters like the outcome in a specific dispute. While she was planning director for Denver, the late Jennifer Moulton used to say, "Democracy means having your say, not getting your way, and most citizens understand that."

Our failure to focus on the issue of governance is partly the result of adjustments made to Euclidean zoning throughout the twentieth century (see chapter 1) and partly the result of media and public focus on short-term concerns over long-term systems. We have a system of zoning that can and does change over time, but it tends to adjust through incremental changes and sometimes loses sight of some big picture goals like effectiveness, understandability, and efficiency.

In addition, media coverage of planning and zoning often focuses on "hot button" issues. It is much easier to cover a vociferous neighborhood-versus-developer dispute at city council, or to describe the planning vision articulated by the mayor at a press conference, than it is to cover how well the zoning system is doing its job. After spending two years improving the performance of a city zoning ordinance and then summarizing the improvements in a one-page press release, it is often an uphill struggle to get any type of press coverage at all. Good governance is usually not newsworthy—even though bad governance is.

So what are the elements of good governance? Volumes have been written on this topic (see the Suggested Reading List at the end of this book), so we will only touch briefly on the subject here. To begin with, of course, good governance means acting within the bounds of the law; the city's actions must be legal. The boundaries of land use law are discussed in chapter 5, so we'll take that as a given for now.

In addition, systems of governance should be "transparent" except when the law requires that specific decisions (e.g., personnel matters, lawsuit strategy) be conducted in private. Decisions should be based on the law and on adopted procedures and criteria, and what appears to be happening in the public hearing should be what is really happening (i.e., the result was not predetermined in a backroom deal). But American government is among the most transparent in the world, and transparency requires nothing different for zoning than it requires for other government actions. The same can be said for accountability. Of course it's important, but America's local governments generally do that pretty well, and the principle of accountability doesn't require anything different for zoning than it does for other activities.

We will not therefore review legality, transparency, or accountability as aspects of good governance that affect zoning specifically. Instead, we will review six goals of good governance that are particularly important to zoning. Those six goals are effectiveness, responsiveness, fairness, efficiency, understandability, and predictable flexibility.

Effectiveness

With more tools in the toolbox, government's ability to control land development has clearly increased since 1916. There is no doubt that PUDs, performance zoning, and form-based zoning give governments a wider range of levers on the future. Some cities have gone further to adopt design review procedures, environmental protection standards, and regulations on the rate and timing of growth, each of which increases the level of control.

Once zoning provisions are adopted, city governments generally assume that they are actually being used and are achieving their intended results. But that is not always true. In the early 1990s, Denver had twenty-one different density bonus provisions that applied to its downtown. To reward builders who did what it wanted, the city had twenty-one different ways of allowing them to build buildings bigger than they otherwise could. But only one of those bonuses—a reward for creating open plazas—was actually being used regularly. The city had granted bonuses totaling more than two million square feet of floor area in return for construction of plazas. Three other bonus provisions had been used once or twice, and the remaining seventeen provisions had never been used. The provisions weren't effective because they clearly were not helping steer the future in the directions Denver wanted. So the city repealed some and recalibrated others to make the reward more attractive to builders.

The question of effectiveness can also arise in the context of environmental controls. During planning for the redevelopment of the Denver Stapleton airport site, the Stapleton Redevelopment Corporation commissioned a study of best practices in environmental planning. One important topic was stormwater runoff. About a third of the Stapleton site was planned for trails and open space, and allowing urban runoff to pollute the streams would harm the biodiversity of the area, compromise the quality of stream corridors as wildlife habitat, and reduce resident enjoyment of streams and trails. Reviewing best practices from around the United States resulted in a very long list of possible actions, only some of which could be addressed effectively through zoning. Many ways to reduce stormwater runoff from potentially polluted sources can best be addressed through controls on agricultural practices and on commercial and industrial operations—as opposed to controls on how their sites are developed.

In the end, that early study recommended that zoning efforts concentrate on two "physical" solutions that could be verified easily by city staff. The first was to require parking lot runoff to be filtered through swales before entering streams, and the second was to require that some commercial and industrial products be under cover when stored outdoors. Part of making zoning effective is deciding which good ideas do not belong in the ordinance, either because their contribution to the goal is minimal or because administration would be complex, intrusive, or expensive. The city's available financial and staffing resources should always be considered when determining the effectiveness of a potential zoning effort. If the city does not have the trained staff or money available to implement a proposed solution, and if it does not seriously intend to budget the money necessary to hire, train, and retain those staff, even the best zoning tool will be ineffective. As redevelopment of the Stapleton site has since burgeoned into one of America's largest new communities, zoning and stormwater regulation on the site have evolved to a much more sophisticated level—but the initial recommendation of two key zoning controls was appropriate for its time.

Many questions about zoning's effectiveness involve the amount of "line drawing" involved. Zoning inherently requires making distinctions among different pieces of land, or areas of the city, or land uses, all of which can be questioned. Zoning novices often question the city's right to draw zoning lines that allow certain building heights and uses on one side of an alley and different heights and uses on the other, but the courts crossed that bridge long ago. As long as the city's determinations have a reasonable basis related to some legitimate government interest, its line drawing will almost always be upheld. The more interesting question is not whether city governments can make these kinds of distinctions but which distinctions are effective in achieving its planning goals. Advocates of performance zoning, PUDs, and form-based zoning have all argued that zoning ordinances make unnecessary distinctions and draw the wrong lines—that is, that Euclidean zoning treats properties or land uses differently in ways that do not promote the good of the city as a whole. Euclidean zoning does have a tendency to breed more distinctions over time (see chapter 1), so it is often helpful to question whether the lines we drew in the past are still useful.

Hint for the future: While cities have proven fairly adept at adding tailored zoning provisions to address discrete community challenges, they have been relatively poor at removing outdated or ineffective tools. The need for distinctions between almost-similar uses or zones should be subject to careful scrutiny. Future zoning should have mechanisms to eliminate regulations that have not proven themselves effective over time and to ensure that its zoning rules are within the capacity of available time, staff, and resources. As development technologies and market desires change, many previously effective provisions can become ineffective, and there needs to be a process for spotting and removing them.

Responsiveness

The whole point of democracy is that elected officials are supposed to reflect the will of the people, subject only to legal constraints and their own judgment about what is in the best interests of the city. There is no doubt that city government is supposed to be responsive, but it is not that simple. Harder questions arise over issues of time and place. The "time" question is whether to be responsive to short-term or long-term interests; the "place"

question is whether to be responsive to the interests of one neighborhood or of the city as a whole. Responding to the immediate wishes of some citizens in a specific neighborhood may undercut programs that promote the long-term good of many others. This is a fundamental tension in zoning: any pattern of land uses and regulations designed to promote the overall prosperity and stability of the city will regularly create impacts that are hard on some property owners, because their property values decline, because they cannot do what they want with their property, or because their surroundings change in ways they don't like.

On a basic level, this issue has been resolved. Both the federal and state courts have concluded that city councils usually have the power to decide whether the hardship is justified (within some limits, which we will discuss in chapter 5). But the fact that the trade-offs inherent in zoning are legally defensible doesn't comfort elected officials who are about to make a land use decision they think is in the best interest of the city, even though it is opposed by a roomful of angry citizens. One challenge for future zoning ordinances is how and when to be responsive to short-term interests while promoting long-term goals.

Zoning also has to address the "place" element of responsiveness. Citizens who can easily see the merit in a rezoning or development approval for land located across town change their minds when the proposed development is in their neighborhood. NIMBYism was already discussed in chapter 3, but it reappears here as a problem of governance. Elected officials need to respond both to the citizens living close to the proposed development and to other residents who know that the city (and even the neighborhood in question) may need the proposed development. The bane of planners' existence is "LULUs," or locally unwanted land uses—facilities that need to be provided somewhere even though no one wants to see them close to their homes or shops.

Hint for the future: Zoning has evolved toward increased responsiveness to those closest in time and place to the proposed changes, but it needs to better respond to the interests of the rest of the citizens and the needs of the future. The increasing competitiveness of the global economy, the need for better protection of the environment, and the need for more sustainable development will require that cities increase the efficiency of land uses and transportation systems, and that will require a shift of regulatory emphasis away from short-term and toward long-term interests. One way of doing this is by periodically updating the ordinance to reflect the changing desires of citizens rather than by politicizing individual development approvals.

Fairness

When I went to law school, I was surprised to learn how many different ways there are to look at fairness. Each side in a public policy dispute can usually cite some way in which fairness requires that he or she win the dispute. Not only is it popular to have fairness on your side, but it is usually pretty easy to do. Much turns on your definition of what fairness requires. The U.S. constitution defines some aspects of fairness, but our system of government leaves wide latitude for states to define what fairness means within their borders. States with Home Rule systems of government (discussed in chapter 5) often leave similar latitude for cities to make their own decisions about what is fair in city matters. So the surprising answer to "What does fairness mean in zoning" is often "What do the voters and elected officials want it to mean?" To look at fairness in zoning, we need to separate the topic into three parts: results similarity, social equity, and procedural fairness.

"Results similarity" means making similar decisions in similar cases. This is a generalized concern that has surprisingly little impact on zoning. Governments typically try to make similar decisions in similar cases, but generations of judges have repeatedly held that land is not fungible—that is, two pieces of land are rarely so similar that the government must treat them the same way. The adoption of PUDs as a zoning tool and the decline in reported cases about "spot zoning" reflect this reality.

In theory, Euclidean zoning districts treat all property within the zone the same way, but in practice they treat different types of property differently depending on environmental conditions, lot sizes, and other factors. Most of the zoning reforms described in chapter 1 enabled government to take into account more and more factors specific to the land, its location, and the values of the elected representatives—all of which make it almost impossible to prove that your land is legally similar to another piece of land that has been zoned differently. History shows that applicants, neighboring citizens, and judges do not really expect that zoning will result in very similar decisions, and results similarity is now almost a dead-end in zoning governance. Although "spot zoning" cases still come up from time to time, and plaintiffs do sometimes win them, those wins are relatively rare.[1] Results similarity is no longer a good yardstick of whether zoning governance is equitable.

Social equity is the second idea of "fairness" that can be attached to many different aspects of zoning. Over the past several years, planners have begun to talk about environmental equity—or the need to make sure that unwanted or polluting land uses are not located primarily in poor neighborhoods. Similarly, although the dominant approach is to limit adult uses to certain zone districts within the city, the various adult use industries (and sometimes the residents of the areas where they are allowed) have argued that this is unfair and that these uses should be distributed rather than concentrated in one area. As a third example, under the federal Fair Housing Act Amendments, some types of group living must be treated as residential uses of land even though they are operated as commercial businesses. As a result, they must generally be allowed in at least some residential zone districts in many cities, but some argue that fairness requires that group living facilities be allowed in all residential districts.

Although strong feelings lie behind these and other social equity arguments, I am not sure that good governance *requires* that zoning ordinances embrace them. Instead, I think good governance requires that the city council conduct an open and inclusive process to determine how these uses will be treated, that they comply with state and federal law, and that they base their decisions on data regarding the impacts of these uses wherever possible.

One reason for the success of group housing advocates has been their ability to find evidence that many types of group housing have few, if any, adverse impacts on neighbors. And although cities have long cited general studies showing that adult uses produce negative neighborhood impacts in the form of litter, loitering, and crime rates, the industries behind these uses have raised the level of discussion by producing studies showing that some uses (for example, bookstores with only a limited amount of adult material and that are not identified by signage as adult bookstores) produce few of those impacts. Most claims that zoning is socially unfair are really claims that decisions about unpopular uses and facilities are made based on criteria other than their real impacts. If that is true, then decision-making processes that focus on documented impacts will result in greater social equity.

Unlike results similarity and social equity, though, the idea of procedural fairness remains an important concept in zoning governance. Citizens expect, and state laws usually require, that similar applications be subject to the same types of review and approval procedures. Those procedures are often spelled out in great detail, including the criteria by which the decision must be made. The focus on procedural fairness, rather than on results similarity, is shown in the litigation strategies of those disappointed by zoning decisions. The first step in most legal challenges is to find a procedural step that was missed or muffed, allowing the challenger to knock out the resulting decision rather than to attack the decision itself. Only if the procedures were constitutionally sound and the statutory requirements were scrupulously followed do plaintiffs challenge the substance of the decision, because governments have wide latitude on that front. When Loudon County, Virginia, adopted a 2003 zoning amendment dramatically reducing the number of homes that could be built in rural areas, it provoked more than two hundred lawsuits. Although plaintiffs were really upset about the substance of the amendment, they went after the procedure used to adopt it, and they were successful. In 2005, the Virginia Supreme Court ruled that the adoption process was flawed and that the revised zoning was therefore invalid.[2]

Although most city governments do a fairly good job of processing similar applications in similar ways, they often fall short on another aspect of procedural fairness: ensuring that unwritten factors do not influence administrative decisions. Most zoning decisions fall within three categories: (1) "ministerial," if the decision is determined only by compliance with objective standards; (2) "discretionary administrative," if they require the staff to use its judgment within boundaries established by city council; or (3) "discretionary legislative," if they are made by the city council within the bounds of the police power.

Rezonings are almost always discretionary legislative decisions, and applicants realize that there is no guarantee that the city council will decide in their favor. That is why the decision was sent to the elected or appointed officials—because it involves legislative judgment as to what is best for the city, and the city council is rarely constrained to make a particular decision. Politics can and does influence this process and applicants who apply for these types of decisions know (or should know) that the answer to their request may be "no."

However, most other zoning decisions are not discretionary legislative decisions. Many are ministerial decisions made by planning staff or an appointed board based on specific criteria. The criterion is usually that the application must comply with the standards in the zoning ordinance. That is how we grant building permits, sign permits, and fence permits. If the application meets the standards in the ordinance, you get a permit; if not, then no permit. For ministerial decisions, the standards are adequately detailed to determine the outcome.

But a wide middle range of administrative zoning decisions are not completely determined by written criteria; they are discretionary administrative decisions. Whether a particular driveway layout will permit adequate access by fire trucks often requires a little judgment by the fire staff. Whether the proposed buffering will adequately protect neighbors from noise impacts also requires some experience and judgment. More seriously, when the fire access regulations conflict with the landscaping regulations, it takes judgment to reconcile them, and most owners would prefer that type of compromise to an outright denial.

Some state zoning enabling acts read as if planning staff are not to exercise any discretion at all—that is, as if all zoning decisions by staff must be completely ministerial. But in practice no ordinance can spell out how every conflict between regulations is to be resolved, so staff has to have some room for judgment. In most ordinances, it is the planning director or zoning administrator who is allowed to make judgments, but in practice, they are also allowed to delegate powers to their employees. Staff numbers make the judgments, but the director remains politically accountable for their decisions. This is not bad—rather, it is good governance. Those who believe a big city zoning ordinance can be administered without making some judgment calls in the process are fooling themselves. Many administrative decisions cannot be ministerial, and trying to make them so would produce a very cumbersome zoning system.

But it is bad governance when politics is allowed to sway administrative decisions. This can happen from various sources. Applicants can pressure (or worse) the director to approve a controversial project, neighbors can pressure (or worse) the director to deny a project that meets the zoning standards, or city council members may have an axe to grind on either side. A planner once told me he got a call from his city manager telling him to "lose the application in a drawer for a while" and not tell his immediate boss about the call or the drawer. Procedural fairness in this case means avoiding undue influence on decisions that are supposed to be made based on professional judgment.

Some cities that scrupulously follow written procedures are lax when it comes to insulating their staff and director from improper influence. Others allow written letters to be sent to staff regarding a particular application—ostensibly to point out factors that staff may not be aware of—but then require that those letters be a matter of public record, that they be circulated to other interested parties, and that the written decision indicate whether the staff member relied on any of those letters when making the final decision. This is slicing things pretty thin—the disappointed party may feel that another opportunity for rebuttal should have been offered—but it does allow for judicial review of the decision and for the staff and director to be held legally and politically accountable for their judgments.

For zoning, the most important benchmark of equity is procedural fairness, and that needs to be defined to include limits on outside influence over administrative decisions. Most ordinances do this in writing, but many cities don't do it so well in practice.

Hint for the future: Future zoning should ensure that similar applications are required to complete similar review procedures and should better insulate administrative and quasi-judicial decisions from improper influence. This is particularly true in the later stages of development approval, after preliminary approvals have been given and investments in reliance on those approvals have been made. In addition, all factors considered in making nonministerial decisions need to be noted in writing so that they can be referred to on appeal.

Efficiency

The evolution of zoning has led to more complex rules, and the resulting regulations often require more time and money to operate. PUDs commonly take a long time to negotiate and also require more staff time to review files to respond to future questions or amendments. It can take time and money to design good performance zoning standards and to measure compliance with them. Form-based zoners would claim that any added time and money spent to understand and comply with a typology of permitted building types and forms is offset by savings from a more flexible approach to uses inside the building. That may be true, but it is too soon to tell whether there is a net time savings.

Efficiency is usually discussed in terms of time and money. But in the case of zoning administration, the time element is more important than the financial costs of actually administering the ordinance. Within any mature city, planning and zoning costs represent a relatively small share of the total municipal budget; zoning administration is an even smaller share. Administrative fees (as opposed to development impact fees) are usually calculated to offset the actual staff expense of reviewing applications, so the application fees themselves are seldom controversial. But if more complex regulations cause cities to spend more time reviewing and approving applications, the efficiency losses to businesses and citizens can be significant. Delaying an approval hearing by one month usually means one more loan payment to be covered before the land can be used as the applicant intends, and an increased risk of losing tenants who are waiting for the improvements to be completed. Multiply those losses by the number of pending applications and it adds up.

In many cities, an increasing percentage of applications cannot be approved by zoning counter staff; they have to be referred to planning staff or design review boards for further review, which usually increases the time required between application and permit. In fact, in some cities the ratio has flipped from a situation where the majority of applications could be approved at the zoning counter to one where more than 50 percent of applications now require consultation with planning, environmental, or design staff before the permit can be issued.

Fortunately, technology has offset some of the decreased efficiency in zoning operations. Aerial photography, computerized maps, and for GIS systems have made it easier to put information in the hands of applicants and opponents of proposed development, as well as planning staff. In May 2004, the American Planning Association reported that e-governance was significantly affecting the administrative costs of planning and zoning. Whereas paper permit applications cost an average of $5 to process, e-permits (permits applied for and issued over the Web) cost an average of $1.65. An estimated 50 percent of local government construction permits are ministerial permits that could be issued this way, but the dollar value of construction authorized by those permits is only 10 percent of the total dollar value of the U.S. construction industry.[3] Much of the remaining 90 percent (or $1.17 trillion in construction) still requires approval through permits that require some degree of discretionary judgment. Technological approaches to the review of applications for those permits have been struggling against increasingly complicated ordinances.

In addition to the time and money required for applicants to get approvals, there are the economic losses to both applicants and neighboring property owners when land use applications experience "surprise endings" late in the process. When an owner receives a special use permit for a gas station subject only to relocation of the driveway by 10 feet (which the owner can do) but the city then inserts a new requirement for design review by a neighborhood design panel, which turns down the project, the government has affected the efficiency of the system by inserting uncertainty. Many states have adopted "vested rights" laws to address this aspect of zoning inefficiency, and these laws will be discussed in chapter 5.

Incidentally, the fact that a zoning decision may decrease some property values is not a sign that the system is "inefficient." Increases and decreases in property values are inherent in the concept of zoning, and courts have been consistently clear that zoning is not legally required to protect the value of each individual property unless there is a state law imposing that requirement. "Highest and best use" of property is and always has been a concept used in real estate appraisal, but it has never been an element of zoning law.

Hint for the future: Future zoning should eliminate unnecessary line drawing among types of uses, zones, and developments that do not differ significantly in community impacts, in order to reduce administrative time required to make and defend those decisions. Review and approval procedures should be simplified as much as possible, and technology should used to put more site-specific facts in the hands of counter staff and citizens. Reviews for compliance with technical standards should be taken out of the public hearing process.

Understandability

One unintended result of the evolution of Euclidean tools is that zoning has become harder and harder to understand. Early in my career, I received advice from an eminent attorney who told me that if I just memorized the Denver Platte River Valley zone district ordinance, I would have mastered something so complex that I would never want for work. Wrapped within one zone district were seventeen subareas, each with its own development  rules and a process by which neighbors had to come together to adopt a subplan before the "real" zoning kicked in. I didn't take the advice, but I later drafted something almost as complex myself.

But zoning ordinances should not be understandable only to lawyers or zoning staff (who usually make the best of a bad situation and learn to live with it); they should be understandable to average homeowners, at least those who have completed high school. Few citizens ever read a zoning ordinance cover to cover, of course, nor should they. The test of understandability is not whether you can hold a picture of the entire ordinance in your mind and see how all the pieces work together, but whether people of average intelligence can find the answers to their questions when they need to. Better yet, two people should be able to look at the ordinances and find the same answers to the same questions. That alone is fairly hard in most ordinances.

Zoning ordinances are difficult to understand because they include some or all of the following:

- Long lists of zoning districts, some of which differ from others in only minor ways.
- Long lists of possible uses, many of which differ from one another in only minor ways and some of which sometimes overlap so that it is not clear what label will be applied to a specific activity.
- Numerous approval procedures, some of which may not be written down or may be administered in ways other than what is written. Often, this is the result of a planning director making a good faith effort to resolve two conflicting requirements, but that rationale and solution are not disclosed to the reader.
- The accretion of new regulations over time and the failure to integrate new material with other, similar material in the ordinance. New regulations about a single type of facility—for example, telecommunications antennae—are often tacked on as a new chapter, even though some of the content addresses permitted structures (which is covered somewhere else in the zoning ordinance), other parts of the text address permitted uses (also covered elsewhere), and still other provisions address review procedures (which are also covered elsewhere).
- Internal inconsistencies among different provisions of the ordinance, leading to the practical impossibility of meeting all the requirements. This is because no one can actually anticipate all of the ways various requirements will combine with different uses on land parcels of

different shapes, sizes, and locations—which is the basic reason why zoning cannot be drafted to eliminate the use of judgment.

- Political compromises that require complicated text to address a very narrow range of problems. Over time, zoning disputes are often resolved by crafting an amendment that "splits the baby" between interest groups. A provision allowing the practice, or disallowing it, would be very short. But many compromises sound more like "If X happens, the rule is A; if B happens, the rule is Y; and if C happens, we'll hold a hearing and make a decision based on the following criteria." It takes a much longer paragraph to describe a compromise than a simple yes or no.
- Separation of zoning-related topics in different chapters of the municipal code (outside the zoning chapter) without good cross-references. For example, some cities put sign controls, parking requirements, and landscaping regulations somewhere else in the city code but fail to provide cross-references showing the zoning reader where to find those materials.
- Failure to explain what you can do if your proposal does not meet the standards in the ordinance, which is one of the most common questions from citizens. There are usually several ways to proceed (e.g., a variance, a special use approval, or a rezoning), but unless the ordinance explains that, opponents think the project cannot be approved and the applicant has to find the way forward through a conversation with staff (which, of course, potential opponents are not privy to).
- Use of planning and zoning jargon rather than plain English.

Understandability is one area where Euclidean hybrid zoning often fails miserably—leading to the impression that only experts can understand zoning.

Hint for the future: Future zoning will simplify land uses and the menu of available zoning districts, and will eliminate ineffective development standards, to improve the understandability of printed versions of a zoning ordinance. The bigger breakthrough will come through the expanding use of Web-based zoning tools that respond to discrete questions and do not require citizens to understand the overall structure of all the zoning provisions.

Predictable Flexibility

The previous five governance topics have been pretty standard—governance 101. Now I'd like to add one that is unique to zoning and not quite so obvious. Good zoning governance requires that there be a good balance between flexibility and predictability in the system. This is an area where the level of discussion needs to be raised several rungs to be more productive.

When a steering committee of luminaries first meets with a consultant to review the city's zoning ordinance, they often say: "All we want is predictability—and flexibility." At one level, this is nonsense. A zoning system cannot be both predictable and flexible on the same point at the same time. My experience is that the speakers really want predictability in some cases and flexibility in other cases. But it is difficult to agree on workable principles about when things should be predictable and when they should be flexible.

For example, on Monday homeowner Mary wants predictability when it is clear that the proposed apartment building on the corner does not meet the minimum setbacks by a foot (she wants it denied), whereas apartment builder Jennifer would like a little flexibility (she wants it approved because the site makes that last foot very expensive to achieve). On Tuesday, Jennifer wears her homeowner hat and wants predictability when it becomes clear that Tom's proposed store expansion on the corner of her block is two parking spaces short of its requirement (she wants it denied). On my most cynical days, I think people want predictability when it favors their interests and flexibility when that favors their interests. In other words, their allegiance is to neither flexibility nor predictability as a guiding principle.

On a deeper level, though, there is wisdom in the desire for both predictability and flexibility, and much of the history of zoning has been an effort to balance and rebalance those two goals. Euclidean zoning was designed to promote predictability. PUDs were designed to give flexibility in design, although if all the details are locked down, the PUD approvals may result in much more predictability about what the future will look like. Performance zoning was also designed for flexibility in approach but predictability in impacts. Form-based zoning aims at more flexibility in uses and more predictability in design. The dance between flexibility and predictability is, in fact, the most constant theme in the history of zoning. And still, on any given day, both citizens and developers (and citizens when they are developers) complain that the results are either too unpredictable or too inflexible.

Good governance requires that we get beyond the words themselves to a better idea of what kinds of things should be predictable and what kinds of things should be flexible. By analogy, this is like designing a "fuzzy logic" transmission for a car. For years, even the best automatic transmissions "hunted" for the right gear when they were climbing slopes. In third gear, the engine was working pretty hard, so the transmission would upshift to fourth, but in fourth the engine didn't have enough torque to maintain momentum up the hill, so it would kick back down to third. This annoyed drivers, who wished the car would just make up its mind. Over time, designers added more gears to transmissions, which solved the problem but made the transmission more complex. A second solution was fuzzy logic, which used a computer chip to recognize when the transmission was hunting and told it to stop, usually by shifting down to third gear and staying there despite the hard work. Drivers were just happy it had stopped hunting. In short, fuzzy logic defined a predictable point (i.e., when the transmission was hunting) and made the transmission flexible with regard to shift points—it bent the usual rules about when to shift, but it did so in a predictable way.

Good governance requires the same approach. It must be grounded in predictability, because knowing what the government will probably do in a certain circumstance is fundamental to both property rights and due process. But it must allow flexibility at defined points in that framework. For example, some Canadian and Indian systems use "tolerance" bylaws to define a range of flexibility (sometimes 5 or 10 percent) around certain standards. Some of those ordinances limit their flexibility to individual properties (like a variance), so that an individual is not required to apply for a variance or prove unique hardship over a 6-inch setback encroachment but a developer cannot design an entire subdivision with 6-inch encroachments.

Hint for the future: Future zoning should recognize the need for judgment in applying zoning regulations, and cities should structure their staffing to make those judgments. Cities should also allow defined degrees of flexibility in applying regulations, clearly define the range of flexibility available to staff and appointed boards, and establish criteria to apply in using that flexibility. In some cases, development standards could vary in predictable ways based on the state of surrounding properties. Predictable flexibility will be particularly important for nonconforming properties and for redevelopment in mature areas.

CHAPTER 5

The Legal Framework for Change

TOMES HAVE BEEN WRITTEN ON THE LAW of zoning,[1] but this is not going to be one of them. To design a better way to zone, we don't need to review all of zoning law—just the framework of constitutional protections that the new system has to respect. There are five basic sources of law related to zoning:

- the U.S. Constitution;
- federal acts adopted by Congress;
- the fifty state constitutions;
- statutes adopted by the fifty state legislatures; and
- the common law that emerges through court decisions.

This chapter reviews only the federal Constitution and laws that affect zoning in all cities, as well as some related common law. We are concerned with both what the federal Constitution and congressional acts say and what they do *not* say, because all those areas of federal "silence" are areas for potential improvements.

Of course, in pursuing a better way to zone, each city also has to comply with its state's constitution, but this book cannot consider each of them individually. Fortunately, many state constitutions have provisions roughly similar to the U.S. Constitution in key areas that affect zoning, especially due process and regulatory "takings" of property. On other topics, such as vagueness and vested rights, the common law has also evolved from similar origins in the state constitutions and federal Constitution. Many points of federal law and common law reviewed in this chapter will find parallels in state law.

In addition, each state has different zoning enabling laws, and cities also have to comply with those laws. But state enabling legislation can and does change much faster than constitutions do. If the federal and state constitutions are the frame within which land use regulation must operate, then state zoning laws are the canvas—and artists can always get another canvas and change the picture. That is not to say that changing state enabling acts is easy. It is often very hard, especially if your profession is not represented by a strong lobby. But state zoning rules change in several states every year. Over the past decades, many states have amended their zoning laws to accommodate PUDs, encourage affordable housing, better protect the environment, accommodate telecommunications facilities, allow form-based zoning, promote Smart Growth, refine vested rights, limit "downzonings," and address a host of other zoning issues that catch legislators' attention.

Between 1994 and 2001, the American Planning Association convened an unprecedented multistakeholder effort called Growing Smarter to craft model state land use acts to replace those based on the outdated Model Zoning and Planning Acts of the 1920s. Drawing on input from numerous planning, transportation, development, and environmental stakeholders, this effort produced two wide-ranging guidebooks offering options for states interested in modernizing their statutes. The premise was that state zoning legislation can and should change. Clearly, state legislators agree with that premise each time they vote to change their zoning laws, which is frequently. So current state laws should not be seen as a straitjacket from which reforms have to extricate themselves.

One key aspect of state enabling law that should be discussed at this point is the amount of freedom granted to local governments to paint their own pictures of how zoning should work. On one end of the spectrum are "Dillon's Rule" states, in which local governments can exercise only those specific powers granted by the state legislature. These states are like paint-by-number pictures; they have to be colored in a certain way, and once they're colored, you will need a different canvas with a different pattern to make a different picture. In Dillon's Rule states, if the zoning enabling act closely tracks existing Euclidean hybrid zoning practices, then changes to the enabling act may be needed before zoning can change in the ways described in chapter 7. At this point, only Alabama, Idaho, Indiana, Mississippi, Virginia, and Vermont are listed as "pure" Dillon's Rule states.

At the other end of the spectrum are "Home Rule" states, which allow their local governments freedom to develop zoning systems within broad parameters set down by the legislature. In this case, the canvas is more like an erasable whiteboard. Local governments have already drawn different pictures within the frame, but the state allows them to change the pictures, so they can simply wipe a part of the board clean and do something different—as long as they stay within the outer limits of Home Rule authority. In Home Rule states, fewer amendments to state legislation may be needed. Thirty-six states have constitutional provisions granting home rule on at least some topics, while another eight states have statutory provisions granting at least partial home rule.[2]

Most states fall somewhere between pure Dillon's Rule states and full Home Rule states; they grant some flexibility to local governments but limit that authority in specific areas. For example, New Jersey limits local authority to ignore regional housing needs, Oregon constrains zoning for development outside of urban growth boundaries, and Florida limits the ability to approve developments of regional impact that may affect neighboring cities.

Finally, constitutional scholars typically divide the powers of government into three parts:

- the power to regulate private behavior and property (the "police power");
- the power to levy taxes; and
- the power to compel property owners to sell their property to the government for public purposes ("eminent domain").

We will limit our discussion to the first of these—police power—because that is the branch where zoning lives. Urban renewal and redevelopment projects often involve the use of eminent domain, but this book will not review practices in that area. Zoning can be reformed with or without changes to eminent domain law. Similarly, property and sales tax reform could have an important impact on the quality of our cities by removing significant temptations to miszone property, but we will not address tax reform. Our concern is with the legal limits on the use of police power to craft a better zoning ordinance.

Due Process

We start with due process because it is the federal constitutional provision that applies most broadly to zoning law.[3] The Fourteenth Amendment to the U.S. Constitution states: "[N]or shall any State deprive any person of life, liberty, or property, without due process of law." Due process has two parts: procedural due process (where most of the action is) and substantive due process (which is rarely violated). In the context of zoning, procedural due process means the rules established to ensure that ordinances are not adopted or used to deprive persons of property without giving those affected a fair opportunity to influence the result. Who is "affected" and what constitutes a "fair opportunity" differs depending on the type of decision being made.

For governments, procedural due process sets up a framework for how laws are made, changed, or applied. For private property owners, procedural due process provides some guarantee that the government must listen to those who will be affected before changing either a law or its applicability to specific land. After a law has been adopted, due process also requires that it not be applied haphazardly or selectively.

The "easy" due process scenario occurs when a government decides to revise its entire zoning text or to add or amend a new provision affecting many property owners. When it does this, the government is using its discretionary legislative powers (see chapter 4)—that is, it is setting a policy or a set of rules that affects many of its constituents. Whether the new or amended law is broadly applied to many people is a key fact; if it looks as if the broad language of the new provisions will truly affect only one or two landowners, a reviewing court may decide that it was really a "judicial" or "quasi-judicial" action, even though it was done by the city's legislative body.

For discretionary legislative actions, the city council can generally meet procedural due process requirements by publishing notice of a hearing to discuss the new law, making the language available to the public in advance, and offering the public a chance to testify on the new law. Individual notice to everyone who might be affected by the new law is not required; nor is it necessary to give an opportunity to cross-examine or rebut anyone who speaks in favor of or opposing the new law. That a general law may affect hundreds of individual property owners does not mean that "individualized" due process is required. Most of the recommendations in chapter 7 address possible legislative amendments to the text of the zoning ordinance, and they would be reviewed under this standard.

In contrast, when the city council makes amendments to the zoning text or map that affect individual properties or only a handful of properties, it is acting in a "judicial" or "quasi-judicial" capacity. It is not making policy for a large number of citizens but instead is acting more like a judge deciding which law (the old zoning or new proposed zoning) will apply to a specific case. When this happens, the city generally does have to give individualized notice to the landowners whose property and zoning are being discussed (and sometimes to their neighbors), often needs to hold a public hearing, and sometimes needs to offer an opportunity to cross-examine or rebut others who have testified in favor of or against the proposed change. City council members are generally not permitted to discuss quasi-judicial cases outside the hearing. The decision needs to be made based only on information presented at the hearing itself, just as a judge has to make decisions based on evidence presented inside the courtroom. If the changes suggested in chapter 7 are going to be applied in ways that will affect only one or a few properties, they are probably quasi-judicial decisions that would need to meet these requirements of individualized due process.

In addition to zoning text and map changes, cities frequently make administrative decisions about minor permits (special use permits, fence permits, sign permits) and variances. These types of administrative actions are either "ministerial," if the decision is determined only by compliance with objective standards, or "discretionary administrative," if they require judgment (see chapter 4). Procedural due process requires that standards for ministerial permits be sufficiently objective so as to determine the outcome of the decision. For discretionary administrative permits, it requires that adequate standards exist to guide the decision maker.[4] Sometimes, procedural due process in discretionary matters also requires that there be a procedure giving at least the applicant (and sometimes others) a chance to be heard. Generally, both ministerial and discretionary decisions can be appealed, usually to a city board or to the courts.

State laws differ significantly on what types of land use decisions require the involvement of the city council, the planning board, the board of adjustment, or a hearing officer. The city council is almost always the decision maker on a zoning map or text amendment, and the board of adjustment commonly decides variances. That's where the predictability of state law ends and each state goes its own way. When state law does not name a specific decision maker, city councils often can delegate the decisions to someone or some group within the city administration, provided that the procedures for delegated decision making comply with the principles of due process.

But what about substantive due process? Regardless of whether you are the government, a property owner, or another citizen, substantive due process requires that the resulting new or changed law not be "crazy." The word *crazy* here doesn't mean that a challenger doesn't like the law or doesn't think it will work. It means that the law logically *cannot* produce the result that the government is trying to achieve. This is a very hard standard to meet, because when a difference of opinion exists as to whether a law will work in a certain way, the courts—as a matter of legal principle—generally side with the government.[5] Only when a plaintiff proves that the new law *cannot* work will she win a substantive due process case.

Substantive due process claims are grounded in the same requirement in the Fourteenth Amendment to the U.S. Constitution that the government not deprive citizens of property except after "due process of law." In essence, the challenger is asserting that although the government may have gone through the proper steps required for procedural due process, the result is nevertheless illegal because there is some nonstatutory reason why the government cannot take that action. In the area of zoning, the claim is usually that the regulation is illegal because, even if the law worked perfectly, it logically cannot produce the result that the legislators were hoping to achieve. Another way of stating this is that there is no "rational relationship" between what the government has done and what it is trying to achieve.

The poster child for substantive due process claims is *Nollan v. California Coastal Commission*, in which a California government agency required a beachfront homeowner to grant public access across the beach in front of the homeowner's proposed replacement house to compensate for the fact that the new house was so wide that inland citizens would no longer see the ocean.[6] Before, they could see the ocean by looking past the sides of the house, but in the future they would not be able to do that. The court held that there must be an "essential nexus" between the goal that the government is pursuing and the regulation imposed on private property. In this case, there was no way that side-to-side access across the beach could compensate for the lack of views from inland properties. Inland citizens whose views were blocked would indeed have to walk to some other place to see the ocean, but better access along the sand on this property would not help them with that view. Interestingly, the court held that it would have been within the government's power to require the house to be narrower, or to prohibit the wider replacement house altogether, because that would indeed have protected the views to the ocean that they wanted to protect.

In addition, courts sometimes find substantive due process violations when it is clear that the government's zoning action was motivated by spite or some other improper motive. Those cases generally involve poor judgment about the enforcement of the ordinance, however, and not the text itself, and they are beyond the scope of this book.

Regulatory "Takings" of Property

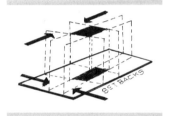

Since the 1980s, the U.S. court system has been flooded with cases claiming that zoning regulations result in a "taking" of private property in violation of the Fifth Amendment to the U.S. Constitution. The actual language of the Fifth Amendment reads: "[N]or shall private property be taken for public use, without just compensation." Volumes have been written to explain what the law is or should be in this complex area, but, unfortunately, much of what is written has a not-so-subtle pro–property rights or pro–government authority bias. Property rights advocates claim that the law in this area is biased in favor of governments and that cities take unfair advantage of the law. Those who support the current levels of government control view the past twenty years of strategic litigation as an assault on basic land use tools that are used fairly most of the time.[7]

The complexity behind takings comes from the fact that it requires judges to compare trends in two very different branches of government law. This book focuses on the government's use of the police power, not on its power to acquire property through eminent domain. But those who claim that zoning regulations take their property (or at least part of it) are asking the courts to agree that the regulation denies them the use of their property as completely as if the government had exercised its eminent domain powers, and that compensation should therefore be paid. The takings battleground is that turf between local government's clear authority to regulate development and the government's clear duty to pay compensation when it acquires property.

Despite the volume of recent takings lawsuits, the law in this area has changed little since the mid-1980s. The basic rules are still these:

- *Denial of every use.* A zoning regulation will be invalidated if it deprives you of *every significant use* of the property—that is, you cannot build, grow, mine, or harvest anything or conduct any meaningful business or residence on the property. These are sometimes called "per se" takings, and they are rare. Even here, though, if the government can show that you did not have a right to those uses under the prior laws of nuisance (i.e., that zoning did not create the problem), the zoning restriction may be upheld.[8]
- *Denial of all reasonable economic use.* A zoning regulation will be invalidated if it leaves you with some uses that sound good on paper but that in fact leave you with no reasonable economic use of the land. Unlike "per se" takings, this usually involves a factual inquiry into the history of your land and your investment in it. The majority of takings cases are in this category.[9] They are difficult to summarize, but the basic framework of the law is as follows:

  - Diminution in property value (even a big one) does not necessarily mean that payment is due.[10] The law focuses on what is left to you after the regulation, not what you paid for the land or the amount by which the value was reduced. Reductions in value of over 90 percent have been upheld without requiring compensation.
  - The property must be considered as a whole in determining whether all reasonable use has been denied.[11] This is troublesome to those who compare regulations to eminent domain actions, because eminent domain law does allow compensation for taking a piece of the property.
  - The taking need not be permanent to earn compensation for the owner. Even if the government revises or repeals a regulation, it may still owe damages if it denied all reasonable economic use during the period the regulation was in force.[12]
  - Cities need to be particularly careful when the regulations require payment of money or dedication of land. The courts see

those areas as particularly ripe for abuse, so cities must be prepared to show that the land or money required is proportional to
the impacts of the proposed development.[13]

- Delays in project review and approval generally do not usually
lead to a taking, unless they were clearly done in bad faith.[14]
To address issues of delay, some states and cities have adopted
laws imposing maximum time limits for application review
or moratoria.

- The fact that a zoning control was in place when you bought the
property does not automatically defeat a taking claim. In the past,
some courts held that a property owner who bought land while
aware of the restrictions on it could not later claim that the
restrictions denied all economic use of the land (i.e., if you
thought the controls destroyed the value of the property, why did
you buy it?). Recent decisions, though, have reasoned that an
unconstitutional regulation does not gain protection just because
the land changes hands; a new buyer can challenge them as well.[15]

- *Improper government motives.* Even if a zoning regulation does not deny
you all reasonable economic use of the property, it may be invalidated if
you can show that the government was trying to achieve a goal it had no
authority to pursue or that it had some other improper motive.
Improper motives can include exacting revenge for your political actions
or speech, attempting to delay you in order to provide an advantage to a
competing developer, attempting to obtain public open space for free,
driving down the value of your land in anticipation of later purchase by
the government, or simply denying successive applications in a way that
suggests maybe you will never get an approval for anything.[16]

- *Interference with reasonable investment-backed expectations.* Some courts
cite this as an additional ground for finding that a taking has occurred,
while others do not. Property owners may acknowledge that the zoning
leaves them with a reasonable economic use of the property and that the
government was not acting from improver motives but then argue that
the government created a reasonable expectation of returns on their
investment and then took inconsistent action after the investments were
made. In *Palazzolo v. Rhode Island*, the U.S. Supreme Court suggested

that even if you cannot prove a denial of all economic use, you may be able to prove a taking by showing that the government's action interfered with reasonable investment-backed expectations in a fact-specific way.[17] Because of the difficulty of showing denial of economic use for an entire property, this alternate theory of takings analysis will probably remain a fruitful field for litigation.

As we work to address the weaknesses of Euclidean hybrid zoning, we can avoid takings challenges by ensuring that landowners are always left with a reasonable economic use of their properties. Generally, this means ensuring that each zone district has a reasonable range of permitted uses that are really possible on the land and paying particular attention to those zone districts intended for parks, open spaces, and environmentally sensitive lands. In the past, open space zoning was used primarily for government-owned land, so it seldom resulted in takings claims. Increasingly, however, it is used on private land—for example to "lock in" open space dedicated as part of a PUD negotiation. One important key to avoiding takings claims is to ensure that zone districts that do not include a reasonable economic use are not used on private property without the consent of the property owner. A second key is to ensure that zoning does not allow public use of private property without the property owner's consent.

The First Amendment

The First Amendment to the U.S. Constitution has an almost mythical quality—not only to lawyers but to American citizens, and not just in the United States but around the world. Law students dream of practicing First Amendment law, but zoning lawyers don't get to do so very often, because the overlap between the First Amendment law and zoning law is relatively narrow. The two main topics of overlap involve freedom of religion and freedom of speech.

Zoning can interfere with freedom of religion when it regulates the size, location, or operation of "religious institutions" or "places of religious assembly," wordy terms used by most updated zoning ordinances to encompass churches, mosques, shrines, temples, synagogues, and other places of religious assembly, all of which are required by law to be treated equally.

Zoning used to allow religious institutions by right in almost all zone districts, with the possible exception of industrial areas and parks. But as zone districts and use lists were divided into ever thinner categories and as mega-churches appeared, this approach fell by the wayside. Cities began to restrict religious institutions— at least large ones—to certain zone districts and to regulate their traffic, noise, and light impacts on their neighbors. From the point of view of some neighbors, noise did not become "not noise" just because it came from church, but some worshipers thought it should be "protected noise." This led to a lengthy debate on how cities could regulate churches, if at all.

To make a long and complicated story shorter, the general conclusion was that religious institutions do not have a constitutional right to be exempt from zoning, but that cities could not single them out for stricter standards than they apply to other places where people gather. In 1993 and again in 2000, Congress adopted laws to codify the general results of prior lawsuits on this topic. The first attempt was invalidated by the Supreme Court.[18] The second attempt (the Religious Land Use and Institutionalized Persons Act of 2000, summarized later in this chapter) has not yet reached that court, but Congress seems intent on adopting a law of some sort in this area and it seems likely that this field will be governed by some federal law in the not-too-distant future. It is wise to be very cautious and evenhanded in regulating these types of uses. In fact, I think the surest way to stay out of trouble in this area is to ask the question, "Do we apply the same rule and procedures to other places where similar numbers of people gather for nonreligious purposes?"

The law on free speech is even harder to summarize, because there are many different kinds of "speech." The main ways zoning may run afoul of the U.S. Constitution are in regulating signs and adult uses. Claims are sometimes made that regulation of building design restricts free speech, but those cases are rare and generally unsuccessful. There is no federal constitutional right to have your building look the way you want it to look.

One way to stay out of trouble in sign regulation is to be very careful about regulating the message conveyed by the sign. Lots of regulations are legal if they are "time, place, and manner" regulations that apply regardless of the message. Although cities can regulate "commercial speech" more than "noncommercial speech" (i.e., political opinions), the line between the two is debatable and the cases are complex. The Highway Beautification Act of 1965 (summarized below) also affects how cities can regulate signs. Because the principles of chapter 7 do not address sign regulation, however, I'm going to resist the temptation to summarize this complex field of law.

Regulating adult uses is another tricky area because it involves not only printed books and magazines but dancing, theatre performances, films, massaging, and other activities that could also occur in a "nonadult" activity. The only thing they all have in common is their subject area, which generally involves sexual activities or some form of nudity. But because restrictions based on the subject matter are difficult to defend, these regulations have to be grounded in some other rational use of the police power. Like most other politically unpopular uses, they are usually restricted to a few zone districts. But this is also true for lots of other commercial uses, so that reason alone does not usually give rise to a constitutional claim. The First Amendment does not guarantee that adult uses have to be free from all regulation. You don't have to allow a family movie theatre in a residential zone, for obvious reasons, so you certainly don't have to allow an adult theater. That part is easy.

But many cities want to go further—they want not only to contain adult uses in certain zone districts but to limit or reduce the number of them. Traditionally, regulations to do that have been grounded in the "secondary impacts" of these uses— that is, cities cannot regulate adult uses based on their message, but they can regulate them based on whether they have specific neighborhood impacts that the city wants to avoid. Some studies have shown that concentrations of adult uses tended to result in more trash, loitering, crime, or declining property values around them, and regulations grounded in those studies have been upheld by the courts.[19] Because the studies addressed concentrations of these uses, the strategy has been to disperse them. Limiting adult uses to a certain zone district, while dispersing them within that district, will limit their number, which is what many cities are trying to achieve.

Note, however, that the legal basis of this approach relies on documented evidence about secondary impacts. In most other areas of zoning, the courts don't question *why* the city council thought uses would have specific impacts, but when free speech is involved the bar is a little higher. This means that if someone can produce studies showing that the secondary impacts do not exist, or that some small groupings do not produce them, the regulations might be overturned. That has been one approach used by the various adult use industries with some success. For example, some studies have shown that bookstores that do not advertise themselves as adult bookstores and that contain only a small percentage of adult materials may not have significant secondary impacts on the neighborhood. According to these studies, the public treats them like other bookstores and behaves the same way in the neighborhoods around them. This may result in cities having to refine their regulations to differentiate among different types of adult businesses and to tie their regulations more closely to documented impacts of those specific types of uses than they have in the past.

For our purposes, however, it does not make much difference. The principles in chapter 7 do not require any specific approach to signs or adult uses and do not involve any new restrictions in either area. Pursuing the better way to zone outlined in chapter 7 will make it neither harder nor easier to comply with the First Amendment than it is under Euclidean hybrid zoning.

Equal Protection

The concept of equality was fairly important in the early zoning debate. Before zoning, property owners were generally treated equally in that they could each put their land to whatever non-nuisance use they wanted. Euclidean zoning held that the city government had the right to divide those property owners into different zones for the good of the city but that property owners in each zone would be treated equally. Owners of land in a residential zone would each be subject to the same rules, even if those rules differed from those applied to owners in the commercial zone. Note that this was a fundamental redefinition of what equality meant in land use, and the courts said that was constitutional.[20]

But over the years, even that degree of equality has been eroded. It is not uncommon for those disappointed by a rezoning to claim that they are a victim of "spot zoning" or that they have an "equal protection" claim against the city, but it is equally common for the city attorney to smile or maybe yawn. The federal constitutional right of equal protection has become largely irrelevant to zoning, except in the three narrow cases discussed below. These days, relatively few equal protection lawsuits are filed, and those that are filed rarely succeed. How did this happen?

There are three answers. First, the right to equal protection enshrined in the U.S. Constitution applies to constitutionally protected federal rights and not to expectations. Owners have federally derived rights to have zoning controls adopted with procedural due process, to pass the test of substantive due process, and to avoid having all of their reasonable economic uses "taken" through regulation, but they almost never have a constitutional right to be in a specific zone district. Zoning regulations are treated as statutory rights that create expectations. You may have expected that existing zoning either would or would not be changed in some way, but that does not create a right grounded in the U.S. Constitution. In almost all zoning cases, a landowner wanting to claim an equal protection violation cannot find a constitutionally protected right that has been denied.[21]

Second, and very importantly, after hearing decades of cases the courts have generally concluded that most parcels of land are unique—that is, it is hard to find another parcel just like the one being considered. This is why results similarity is not an important part of zoning governance (see chapter 4). Even if two parcels of land look, smell, and taste the same, the real estate mantra of "location, location, location" applies. Location is so important to the viable uses of land and to land value that direct comparisons of land parcels in different locations are always subject to attack. Inherent in the concept of zoning is that zone district boundaries will have to be drawn, usually along a street, alley, river, railway, or parcel boundary. Parcels on opposite sides of the line are likely to be very similar. By agreeing that zoning is constitutional, the courts have essentially agreed that those lines will be upheld as long as they're backed by rational reasoning, in effect allowing cities to treat geographically and environmentally similar parcels of land as legally different from one another. That is why claims that two parcels are so similar that they have to be zoned the same way almost always fail.

The evolution of zoning tools made it ever easier to recognize differences between different parcels of land and to give them different consequences, and there is no logical end point to this process (see chapter 1). New zone districts could be created to recognize any rational grouping of uses, so the principle of equality got applied to ever narrower and more homogeneous groupings of uses. Euclidean hybrid zoning is satisfied as long as, for example, you are treated the same as other property in the R-1x zone district, and if you are not, there is no reason the city cannot create an R-1x.5 district. Or they could get the same result in other ways. Let's walk through an example.

There were four parcels of land with ten houses each in the "Residence" ("R") zone. Forty houses all zoned R. Then city council amended the text of the zoning ordinance, with a public hearing, to allow parcels nearer the commercial area to be used for offices while those farther away could not. That was rational and therefore legal. Although city council did not change the zoning map to redesignate the parcels, we'll think of the two parcels (twenty houses) near the commercial area as being "type 1" and the other two parcels (twenty houses) as "type 2" properties. Then council adopted a rule that properties near the river could not be redeveloped as apartments—they did not want large numbers of people living in a potential flood area. One type 1 parcel and one type 2 parcel were near the river and subject to the new restriction. That was very closely related to public safety, so it was legal too. Again, council did this through an amendment to the zoning text (not the map), after a public hearing. We'll think of the two river parcels (with twenty houses) as being a new "type F" (for flood risk). Voila, within a single R zone, the city now had four sets of zoning controls for four parcels: ten houses each of types R(type1), R(type1/typeF), R(type2), and R(type2/typeF). This is shown in the accompanying illustration.

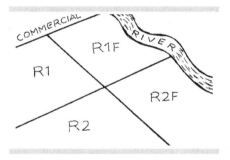

The mechanism for applying different controls really doesn't matter. The city could have come up with a new zone district each time it wanted to apply a new regulation to some (but not all of) the properties in a zone district. But that would have made the zoning map harder to read, with lots of different colors and hatching. If and when the actions were challenged because all the R houses were not subject to exactly the same standards, the city would say: "Look, Judge, we are treating all people in the 'close to commerce' class the same and all those in the 'close to the river' class the same. We've upheld the idea of equal treatment within rational classes of properties, and we used the same due process we would have used if we had created new districts, so why make us create a new zone for each distinction?" And the judge would generally agree.[22] Logically, of course, there is no stopping place. Land could continue to be distinguished by a growing list of characteristics (e.g., geological, historical, fire risk, or just architectural style).

The third reason was that when PUD zoning became common, it was clear that you could custom design your zone district through negotiations with the city, so why get hung up about individualized effects of zoning controls in the other zones? In recent years, some zoning ordinances have even included provisions saying things like: "This zone includes both hillsides and flatlands, and you can build different things in those two subareas. But we don't have the time or money to survey where the line between the two is right now. When you get ready to file an application or you want to sell your property to someone who wants more certainty, we will come out and determine which part is which (based on slopes and soil types and vegetation), and that will determine where you can build what." Courts have upheld this type of language.[23] For all of these reasons, the view that "equal protection" requires similar results lost its place at the zoning table.[24]

This sounds terrible, but it really isn't. To start with, many property owners use PUDs, variances, and special use permits to individualize their zoning controls anyway. There is not a lot of hue and cry for greater uniformity, and courts have found that measuring zoning equality is like measuring puddles of Jell-O.

There are three exceptions to the general irrelevance of federal equal protection rights in zoning. The first is "class-of-one" complaints. When property owners can show that the effect of the city's regulations is to single out their one property for stringent standards and that no rational reason for the decision exists, they can still get the court's attention.[25] In recent years, there seem to be more cases in this class—more cases where the government appears to be singling out one or two landowners for different treatment without an adequate explanation for why it was done.[26] I think this just reflects the end game for individualization of zoning controls. You can proliferate zone districts and controls to apply to ever narrower segments of the city, but when you end up addressing just one property owner, the courts may say: "Time out. Equal treatment is meaningless if there is only one property being compared."

Perhaps that is what the law should be concerned about. Although equality of the land itself is hard to come by, the law should prevent one person from being singled out for unique burdens—unless, of course, those burdens are inherent in the land itself. If you bought the only hillside with a 75-degree slope and unstable soil, your complaint that the city's seismic hazard ordinance singles you out for unfair treatment may sound hollow. There are plenty of cases in which the court says, in effect, "If you buy a swamp, you own a swamp. Don't expect it to be treated like dry land." So some class-of-one challenges fail.

Second, regulations that start to regulate *who* can live in different types of housing may be vulnerable to a claim that they violate federal equal protection rights or privacy rights grounded in the Fourteenth Amendment. Attempts to restrict housing to families or to restrict who will be considered part of the family are on particularly shaky ground.[27] The same applies wherever zoning bumps up against a federally recognized civil right or a class of persons with federal protection.

Third, evidence that the government has singled out a landowner for selective enforcement of the law or for malicious or punitive reasons can still succeed on equal protection grounds.[28] This third exception deals not with the substance of the zoning ordinance, however, but with questionable political decisions about how to enforce the ordinance, which are beyond the scope of this book.[29]

Perhaps more importantly, as courts have become less concerned with whether substantive zoning provisions treat specific parcels "equally," they have given more attention to the procedural fairness of zoning decisions. Courts seem to have decided that the way to avoid unfairness in applying different zoning regulations to apparently similar pieces of land is to examine why and how they were adopted. Concern with the adequacy of notice, the fairness of public hearings, the avoidance of discussions outside the hearing room, the factual basis for the decision, and the absence of suspect motives has picked up the slack from concerns about the equality of land parcels.

All of the above discussion concerns the federal constitutional right to equal protection. Some state constitutions grant broader rights to equal protection than those contained in the U.S. Constitution, and an ordinance that survives federal scrutiny may fail state scrutiny. This is an area where a good understanding of state law is crucial, because selective or unfair application of zoning laws often gets caught on state, rather than federal, grounds.

Vested Rights

Many Americans have a general sense that it would be unfair for the government to change its zoning laws after a developer has moved ahead with a legal development, but the law in this area is more complex than that. This is an area controlled primarily by state enabling acts (not federal law) and by the common law that has evolved over the centuries.

The issue is tougher than it sounds because there is wide disagreement about how far a developer needs to go before the rules of development get "locked in." Is it enough to have bought the land? Paid an engineer to lay out the site on paper? Paid an architect to design the building? Arranged a construction loan? Pulled a building permit for the foundation of the first building? Pulled a building permit for all of the first building? Actually built the foundation?

Before we review the substance of vested rights doctrine, note that this is a "pipeline" issue and that it is very easy to avoid legal troubles in this area. Pipeline problems affect only those projects for which specific applications have been filed before the rules were changed. There is almost no question that zoning text changes can apply to properties where specific applications have not yet been filed, but problems occur when cities try to "catch" unpopular developments through zoning text changes even though the application has been filed. If the city were to adopt a clear policy that all zoning text changes will affect only applications filed after that date, virtually all of the lawsuits based on vested rights would go away. However, that would require elected officials to see the long-term credibility and predictability of the zoning system as more important than responsiveness to short-term complaints (discussed in more detail in chapter 7).

The term *vested rights* is commonly used as shorthand for "I should be able to complete my development under the old rules," but again the law is more complex. Many states have passed detailed laws defining exactly when the old rules get "locked in" for purposes of a particular development. In general, those laws set a time in the development process after which the city cannot apply some kinds of new regulations unless the developer is compensated for any resulting damages. The government's power to change the rules is not taken away, but it has to pay for the exercise of those rights, just as it does when it buys private land.

However, in the absence of a state vested rights law (or alongside one, if it exists), there is the common law doctrine of vested rights. In general, it states that property owners are entitled to rely on the development rules as they are on the date they actually started building the building. Buying the land and filing an application for a permit are generally not enough under common law, even though "soft costs" for engineering and architecture may have been incurred.[30] Construction must have started (i.e., "hard costs" must have been incurred), and in some states the construction must be of something beyond the foundation. I think this rule is a carryover from days where preconstruction soft costs were fewer and less expensive—days when the applicant had not spent a lot of money (except to purchase the land) before getting a building permit. The move toward vested rights statutes that set the magic date at the time of application rather than the building permit reflects the reality that zoning, engineering, design, and environmental controls now require significant investment prior to the issuance of a permit and actual construction.[31]

Although disputes over vested rights are relatively rare, they do illustrate a weakness in the current zoning system. These disputes often arise because zoning ordinances are unclear or inconsistent about what can be developed. What applicants view as legitimate business opportunities the neighbors may view as a loophole that should have been closed before the application was filed. Even though elected officials may sympathize with the applicant and like the proposed development, when faced with a roomful of angry voters the temptation is strong to change the rules and make the voters happy. When this happens, it creates economic inefficiency that could have been avoided. Zoning ordinances should be designed to make this hard to do, and the best way to do this is to build in vested rights provisions and a program of periodic zoning review. The more zoning is treated as a land management system that needs to be kept current—in terms of market demand, development models, and citizen preferences—the more the temptation to make postapplication changes can be avoided.

Vagueness

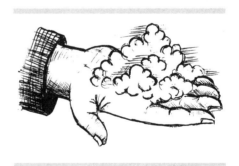

Even if a zoning regulation is adopted with adequate procedural due process and it passes the "not crazy" test of substantive due process, it may be invalid if it is worded so vaguely that a reasonable property owner cannot determine how to comply with the law. A law that is too vague for citizens to understand is probably also too vague for the courts to review when the city's actions are challenged. If the law doesn't clearly state what is "good enough" to get an approval, then how can an appeals board or a court decide whether the enforcement officials overstepped his or her bounds?[32] Although citizens are often confused by the wording of zoning ordinances, that alone does not necessarily make them unconstitutionally vague; in fact, it is fairly rare for a zoning law to be invalidated on these grounds.[33]

My own personal favorite example is the use of the word *appropriate* in development standards and design guidelines. Appropriate according to whom? You say it's not appropriate, and I say it is. The word *compatible* is another good candidate for this honor. Compatible according to what criteria? Nevertheless, courts have upheld the use of standards involving the use of both "appropriate" and "compatible." When challenged on vagueness grounds, cities that use these terms succeed when they can show the court that the zoning ordinance, taken as a whole, has enough detailed content to "fill in the blanks" as to what will be held appropriate. Better yet, cities survive the challenge when they can point to a definition of those terms that fleshes them out—for example, by saying that "compatibility" includes similarity in height, bulk, setbacks, materials, or roof shapes (or two or three of those five). With that kind of additional guidance, zoning officers can make some reasoned judgments and courts can review whether those judgments were sound. The planning staff reviewing applications still usually get the benefit of the doubt, but they have to have a leg to stand on; they cannot be making things up as they go along without any guidance.[34]

Vagueness cases may also turn on how the city has enforced the requirement in the past. In some cases, design and development standards that would have passed the vagueness test on their wording alone have been invalidated where plaintiffs could show that the results had been random. Showing a judge the clear wording of the ordinance and then pictures of wildly different developments that have been approved (or very similar ones that have been denied) may lead the judge to conclude that the standard is unconstitutionally vague "as applied." Some lawyers claim that these decisions should instead uphold the standard and then invalidate the action as arbitrary and capricious enforcement, but they are nevertheless sometimes reported as vagueness cases.[35]

This is one area where we need to pay attention as we think about a better way to zone, because one way to insert more flexibility into zoning ordinances is to use more general terms and standards. The terms that are used will need to pass the vagueness test, and the best way to do that is to define the factors to be considered in applying each term. This requires some degree of care in drafting standards—particularly development and design standards—but the extra effort will pay rich rewards down the road.

Preemption by State and Federal Law

The six topics above cover most of the constitutional limits on our search for a better way to zone, as well as the common law of vested rights. But one more category of restrictions applies to all U.S. cities and is often ignored in today's zoning ordinances. In a small but growing number of areas, local zoning powers are being preempted by state or federal legislation. In Dillon's Rule states, the state laws clearly constrain local zoning powers. In Home Rule states, the city governments have more latitude, and there is room for argument (and plenty of real argument) as to whether the state mandate in fact binds local government. Areas of state preemption vary widely from state to state, and reviewing them all is beyond the scope of this book.

Federal law is a little clearer. In those limited areas where Congress has inserted itself in land use, it generally claims a right to regulate under the Commerce Clause of the U.S. Constitution, and its powers have generally been upheld. The significant areas of federal intervention in land use law are summarized below in roughly the order they affect zoning decisions. Those listed at the start of the list tend to come up regularly, while those listed later affect zoning decision less often.

- The Telecommunications Act of 1996 limits local powers to restrict telecommunications antennae, dishes, and other facilities in certain ways in order to encourage the availability of services and competition in the industry.[36] It also prevents local governments from making decisions about siting of telecommunications facilities based on possible electromagnetic effects if they meet federal standards.
- The Religious Land Use and Institutionalized Persons Act of 2000 (RLUIPA) generally prevents local governments from singling out religious land uses for extra levels of control that do not apply to other places of assembly.[37] Although more than a hundred suits have been filed citing RLUIPA, the act has been upheld by the Eleventh Circuit Court of Appeals.[38] Provisions of the act addressing the rights of

institutionalized persons have been upheld by the Supreme Court, but provisions addressing land use have not yet been heard by that court.[39]

- The National Manufactured Housing Construction and Safety Standards Act of 1974 sets standards for adequate construction of mobile homes built since the 1960s and prevents local governments from adopting different construction standards or from subjecting mobile homes to building codes applicable to stick-built houses.[40] Although the act clearly targets construction standards rather than zoning practices, there has been litigation about whether it requires manufactured housing to be permitted in residential zone districts.

- The Americans with Disabilities Act of 1990 includes provisions requiring that "places of public accommodation" (i.e., places where the public is likely to be present, as defined in the act), commercial facilities, mixed-use facilities, and religious institutions meet federal standards for accessibility of the building and various facilities on the site.[41]

- The Fair Housing Amendments Act of 1988 addresses discrimination in the sale or rental of housing to persons with certain "handicaps," as defined in that law.[42] However, it also has provisions creating liability for "otherwise mak[ing] unavailable" housing to such persons (which could happen through zoning provisions) and requires that cities make "reasonable accommodations in rules, policies, practices, or services, when such accommodations may be necessary to afford [a handicapped] person equal opportunity to use and enjoy a dwelling."

- The Highway Beautification Act of 1965 requires that states receiving federal highway funds establish a program to control various types of signs near interstates but allows local government to override those controls in commercial and industrial areas.[43] In other types of zone districts (notably residential or open space), state controls apply.

- The Clean Air Act requires states to adopt and implement State Implementation Plans to meet federal air quality standards.[44] Although it does not mandate specific local zoning actions, states sometimes consider whether zoning needs to be changed or limited in order to reduce pollutants, particularly vehicle emissions related to the number of lane miles built or auto miles traveled.

- The Clean Water Act authorized the Environmental Protection Agency

(EPA) to establish acceptable effluent levels for water pollutants and established a system under which EPA could delegate some of the implementation authority to state governments.[45] Section 404 addresses permitting of alterations to wetlands, a source of great controversy and uncertainty as to the types of lands and wetlands covered. Like the Clean Air Act, it does not require specific zoning provisions, but zoning changes could be one tool considered by state and local regulators to help meet federal water quality standards.

It is usually not the city government's job to enforce federal laws, and some state laws that preempt local authority do not impose an affirmative obligation on the city to implement or enforce them. Still, most property owners want their buildings to be legal, and those who violate federal laws in their development risk enforcement by federal authorities. When enforcement suits occur, the cities that approved the violating development sometimes get drawn into them. Many property owners are not even aware of these areas of state federal authority. They assume that the city controls development, and the city does nothing to change that perception.

At a minimum, cities should cross-reference the applicable federal laws on their Web sites and on their forms (preferably e-forms). Occasionally, city attorneys object that acknowledging a federal law that purports to control development implies city agreement that it applies or obligates the city to enforce it, and they do not want to do that. I think this is poor governance and a significant source of confusion to the public. In many cases, courts have already determined that the federal laws listed above apply to local governments and to private property owners within their cities. The small (and, I would say, theoretical) benefit to cities in not acknowledging those laws is clearly outweighed by the value to the public of knowing what laws apply to their land and being able to avoid legal challenges from the federal government.

Now that we have reviewed the legal framework that defines the outer edges of zoning powers, let's move on to consider how Euclidean hybrid zoning could be transformed, over time, into a better way to zone.

CHAPTER 6

What Have We Learned?

SO WHAT HAVE WE LEARNED FROM THIS grand experiment with zoning? I think there are eight lessons that, taken collectively, point the way toward a better way to zone.

Eight Lessons

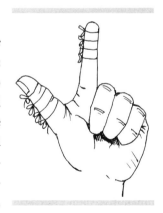

The first lesson from the past ninety years is that *the Euclidean zoning foundation—the basic idea—is both very durable and clearly flawed*. On the one hand, no one has really managed to replace the fundamental concept of use controls, box controls, and variance procedures, although box controls have been refined into more detailed form and design controls sometimes. On the other hand, we remain almost continually dissatisfied with the zoning tools we have. Citizens, planners, legislators, and designers have been trying to fix it, expand it, limit it, or change it ever since 1916, and we are still working on it.

As a result, it is not surprising that almost all so-called Euclidean zoning systems used today are actually hybrids that draw on the major innovations of the past ninety years. Some parts of the regulations incorporate performance measures, some areas of the city are subject to fairly detailed design or form-based controls, and there is almost always the ability to cut your own deal through the PUD process. But most of these non-Euclidean improvements explicitly or implicitly rely on Euclidean zoning as a backstop. They show up as islands in a sea of Euclidean zoning. Some cities have more islands of exceptions than they have basic Euclidean water around them, so maybe we should say they represent dry land in a Euclidean delta. In either case, the system still relies on the water of Euclidean zoning to make sure all the territory is covered. The improvements on Euclidean zoning over the years still don't answer all the questions about property and development, and they implicitly assume that the parts of Euclidean zoning that they did not change are still in effect.

Future zoning will therefore need to build on the Euclidean hybrid foundation. The past ninety years of work have not been in vain, but the resulting hybrid is not well suited to the needs of today's mature cities. Future zoning needs to be a better mix of the Euclidean systems and the alternatives presented to date (plus new innovations we have not even thought of), and it needs to keep up-to-date with changing cities better than it has in the past.

The second lesson is that *as the Euclidean hybrid zoning systems have gotten more complex, the amount of time and money required to administer them has also increased.* Planning and zoning departments now need more specialized skills. They often need to know how to measure adverse impacts like noise, glare, emissions, vibration, and wind, which could require training in how to use specialized equipment. They need to be able to review design details for specialized areas and to refer back to the files to pull out an increasing number of PUDs and compare the proposed development to the standards in lots of one-off approvals.

Future zoning will need to be simplified by eliminating outdated controls that are ineffective or inflexible, by eliminating distinctions that are unrelated to actual impacts, and by limiting the use of labor-intensive tools to important situations. Overreliance on PUDs will need to be reduced. We also need to make the quantum leaps in efficiency available through Web-based tools.

A third lesson from the past ninety years is that, *although the structure of Euclidean zoning is not inherently rigid and detailed, it has a tendency to become rigid and detailed over time.* This is probably because the politics of neighborhoods leans toward predictability, which leads to ever-finer use distinctions and design controls. In the process, distinctions among uses seem to have gotten disconnected from their actual impacts. Variances have always been intended to inject a dose of flexibility, and they have been used much more often than we originally thought would be necessary. All major reforms of the original Euclidean idea have been touted as more flexible than Euclidean zoning with variances. Performance zoning loosens up on physical parameters, form-based zoning lightens up on uses, and PUDs allow you to negotiate just about anything.

Future zoning will need to accommodate the need for flexibility better than our current zoning tools. More importantly, future zoning will need to satisfy the yearnings for both predictability and flexibility in politically acceptable ways.

Fourth, *many of the assumptions behind the Euclidean model have proven false.* In many cases, the assumptions paid too little attention to how mature, already-developed cities operate. They assumed one-time zoning ordinance adoption, with variances and nonconformities as minor issues. But as zoning ordinances continue to be amended, the need for variances and the number of nonconformities increase. Uses and structures that do not meet zoning requirements remain in place for decades. It turns out that one-size-fits-all development standards do not work well and that greenfield development standards are often counterproductive when applied to mature areas because they discourage reinvestment and redevelopment. In short, the basic Euclidean hybrid system focused too much on guiding new development, which is treated as a city design problem, and too little on promoting reinvestment and renewal of older areas, which requires more focus on managing and improving what you have.

Future zoning will need to acknowledge that the standards we want and need to apply to older developed areas are not the same as those we need to apply to new development areas. It will also have to address nonconformities more realistically and more flexibly than zoning has in the past.

The fifth lesson is that *the pressures exerted on zoning decisions by market forces, by politics, and by municipal finance restrictions have increased dramatically.* The politics behind zoning have been strongly influenced by growing demand for attainable housing, which puts a premium on higher density or cheaper land. Zoning has also been influenced by tax caps that create biases in the system toward zoning for commercial development. The growing importance of transportation systems has also driven many zoning decisions as voters demand mobility but resist road expansions in their neighborhoods. Neighborhood resistance to change has increased, particularly to uses that will increase traffic or might reduce the average home value in the area. Again, this discourages development of attainable housing. Some of these forces were not anticipated when basic zoning tools were designed, and others have turned out to be more powerful than anyone anticipated.

To be effective, future zoning will need to be better able to resist or avoid some of the powerful political and market forces that have biased land use decisions— particularly those biases that lead to narrow-minded or short-term decision making.

The sixth lesson is that the changing structure of the American economy is making it more difficult for many citizens to afford housing, and *zoning often compounds the problem of providing attainable housing through regulatory barriers or rigid definitions of permissible lots and housing types.* Although traditional zoning approaches address different types of housing, most are not linked to serious analysis of attainability for both current and anticipated residents of the city. Some cities have innovated by allowing creative lot arrangements, clustering of densities, and more flexible approaches to housing, but those new ideas have still not allowed the supply of attainable housing to rise with demand. NIMBYism has compounded this problem, because building more attainable housing often requires housing that will differ in size, density, or appearance from development around it.

Future zoning will need to pay more careful attention to the combined impacts of regulations and standards on the affordability of housing and will need to allow significantly more flexibility than we do now. In addition, future zoning will need to incorporate procedural changes to make it easier for attainable housing to be approved and built.

Seventh, as it has evolved, *Euclidean hybrid zoning has become disconnected from some important aspects of good governance.* Procedural fairness has been compromised because administrative decisions have not been shielded from improper political or personal influences. Zoning ordinances remain difficult for the public to understand; almost no one outside of city government, zoning lawyers, and very committed citizen activists can explain how the system works. And most zoning systems are inefficient because increasing complexity requires more staff and, sometimes, longer reviews. Some systems politicize later stages in the approval process, which feeds NIMBYism and increases economic losses through surprise endings. Predictable flexibility has not been achieved, as both citizens and developers continue to be upset by both overrigidity and unpredictable outcomes.

Future zoning will need to take into account the time and effort required to run the system, which appear to be increasing without a commensurate increase in quality of our built communities. It will also need to focus more closely on understandability to citizens, to encourage involvement when standards are being established, and to limit opportunities for political decision making late in the development review process.

Eighth, *zoning remains a mostly static tool.* If we are lucky, it is tied to a clear picture of a desirable future developed through good planning. If we are unlucky, it is not tied to a planning vision, but buried deep in those regulations is an implicit picture of the future that zoning is promoting—one that may not have had the benefit of public discussion and debate. Because it is static, we spend a lot of time amending and re-amending zoning to catch up with an ever-moving vision of the future. We are making planning less static all the time, however. Market opportunities and our understanding of the environment change fast enough that we no longer use static physical plans to create detailed snapshots of the city's physical development. For the city as a whole, we do "vision" or "strategic" plans. The physical details are left to be filled in by smaller-scale neighborhood plans or, where those plans don't exist, by zoning regulations. The result is a dynamic plan that changes as opportunities arise, tied to zoning that is stuck on fixed standards—standards that are often anchored in a prior rigid snapshot.

Future zoning will need to become more dynamic so that it can anticipate some degree of changed circumstances and adjust to them in predictable and politically acceptable ways. Many types of development standards can be made automatically adjustable to changed circumstances in the surrounding area and, therefore, more efficient to administer and more supportive of investment and reinvestment in mature cities.

Focusing on the Process of Zoning Change

To respond to these lessons, we need to focus on the *process* of zoning change rather than on a fixed "model" of what correct zoning looks like. The better way to zone described in chapter 7 is not a model ordinance but a guide to healthy zoning change over time.

Larger cities rarely adopt mandatory model zoning ordinances, even though several are already available, including *A Unified Development Ordinance*, the *SmartCode*, and the *International Zoning Ordinance*

(2006). All of them contain good provisions, and that is what big cities generally use them for—as good templates for addressing specific problems. Big cities usually pick, choose, revise, tweak, redraft, and then adopt those provisions that look as if they will work, and they leave the rest of the model alone. Some smaller cities do indeed adopt model codes as a whole, but even that is rare. Even in small cities, model regulations are generally adopted only for key areas where the city wants to see innovation or a different pattern or quality of development.

The reason model codes are used as tool kits to draw from—rather than as systems to adopt—is simple. Most of our urban areas are already developed. They are not blank sheets of paper on which the future can be sketched to our liking. They represent tens of thousands of properties and owners that did not develop according to any pattern book. They are messy, not in a pejorative sense but because the development patterns are a bit of this and a bit of that. Some prezoning development, some development under Euclidean zones, some PUDS, maybe pockets of form-based or traditional neighborhood development, all seasoned with a strong dose of variances and special use permits that make it very difficult to see any pattern at all. And that is OK. We long ago abandoned the idea that zoning would produce uniformity, even within a given district. "Messiness" in the built environment—particularly in older areas where time and change have had longer to operate—means that it is difficult to impose a pattern on them after the fact. Designers like to do that, but it can be taken too far and it can cause problems.

In the mid-1990s, I worked in St. Petersburg, Russia, and met with several municipal officials. Prior to the fall of the Iron Curtain, city planners in Russia had lots of power (and economic planners had even more). In fact, the planning director was called the chief architect, and he treated his city almost like a bar of soap ready to be carved into a beautiful pattern. For historic structures, this meant complete control over both the exterior and the interiors as well as over everything that could be seen as you looked out from the historic building or viewed the building from surrounding properties. They had complete control based on rigorous design analysis—at least in theory.

Surrounded by the imperial avenues, ornate palaces, and elaborate churches of Peter the Great's capital, it was easy to see the benefit of that approach. But most of the memorable buildings were built hundreds of years ago, long before the communist approach to land use and long before the postcommunist systems of private property, real estate development, and financial institutions that

Russia has seen since 1990. The more modern parts of St. Petersburg— Petrograd and Leningrad—are much less impressive. Total control based on an idealized model did not produce quality. But planners in Russia still had a hard time adjusting to a world in which they could not impose a very detailed preferred pattern on the city.

The truth is that zoning for mature, built-up areas should be one part design pattern and two parts land management. Large redevelopment projects may provide an opportunity to reinvent an area to match a detailed master plan, but those projects are the exception rather than the rule. The bread and butter of zoning in mature cities—U.S. as well as Russian—is small-scale, one-owner applications to expand, change, rebuild, or replace a single building or to change the uses inside it. The pattern of development depends primarily on which owners decide to replace or rebuild their buildings and when they get around to doing it.

Early in my career, I fell into the trap of thinking that you could impose a beautiful design through zoning. I believed that the best future was one in which you drew a pretty picture of how the world should be (preferably with the consent of the property owners). Once you had the picture in focus, you pressed the shutter and "locked in" the standards to make the picture come true. But life seldom turns out like the picture you envisioned, and that is true both for the city and for private developers. Ask any owner of a significant multibuilding PUD how many times it was revised before the last building was competed. The larger the scale of the development, and the more time elapses, the more revisions you get. City zoning ordinances have the biggest canvas of all—they purport to regulate the entire city over a long time period—and that means that lots of things are going to change in unexpected ways.

For all of these reasons, it is a mistake to think of zoning as a fixed model of uses and standards and forms that will work well over time. The only sure thing about zoning is that what we need it to do will change over time. Instead of aiming toward a fixed model, it helps to think of zoning reform as a *process* guided by principles that will make it more effective, easier to understand, and more durable over time. Chapters 7 and 8 outline a process approach to reforming Euclidean hybrid zoning and describe how to get started on the road to reform.

CHAPTER 7

A Better Way to Zone

THIS CHAPTER CONTAINS TEN PRINCIPLES to guide the process by which zoning for large, mature cities can be improved. They are based not on a designer's picture of the future (because one size—or even six sizes—does not fit all) but on a governance picture of the future. They acknowledge that zoning change tends to be evolutionary rather than revolutionary, because most property owners have at least a passive interest in the current rules and many of them do not wake up in the morning yearning for change. These ten principles respond to the lessons of the past—not just individual mistakes but the pattern of mistakes and corrections that has led us to current Euclidean hybrid zoning. It is these "meta-lessons"—the big lessons behind the smaller corrections—that we need to learn and remember as we revise the zoning ordinance.

The ten principles of a better way to zone are:

1. more flexible uses;
2. the mixed-use middle;
3. attainable housing;
4. mature areas standards;
5. living with nonconformities;
6. dynamic development standards;

Table 7.1: Ten Key Changes to Euclidean Hybrid Zoning

	More Flexible Uses	Mixed-use Middle	Attainable Housing	Mature Areas Standards
FAILED ASSUMPTIONS				
A Few General Rules		✔	✔	✔
Separate the Uses	✔	✔		
Greenfield Standards			✔	✔
Variances Will Be Rare	✔	✔		✔
Nonconformities Go Away	✔	✔		✔
Static Rules				
Zoning Is Technical				
NEW LAND USE DRIVERS				
The Market	✔	✔	✔	✔
Tax Caps		✔		
Transportation Systems	✔	✔		
NIMBYism	✔	✔	✔	
GOVERNING WELL				
Effectiveness		✔	✔	✔
Responsiveness		✔		✔
Equity			✔	
Efficiency	✔			✔
Understandability	✔	✔		
Predictable Flexibility	✔	✔		✔

     7. negotiated large developments;

     8. depoliticized final approvals;

     9. better webbing; and

   10. scheduled maintenance.

Table 7.1 summarizes how these ten principles respond to the critiques in chapters 2, 3, and 4. Each section of this chapter includes a discussion of the specific ways these ten principles will improve zoning. In addition, each section

Living With Non-conformities	Dynamic Development Standards	Negotiated Large Developments	Depoliticized Final Approvals	Better Webbing	Scheduled Maintenance
	✔	✔			✔
✔		✔			
✔					
✔		✔			✔
✔					
	✔				✔
		✔	✔		
	✔	✔			✔
	✔				
	✔	✔			✔
	✔	✔	✔		
✔		✔	✔		✔
✔		✔		✔	
			✔		
	✔		✔	✔	✔
✔			✔		
	✔		✔		

includes a brief discussion of how the principle complies with the legal framework of zoning outlined in chapter 5.

I make no claim that the reforms described in this book can be adopted under existing state statutes. In some cases, they may require changes at the state level, but history shows that the state canvas can and does change. You will need to consult with a zoning lawyer licensed in your state to confirm whether and how the principles in this chapter can be applied under your state constitution and enabling acts.

More Flexible Uses

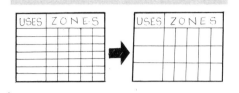

To understand the first two principles in this chapter, we first have to
envision how Euclidean hybrid
zoning identifies permitted, condi-
tional, and prohibited uses in each zone district. Old-style ordinances listed each
permitted and conditional use over and over again in a separate list for each zone
district. Newer ordinances generally save ink and trees by listing them all in a
table. The left-hand column of the table contains the full list of possible uses that
may be allowed in different zones—generally one use per line. Each column to
the right lists a different zone district available in the city. The table includes
symbols in each "cell" (the intersection of a line and a column) to indicate
whether each use is allowed by right, conditionally allowed, or not allowed in
each district. Even when old-style ordinances do not have a permitted use table,
some planner invariably has a homemade table in a desk drawer somewhere, just
because it is a useful thing to have.

The first principle is to lighten up on the left-hand column of permitted uses.
Many zoning ordinances contain pages and pages (and pages) of narrowly defined
uses (see chapter 2). Usually, the longest lists are in the heavier commercial zones
applicable to downtowns, shopping centers, and along major arterials. When I
worked for the City and County of Denver, the list of uses for a single zone
district—the downtown B-5 district—had eighty-three permitted or conditional
uses (plus two categories allowed anywhere in the city). The first use was listed as
"a"; when the single-letter alphabet ended, they went on to "aa" and so forth until
the last use appeared pages later as "eeee."

Some large city zoning ordinances went further. They crafted their lists of nonresidential land uses to match either the 1987 list of Standard Industrial Classification (SIC) codes or the North American Industry Classification System (NAICS)
codes, which replaced the SIC codes in 1997. There are twenty-four two-digit
NAICS Codes, which are further divided into ninety-six three-digit codes and then
even further into four-, five-, and six-digit codes describing very specific activities.
A single three-digit code—NAICS code 311, which includes food manufacturing—
is divided into a total of seventy four-, five-, and six-digit codes reflecting specialized activities. When they used the NAICS codes as the basis for listing permitted

uses, cities often used a mix of general (two- or three-digit) headings for some activities and were very detailed (four- or five-digit) headings for activities that were unpopular or anticipated to have serious impacts. However, both the SIC and NAICS classification systems were created by the U.S. Census Bureau to count enterprises of similar types, and researchers use them to make sure they are studying identical or similar industries. They were not created to serve as a basis for zoning and they are not well suited to that purpose.

A better approach is the Land-Based Classification System (LCBS), developed with the assistance of the American Planning Association.[1] This system, which was created specifically for planning-related activities, evaluates properties in terms of activity, function, structure, site, and ownership. It is designed to promote a common language for geographic information systems (GIS) so that planners from different cities can compare data with some confidence that they are talking about the same thing. However, the LCBS authors acknowledge that "there can never be a one-to-one match between zoning districts and land-use categories, in so far as it relates to land-use data. Land uses in zoning refer to multiple land-use characteristics, not just activity, structure, function, ownership, or site development character. To regulate land uses, zoning districts employ generalized groupings of multiple land-use characteristics, and such groupings are a function of each community's prerogative."[2]

In other words, the LBCS was not intended to define zoning use categories, because zoning should be based on groupings of uses that *matter* to the city and those will always differ among cities. The solution is to

- combine the list of permitted uses into fewer, broader categories based on real impacts
- control the scale of the activity, which really does have an impact
- adopt performance standards that control the external impacts of land use activities—often by regulating how they are operated rather than how they are built.

Deemphasizing uses, and reemphasizing scale, is another idea where form-based zoners got it right.

The three best places to start looking for ways to simplify uses are the lists of retail, service, and industrial uses. Although some large-format retailers need to be treated differently (e.g., car dealers, big box retailers, home/garden suppliers, and furniture stores), most small-scale retailing has very similar impacts. There is very little difference among the land use impacts of a bookstore, a music store, a pet store, a sporting goods store, and a hardware store of the same size. Allowing the owner to replace one with another, without getting permission from the city, generally helps keep the building occupied and promotes economic stability. Retailing can be grouped into a few general categories; some cities use only "small" (under 5,000 square feet), "large" (5,001 to 75,000 square feet), and "special" (including large-format stores, "warehouse" sellers, and those with big outdoor sale or display areas).

Service uses are also good targets for consolidation. Long lists of service providers often can be collapsed into just two general uses: personal services and business services. Again, impacts related to specific uses within these categories can be addressed by regulations that target only those uses. For example, if courier services like FedEx are causing specific impacts (lots of trucks coming and going), they can be addressed through use standards targeting that specific activity; it doesn't require another listed use.

It also helps to review industrial use lists. The older the list is, the more likely it is that the industry has found a "friendlier" way to operate or a new technology that avoids the feared impacts. Some cities have changed from having literally scores of listed industrial uses (sometimes more than one hundred in NAICS-code ordinances) to only a handful. Some cities now operate with only a "general" (no anticipated external impacts; limited truck traffic) industrial use and a "heavy" (external impacts; heavier truck traffic) industrial use. Some add a third category for "special" industrial activities, which generally includes those that use dangerous chemicals, ship dangerous products, or know in advance that they cannot meet operating standards on noise or odor.

Those who oppose the idea of fewer, broader uses—or of mixed use in general—sometimes cite examples of hot button uses that you would not like to find hidden in a broader category. The usual examples include bars, pawn shops, day labor halls, fast-food restaurants with drive-through lanes, adult theaters, massage parlors, and payday check cashing services. Some neighbors get apprehensive about the possible impacts of these uses, even though studies show that in some cases the impacts are no greater than other uses in similar categories. In other cases, the feared impacts could be better addressed through a business licensing program—that is, if you generate those impacts, you lose your license to operate, even though the activity itself is still allowed in the zone. In still other cases, the key is better enforcement of operating standards. The best way to address noise and loitering issues may be to enforce those noise and loitering ordinances rather than to prohibit uses that may or may not create those impacts.

But sometimes these arguments do not prevail and neighborhoods want specific uses carved out from larger, general categories so they can know that specific uses will *not* be included. They may want to know, for example, that "personal services" will *not* include a massage parlor. If that happens, carve it out and give it a separate use name. But the fact that you have to carve massage parlors out of personal services does not mean that you have to similarly identify all other specific types of personal services in the permitted use table. Allowing these occasional exceptions for the sake of neighborhood comfort that an unwanted use will not occur nearby is a small price to pay for the simplification that broader land use categories brings to the ordinance.

Once the list of permitted uses has been consolidated into a broader, more flexible use list, two related issues need to be reviewed and refined in order to avoid unanticipated impacts on the surrounding neighborhoods. Those two issues are scale and parking.

There are three basic ways to address the scale of activities to ensure that they fit into the fabric of the city around them. The first is to include a size (or traffic) limit on the use itself—like the example of a "retail, small (under 5,000 sq. ft.)" use discussed above. The second is to include a use-specific regulation cross-referenced to the use. For example, there could be a single "retail, general" use cross-referenced to a regulation stating that "in the B-1 zone this is limited to 5,000 sq. ft.; in B-2 and B-3 it is limited to 60,000 sq. ft." The third solution is to separate zoning use designations from scale controls altogether. For example, you could have a B-1 zone district listing uses without any size controls or cross-references, but each time the B-1 zone is applied, it is paired with a set of scale standards controlling the size of development. So you could have B-1/S (for small), B-1/M (for medium), and B-1/L (for large). That may reintroduce some of the detail that you removed when you consolidated uses into broader categories, but this time the details are more closely related to actual impacts.

Most cities interested in simplifying their ordinances follow one of the first two approaches (i.e., use names that include maximum sizes or a use-specific regulation allowing different maximum sizes in different zoning districts). Although the third, "modular" approach is conceptually sound—and it should theoretically be easier to mix and match use and scale modules to fit the existing fabric of the city—developing the scale modules takes some hard work. For example, the scale modules not only need to address the maximum (or minimum) sizes of individual buildings but sometimes also need to address size limits for individual uses (e.g., retail cannot exceed 5,000 square feet regardless of the size of the building it is in) or overall commercial developments (e.g., neighborhood commercial areas will not exceed 2 acres of land area). This can get complicated both to develop and to explain to the public on an ongoing basis. But it is a viable approach that may yield more control.

Parking is the second issue related to a shorter and more flexible list of uses, because two uses within the same category may have different parking needs. For example, doctors' offices often experience a higher volume of clients each day than accountants' or lawyers' offices, so their parking needs are greater. In the past, these differences in minimum parking requirements were often used as a reason to split use definitions into ever-thinner slices. We assumed that if parking requirements were different, then the way to handle it was to define different uses. But there are other ways to approach this issue.

The obvious one is to keep different parking requirements for uses that really do have different needs—even if they fall within the same broad use name. The defined use can be "offices," while the parking requirements can require different amounts of parking depending on the type of office. In the worst-case scenario, an applicant who wants to shift from an accountant's office to a medical office may find that the site contains too little space to satisfy minimum parking. But that can often be addressed by allowing more flexibility for off-site and public parking to meet the need. And if the office is located in a multitenant office building or a multibuilding campus, then the higher parking requirements need to be met by the building or campus as a whole, not by each individual tenant. As some offices shift to more parking-intensive uses, others go the opposite way, and the building or campus owner can be responsible for keeping the buildings as a whole in compliance.

A second solution is to operate a modular zoning system in which parking requirements "modules" are assigned based on the overall parking availability, congestion, and transit availability in the area (like the module regulating development scale discussed above) rather than having a fixed requirement for each individual use. A third

What Does This Fix?

More flexibly designed uses would address the failings of Euclidean hybrid zoning by:

- simplifying the structure of the ordinance;
- better acknowledging market forces that encourage replacement of commercial and industrial with somewhat similar uses over time;
- allowing landowners wider latitude to match uses to the available capacity in transportation systems;
- reducing the need for approval to substitute similar uses, thereby increasing government efficiency and reducing opportunities for NIMBYism;
- promoting the goal of predictable flexibility, because the boundaries of the broader uses would still be defined but there would be more flexibility to accommodate different activities within those boundaries; and
- avoiding distinctions among similar uses, which increases understandability to the public.

---

option would be to operate a permit-based parking system that requires applicants to get an administrative permit (again, with needs tailored to overall neighborhood conditions and transit) rather than linking parking requirements to specific uses.

Is It Legal?

The use of broader and more flexible uses fits easily within the legal framework outlined in chapter 5. Any rational regrouping would conform to substantive due process requirements, and procedural requirements would be no different than for any other type of zoning text amendment. Introducing more flexibility into available uses would tend to reduce the likelihood of takings and vested rights claims, since they represent loosening of existing controls. Because there is no constitutionally protected right to any particular grouping of land uses, or to the separate identification of particular uses, equal protection is not an issue. The groupings themselves do not implicate First Amendment rights, and grouping religious institutions with other facilities for public assembly might reduce the likelihood that they would be subject to special restrictions in violation of the Religious Land Use and Institutionalized Persons Act. Where state or federal regulations affect specific uses, the new use listing should be consistent with those controls, but that is true of all amendments.

145

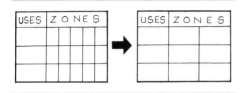

The Mixed-use Middle

In the future, zoning will put more attention into allowing or requiring appropriate mixes of uses and less attention into separating them. My point in the previous section was that there are usually too many *lines* in the zoning use table. The point here is that there are often too many *columns*—that we have created more types of zoning districts than we need. Again, the reasons are generally historical. Someone envisions a new type of development area, and the structure of zoning encourages us to see that as a new zoning district, so we create one. In some cities, this is the first response to a new development idea—"Got a new idea . . . need a new district"—even though there are other ways to accommodate the change. Over time, these new districts proliferate, and each one lives on, even when the reasons for its creation have disappeared.

When zoning was young, we thought in terms of a three-way distinction among residential, commercial, and industrial districts. Over the years, this simple typology expanded to include open space districts, public/institutional districts, mixed-use districts (generally meaning residential plus commercial but not industrial), and business park districts (generally meaning "clean" industrial and heavier commercial but seldom residential). We also gained a host of specialized districts (like airport, landfill, theater, or loft districts) related to the specific needs of the city.

But the availability of four commercial districts, three mixed-use districts, and three industrial districts does not necessarily make it easier to decide where a building combining, for example, offices, Internet drug sales, and drug manufacturing belongs. One great lesson of the past few years, especially since the advent of Internet-based businesses, is how blurry the lines among multifamily residential, office, institutional, commercial, and light industrial zones have become (see chapter 2).

Although most of the debate on form-based zoning has focused on the mixing of residential and commercial uses and districts, the same debate should be happening for the commercial/industrial boundary. Form-based zoners focus on ensuring that the scale of residential and commercial buildings does not differ significantly from that of other buildings around them and ensuring that good design is used to transition between the two. It turns out that the same should be done at the other end of the zoning spectrum. Most large-format industrial and commercial buildings (other than some retail and entertainment uses) tend to spread themselves apart and discourage walkability. Small-scale commercial uses may need walkability or closeness to the street to survive, so it may be difficult for them to make it in a large-format setting. On the other hand, inserting a large commercial or industrial facility into a street front setting with smaller surrounding uses may destroy the walkability those uses need to survive. In the end it is more important to think of business areas in terms of the scale of permitted buildings rather than the commercial or industrial labels of the activities within them.

But if the residential/commercial dividing line can be crossed successfully and the commercial/industrial zone distinction is disappearing, what kinds of zones will be left? I believe that, in the future, zoning will move toward only three types of districts: pure residential districts, mixed-use districts, and special purpose districts.

SF Resid	MF Resid	Commercial	Institutional	Industrial	Special

SF Resid	MF	Mixed Use		Special

With due respect to those who believe we should all live in mixed-use neighborhoods, a large proportion of America's population doesn't want to do so and is not likely to be persuaded otherwise. The desire for a single-family home on a single plot of land surrounded by other single houses on single lots runs deep in our history (and, incidentally, it runs deep in other countries too). Residential suburbs were not a mistake; they responded to a very real and financially powerful market demand. I think this trend will continue for at least two reasons: perceptions of investment security and the desire for elbow room.

For most Americans, their home is their largest single investment, and many think that the best way to guarantee the value of that investment is to make sure it is surrounded by others like it. This is not necessarily so, of course. There are plenty of counterexamples where homes in mixed-use New Urbanist or loft developments are appreciating faster than suburban homes, but those are still perceived to be outside the mainstream of consumer demand. I wish this were not true, but I think it still is.

Since the 1990s, my hometown of Denver has been blessed with three major infill communities that have helped attract middle-income homeowners back from the edges of the city. In the downtown area, mixed-use zoning in the Platte River Valley has allowed mid- and high-rise lofts, condominiums, and apartments to coexist with townhouses, office buildings, parks, and a smattering of commercial uses. A few miles away, the 1,800-acre Lowry Air Force Base was closed and redeveloped with a mix of high-quality residential, commercial, and educational/institutional uses through a fine-grained application of Denver's standard zoning districts. Biggest of all is the former site of Stapleton International Airport, where 4,700 acres of land are being redeveloped under PUD zoning for residential, commercial, entertainment, industrial, and open space uses. A site that big has room for everything. Incidentally, Denver also had *another* 4,500 acres of development land in the outlying Gateway development area, but I want to focus on infill development.

These three developments have been wildly successful. Residential lots in some areas of Stapleton were even awarded by lottery. But you have to look closer for the real story. Between 2000 and 2006, these three big developments were estimated to represent half of the net increase of the housing units increase in Denver's housing stock but only 6 percent of housing growth in the Denver metro region.[3] Yes, this is a strong showing as well as a source of pride to New Urbanist planners, who have been saying for years that there was demand for these smaller-lot, closer-to-mixed-use products, but it is not enough to turn the market tide. Most new housing starts were still in single-family areas on the edges of the city.

Perhaps just as importantly, although Lowry and Stapleton are marketed as mixed-use neighborhoods—and they are in fact mixed-use, compared to most suburban areas—most of the individual homes are located in zoning categories that allow residential use and little else. Lowry has reserved a full 52 percent of its land as open space, but of the remaining development lands, 72 percent is in zoning categories that allow almost exclusively residential uses. The magic behind Lowry's success is in the fine grain of zoning districts that allowed business and offices (as well as open space) to be within walking distances of many homes. But most Lowry residents bought homes in zone districts where only homes could be built.

The discussion above is not a critique of mixed use or New Urbanism or Smart

Growth, all of which I support. The point is simply that many buyers who want a "mixed-use" neighborhood nevertheless buy houses in areas where they are sure that the lots around them will be developed with houses—and only houses. They want all those walkable amenities close by, but not next door. For this reason alone, we will continue to need some purely residential zones.

But there is a second reason. There seems to be a strong market demand for single-family lots—even small ones—for the kids or the grandkids to run around, and developable land is sometimes in short supply. New Urbanism, cluster developments, and Smart Growth have shown us that the yards can be smaller and that some percentage of households with children will agree to live without a yard at all, but real estate agents will tell you that the desire for a private yard is still deeply engrained. Wanting a private yard is not the same as wanting to live on the edge of the city or in a suburb; surveys show that many buyers prefer more central, walkable locations (the New Urbanists were right about that) but also that the yard is still part of the dream. Providing private yards—even small ones in central areas near transit—means building single-family homes or townhomes, and that limits the density of housing you can get on any given parcel of land. That in turn tends to limit the ability to provide offices, shopping, and other services close to the housing.

Many local governments interested in mixed use have run into the dilemma that the nonresidential parts of a mixed-use community are often financially viable only after homes have been built and the buying power and potential office users have moved into the community. To make sure that the mix of uses actually happens, good sites need to be reserved for the nonresidential uses that happen later. These later uses often want to be along roads or transit corridors, and the yard-buying residents don't want to be along those roads, which means that the houses get pushed into the interior of the site and somewhat separated from the later, nonresidential part of the mixed-use project. The point is that the desire for private yards tends to segregate land uses on the developing edges of the city, which is another reason why pure residential zone districts will probably continue to be needed.

Sure, this pattern can be broken. A creative developer with a long time horizon can decide to subsidize nonresidential development in a true mixed-use pattern—that is, really mixed in so that it is walkable from the housing and happens at the same time as the housing. Developments with a truly extraordinary open space system interwoven with multifamily housing may find a greater share of the market willing to give up private yards. But those are still minority situations, and most cities cannot choose to work with only creative, patient developers. Cities have to take property owners and developers as they come, and many developers try to reduce the risks inherent in their business by using short time horizons and specializing in a single product.

The second major type of zone district will be mixed-use zones. This is the logical outcome of the eroding boundaries between the traditional residential/commercial, commercial/institutional, and commercial/industrial categories. Most cities that want to explore the popular territory of mixed uses do that in one of two ways: by "injecting" mixed uses into existing zone districts or by adding on new districts. Injecting mixed use happens when cities review their permitted use tables and ask the "Why not?" question: "Why don't we allow this commercial use in that multifamily zone (or vice versa)?" Often, there is no good reason for keeping the commercial use out as long as the scale of development is compatible, so they add permitted or conditional uses to loosen up on purely multifamily residential or commercial zones near the boundaries of those categories. For example, the city might decide that there is nothing wrong with a restaurant in a multifamily apartment zone provided it does not have a drive-through facility, so that use is added by changing the existing use table.

The injection approach is time consuming though, and changing existing districts risks the wrath of residents who don't want any changes, so other cities opt for the "add-on" approach. Instead of revising the existing zone districts, they create text for a new mixed-use zone or two so that they are available if and when they are requested by a property owner. This is tougher than it sounds at first blush. There is a wide gap between simplistic rhetoric about mixed use and the reality of making mixed-use zoning work. More than occasionally, I meet a developer who thinks allowing mixed use just means creating a new zone district where all uses are either permitted or conditional use and then letting the market sort out what will really happen on the site. It's not that simple, because uses really *do* matter, and some uses actually *do* interfere with one another. If the market truly did control the impacts of development on neighboring uses, we would have shelved zoning long ago.

At a minimum, cities need to think about what types of mixed uses they want to see. Generally, even mixed-use districts have a predominant character—residential, commercial, or even industrial. By thinking through whether the area is a fundamentally residential district where compatible commercial should be allowed, or a predominantly commercial/industrial area where some types of residential development can fit in, most of the obvious impacts can be controlled. This discussion often leads to much improved communication about what the different stakeholders really mean when they say they want mixed use, and to the creation of at least two mixed-use zones—one with a predominantly residential character and one with a nonresidential character. Many cities go on to create more than two mixed-use districts.

The question of scale should be a very important factor in these discussions. Careful discussions of mixed use often result in different mixed-use districts for low-density/horizontal/neighborhood-scale development and for higher-density/vertical development. A third key issue is whether these districts *allow* mixed use or *require* it. Fairly often, it turns out that the builders want it to be available whereas planners want it to be mandatory. Sometimes the compromise is that it is mandatory around transit stops but voluntary in other contexts. For all of these reasons, it is unlikely that only one mixed-use zone is needed. The more time cities take to discuss these issues with neighborhoods and stakeholders, the more likely they will be to decide that multiple mixed-use zones are needed and to design them to achieve the right goals.

The better way to zone is to include a broad middle range of mixed-use zone districts that occupy the majority of the zone district spectrum. Although "pure" residential zone districts will still exist for both single-family and multifamily development, they will be joined with residential mixed-use zones, and most multifamily development will in fact occur in the mixed-use variants. Mixed-use zones will also replace that portion of the zoning spectrum now occupied by commercial districts and light industrial districts. Within this spectrum, there will be different districts distinguished by the intended character of the area (predominantly residential or nonresidential) and the scale of permitted development (low-rise versus vertical), but not by outright prohibitions on residential, commercial, or industrial development. I think the total number of zones needed to accommodate both historical and preferred patterns of mixed use will be smaller than the number we now use to cover the spectrum from multifamily to light industrial zones.

The third major category of zone districts will be special purpose districts, and their number and type will vary from city to city. This category may include heavy industrial districts, industrial-only districts, large-format districts (where buildings with large horizontal footprints are allowed), airport districts, open space

districts, hospital/university/institutional districts, historic districts, adult entertainment zones, open space districts, and others. Most large cities have historical
patterns of development or special places that they want to either protect or change,
and there is no single pattern of zones that will respond to these one-off situations.
Some cities insist that they don't need open space districts (parks are permitted
everywhere, and required open space is protected in some other way), while others insist that they need no less than three open space zones. Some cities put their
airports in agricultural zones, others put them in industrial zones, and still others
create a specific airport zone. Diversity of practice in these special purpose districts should continue.

In the past, some of these special areas have been addressed through overlay
zone districts, and that should also continue. Historic character districts often
require detailed controls that apply only in a specific area, but many cities decide
they can be "overlaid" on whatever base districts already exist. Not every development concern needs to be embodied in a new base district. The logic behind overlay zones is often compelling, and the spread of mixed-use zoning to dominate the
center of the zone district spectrum will not undermine that logic.

Note that the combination of fewer use "lines" and fewer zone "columns" means
that the structure of the permitted use table—which is the heart of most Euclidean
mixed-use ordinances—would be simplified, a result whose positive impacts would
ripple through other parts of the ordinance.

Is It Legal?

The replacement of some multifamily, commercial, institutional, and light industrial districts with fewer mixed-use districts based on character and scale falls well
within the constitutional framework of zoning law outlined in chapter 5. Com-
plying with the requirements of procedural and substantive due process and avoiding unconstitutional vagueness are no more difficult than they are for the current
lineup of zone districts. As with broader use definitions, mixed-use zone districts
tend to add flexibility for property owners, so they are unlikely to raise charges
that property rights have been "taken."

Because the definition of broader zone districts does not directly affect either
religious institutions or signs, this change is unlikely to result in claims under the
First Amendment, but religious institutions should not be singled out for more
limitations or restrictions than other places of public assembly. Replacing exist-

152

What Does This Fix?

Restructuring zoning to recognize the mixed-use middle would address several critiques raised in chapters 2, 3, and 4. In fact, it responds to more of those critiques than any other single recommendation.

- Fewer, more-flexible zone districts would tend to simplify the ordinance by eliminating some ambiguous distinctions between heavy commercial and light industrial zones.
- More mixed-use zone districts would reverse the bias toward separation of uses.
- It would reflect the fact that many nonconforming uses in older areas of the city are not going to leave—and should be legalized instead of pressured to change.
- It would reflect market forces promoting transit-oriented development, integrated neighborhood shopping, and flexible business parks.
- It would address the problem of tax caps by allowing cities to accept small-scale, tax-producing commercial and retail activities in a variety of mixed-use areas, rather than overmapping for single-purpose commercial or industrial zones in the hope that those uses will come.
- It would reduce pressure on transportation systems by allowing workers to live closer to jobs and allowing landowners to better tailor their building to available transportation capacities.
- By reducing the needs for rezonings, permits, or approvals for small-scale commercial and retail, it would reduce opportunities for NIMBYism.
- By better matching the types of neighborhoods planners and citizens want to see built, it would increase government effectiveness in meeting its planning goals.
- By providing more internal flexibility for uses while defining the outer boundaries of the mix in each area, it would promote the concept of predictable flexibility.
- By providing zoning tools that match citizens' perceptions of the mixed nature of many areas, it would improve general understandability of the ordinance.

ing districts with new districts can be done without violating vested rights—no one has a common law right to have their existing zoning continue—but those who have already filed applications under the existing districts should be allowed to complete them. Finally, the definition and grouping of zone districts are seldom topics of state or federal preemption, but in some cases, older state enabling acts speak explicitly of using zone districts to separate uses, and those acts might need to be amended.

Attainable Housing

Housing affordability is one of the five new land use drivers identified in chapter 3. Although good zoning can be part of the solution to this problem, zoning can also make the problem worse. A 1998 study of regulatory barriers to affordable housing in Colorado identified five separate types of barriers, and that list included zoning and subdivision controls.[4] The other four areas were development processing and permitting (which overlaps zoning), infrastructure financing mechanisms, building codes, and environmental and cultural resource protection tools. All regulatory barriers are by-products of trying to promote some social good, and few would support simply waiving the building code or repealing environmental laws for the sake of attainable housing. But the findings of the report do point toward areas where city governments should make sure they get the trade-offs right, because getting it wrong creates an inefficient burden on housing prices.

Within zoning and subdivision controls, the Colorado study identified four specific types of barriers:

- minimum house size, lot size, or yard size requirements;
- prohibitions on accessory dwelling units;
- restrictions on land zoned and available for multifamily housing and manufactured housing; and
- excessive subdivision improvement standards.

The third and fourth items on this list are outside the scope of this book, the third because it involves district mapping decisions rather than zoning text, and the fourth because it involves subdivision rather than zoning. The first two, however, are clearly relevant to our search for a better way to zone.

Across the United States, the legal obligations of local governments related to affordable housing vary significantly. Some states, including New Jersey, California, and Oregon, require cities to draft housing plans based on both the existing and the anticipated population of the city. Other states have no such requirement. But whether or not it is required by law, comprehensive plans are supposed to be based on population projections. Unfortunately, few cities go to the added effort to identify the likely income ranges of the existing and anticipated residents. In addition, the resulting plan often gets disconnected from the projections themselves. By the time the plan is adopted, it is often clear that the preferred types and densities of development cannot accommodate the number of people who are likely to move to the city and will likely not be affordable given their anticipated income levels.

Even if the plan does a good job accommodating projected growth with housing types appropriate to expected income levels, there is often no requirement that the zoning ordinance be modified to reflect the plan. In this area, the approach sometimes seems to be: "Don't build it and they won't come." It is interesting to see how far practice has diverged from theory in this fundamental area of planning. If we do not take seriously the need to accommodate housing for our people—people who earn what our citizens really earn), what do we take seriously?

Of course, the predictable need for attainable housing over the long run does not mean that zoning must allow *new* housing to be built at prices affordable to median wage earners. For all larger cities, the new housing built in any decade represents only a small fraction of the total housing stock. The relevant question is whether a median wage earner can afford a *median* rental or ownership unit, not a new one. In many U.S. cities, it is difficult to live and work without owning at least one car, and lots of people would like to buy a new car, but we don't try to regulate car prices so that they are affordable to median wage earners. Those who cannot afford new cars buy used cars, and the same is true for housing. But the sales price of new housing is still relevant because it can pull that median price figure up or down. In large, mature cities, if the median house price is above the affordable level for a median family, the zoning ordinance should clearly contain some tools to promote more attainable housing.

Ideally, of course, our cities' plans would accurately reflect anticipated housing needs for different income groups and then zoning would be changed to allow those types of housing to occur. But even if zoning does not actively encourage construction of attainable housing, planners need to ensure that zoning ordinances do not place unnecessary barriers in front of reasonably priced housing. Affordable housing professionals know that meeting the housing needs of poorer citizens often requires direct or indirect subsidies to operate fairly complex affordable housing programs. The need for those programs is beyond the scope of this book, but removal of regulatory barriers is not.

The most obvious regulatory barriers to the affordability of single-family housing are minimum lot sizes, minimum dwelling unit sizes, and maximum densities of development. Unfortunately, discussion of these zoning parameters often degenerates into a "numbers game." I have worked in cities where the magic number was 5,000 square feet—as in "We will not approve any single family lots smaller than 5,000 square feet"—and in other cities where the magic number was as high as 1 acre. But most members of the public cannot visually identify lots that are bigger or smaller than these numbers. Designers regularly fool participants in public meetings by showing attractive housing that compares favorably with the audience's homes and then telling them the density shown on the drawings is actually 50 percent higher than their neighborhood.

When apartments and condominiums are discussed, the situation is even worse. Few members of the public can visualize the difference between 14 and 28 units per acre or the types of housing that can be built within those limits. The debate about the right number has become separated from discussion of what will fit into the community and promote greater affordability. And of course, the numbers game feeds the NIMBY machine. Focusing on numbers allows neighborhoods to draw a line in the sand and rally support or opposition around that line, regardless of whether anyone understands the line or how it will affect community quality.

To produce housing that working people can afford, a better way to zone will need to include two types of changes. First, it will have to get away from the density/intensity numbers game—or at least move the battle to numbers that make more sense. Higher densities are often opposed on the basis of additional traffic or schoolchildren that will need to be accommodated. Those are valid concerns, and it would be much more helpful to debate the available capacity of roadways and school systems and the costs of expanding them. A debate over the fiscal impacts of the proposed development would also be an improvement, even though the vast majority of housing will still be built in ways that generate net costs to the community. This is a key fact: you probably cannot house the United States on a "breakeven" basis. Residential growth is usually not able to pay its own way. So deal with it, and move toward intelligent trade-offs between housing attainability and service costs.

As the Denver area has grown rapidly in the past twenty years, the flat, serviceable lands on the east side of the metro area (farther from the Rocky Mountains) have become a magnet for single-family housing. Much of that land is in the suburb of Aurora, which at times has felt that it was drowning in a sea of applications for ever smaller residential lots. One application called for almost eight hundred 3,500-square-foot lots rolling across the land in a grid pattern with no thought to the terrain or any sense of community. Anyone who wants to do that is building a future slum, not because the lots are too small but because too much of any good thing is a bad thing.

After holding the line on a 6,000-square-foot minimum lot size for several years, in the late 1990s Aurora commissioned a study to see how smaller lots could be permitted without compromising community image or fiscal health. The result was a set of regulations that allowed some lots in a development to be as small as 4,700, 4,200, or even 3,700 square feet depending on the location of the garage and access to it. Each design built in features to ensure privacy from neighbors. The secret for Aurora was to allow smaller lots as a part of a mix that allowed more varieties of housing: no more than 35 percent of the lots in the development could be small lots. While they were at it, Aurora adopted regulations requiring all builders to begin by looking at the natural features of the land (not the hoped-for yield of dwelling units) as the starting point in subdivision design, and to organize all large subdivisions into distinct neighborhoods. Not only does that better address the housing affordability issue, but it closed the door on "grind-'em-out" eight-hundred-lot subdivisions. It opened the door to innovation and better design, and in the years since then Aurora has continued to refine and improve the regulations to permit even more creativity.

The City of Santa Cruz, California, took another approach. It hired a team of architects and developed ready-made plans for attainable housing that would meet city regulations. The result was not only affordable but attractive. No one is required to use the designs, but those builders who do use them receive expedited processing because there is no time lost confirming compliance with city standards.[5] Austin, Texas, tried a third approach. Its S.M.A.R.T. ("Safe, Mixed-income, Accessible, Reasonably-priced, Transit-oriented") Housing program gives builders eight options for producing more innovative housing products. Those options include single-family cottage lots, single-family urban lots, a small-lot amnesty, secondary apartments, residential infill, mixed-use buildings, a neighborhood corner store, and a neighborhood urban center. Builders who use the options also benefit from expedited approval processing and waivers of some fees.

Small lots and prepackaged designs are not the only example of innovation, of course. Over the past decades, the building community has brought us "Z-lots,"

"L-lots," cluster subdivisions, live-work units, loop lanes, auto courts, shared driveway subdivisions, assisted living facilities, and mixed-use mixed-income developments.

In addition to allowing smaller lots, our better way to zone will also allow housing developers to be more creative in the housing products they supply. Fortunately, the American housing industry is intensely competitive, and there is every reason to believe it can develop products to meet needs if allowed to do so. The painful news for neighborhoods is that promoting attainability may mean allowing smaller lots and higher densities in built-up areas, and particularly near transit lines. The good news is that there are lots of creative ways to do that.

The United States is generating new households faster than it is gaining population. The old, the young, and singles of all types are choosing to live in smaller, separate households rather than living with either their parents or their children. Not only has this produced demand for smaller single-family/apartment/condo units, but it has also created demand for small units attached to or built into single-family homes. Originally called "granny flats" or "mother-in-law" units, these accessory dwelling units (or ADUs) often have separate entrances, kitchens, and bathrooms so that someone can live close to the family. In recent years, the children-returning-home-after-college phenomenon has been feeding this demand. Just because the children have left does not mean they will not be back someday, and those who return will not want to live in their old bedrooms.

ADUs are only one example of new products. What about manufactured homes, whose growing popularity shows that they are often considered good value for the money? Even before World War II, innovators began envisioning a house that could be built on an assembly line like a car. In the early postwar years, Swedish-born Carl Strandlund convinced the U.S. government to put up $40 million to capitalize an effort to mass produce the Lustron House. But the effort fell into bankruptcy after only a few years, having produced fewer than 2,500 prefabricated houses. Lustron failed because the capital costs of developing the factories themselves were very high. Either those costs had to be passed on to buyers in a more-expensive-than-hoped-for housing unit, or builders had to accept a very long payback period for the up-front investments, or both.[6]

Fortunately, it turned out that we were not dependent on government-sponsored development programs to reap the savings of manufactured and modular homes. Despite the failure of the Lustron experiment (and others), the American economy kept on doing what it does best—it allowed the private sector to

Manufactured Housing Terms

This is an area where confusion is often sown because "hot button" words are bandied about loosely and are often poorly understood. To avoid that problem, we need to clarify how many current zoning ordinances define certain key terms.

- "Mobile home" generally means a home that is originally designed to be moved from place to place on wheels but that is not a recreational vehicle and does not meet the requirements of the Manufactured Housing Act of 1974 (generally meaning a home built before 1976).

- "Manufactured home" generally means the same thing except that it meets the requirements of the Manufactured Housing Act.

- "Modular home" means a home that is not designed to be moved on wheels and that is built with the same general materials used to build stick-built homes but with some or all key components built off-site and then transported to the site for assembly into a home.

- "Single-family detached home" means just what it says, but the term is being used more and more to include both modular and manufactured homes provided that they meet all zoning requirements that would be applicable to a stick-built home. Often, the term explicitly excludes "mobile homes" (pre-1976 units) because they were not subject to generally accepted safety standards and are therefore fundamentally different from dwellings that were subject to approved safety standards.

have at it, rewarded winners, and allowed the losers to start over—so that today we have an unprecedented variety of manufactured, modular, component, and kit housing products available that meet either the building standards of local building codes or the federal Manufactured Housing Act.

The language of the Manufactured Housing Act clearly focuses on building standards and not zoning. But since it was passed in 1974, debate has continued over whether language requiring that manufactured housing be treated as the equivalent of stick-built housing for building purposes also means such housing must be treated the same for zoning purposes. The manufactured housing industry has sometimes insisted that the act should be read that way, but the courts have been largely unpersuaded.[7] This has allowed cities to maintain some "manufactured home–free" residential areas, which is clearly in line with the wishes of many voters. Incidentally, several states have weighed in on the side of the industry to enact state laws limiting local ability to keep manufactured homes out of residential zones.

In the past, opposition to manufactured housing was often supported by complaints about appearance, building quality, and impacts on surrounding property values. But there are now both manufactured and modular products that are almost impossible to tell from stick-built homes. To address the appearance issue, some cities adopted regulations stating that all housing had to be at least 25 feet wide (i.e., wider than a double-wide mobile home constructed from two 12-foot-wide sections); in response, the modular industry delivered 16-foot-wide sections that could be assembled into a 32-foot-wide home. Other cities said the roof pitch had to be more than 3:12, which would make the roof too tall to fit under interstate highway bridges. The industry responded with hinged roofs, which could be tilted downward in transit and back upward when they arrived at the site. Some cities required a "real stone" foundation or a "real brick" facade, so the manufactured and modular builders developed products that delivered those appearance items. And they still undersold some of their stick-built competition.[8]

In fact, it is going to become more and more difficult to defend the lines that currently divide modular, manufactured, and conventional stick-built housing from one another. Because of the efficiency of modular construction, many "conventional" builders are now incorporating modular parts. The use of prebuilt modular trusses is now common, and the use of prebuilt kitchen and bathroom components is on the way. At what point does a stick-built home become a modular home, and how much effort should we spend debating that question?

Some of the changes in the auto industry have followed a similar trajectory. In the 1960s, Japanese cars were "cheap," but by the 1980s we had decided they were as good as or better than others. Then it was the Korean cars that were "cheap," but that gap has rapidly narrowed, if not disappeared. It also became increasingly difficult to tell just what was a Japanese or Korean car. First, components of foreign cars were built in the United States, and then entire cars with foreign names—lots of them— were U.S. built. Pundits quipped that if you wanted an American car, you would have to decide between a Ford built in Canada and a Honda built in Ohio. Although the manufactured and modular building industries cannot substitute capital and technology for labor as readily as the auto industry does, they can do so to some extent, and they will provide increasingly stiff competition for conventional builders.

In the face of continuing pressure for housing affordability and steadily improving manufactured home quality and variety, these barriers will erode. The economic advantages of manufactured and modular homes are often real. Over the next twenty years, we will see a steady stream of communities looking for ways to encourage affordable housing that fits in with existing neighborhood character and concluding that it is not wise to keep manufactured or modular housing out of as many zoning districts as they do now. The number of residential zone districts that keep these products out will decline, but they will not go away completely.

Although changes in future zoning ordinances to allow smaller lot sizes and higher multifamily densities will be visible, changes to allow more modular and manufactured housing will be less so. Instead of adding something to the zoning ordinance, these changes involve deleting things—namely, the barriers that keep modular and manufactured housing out of some zones. Or there could be a mix of barrier removal and new requirements. Following the Aurora, Colorado, approach to small lots, some cities may remove the barriers to allow for a wider range of housing products and then require a mix of those products in order to allay fears about having too much of any one type of housing. Yes, the greatest efficiencies of production and the largest potential reductions in housing price may come when builders build large amounts of the same thing, but most cities learned long ago that this did not produce good neighborhoods.

This is an area where the pure economics of housing runs into the other goals of great cities. Maintaining the status quo will mean losing ground on housing affordability, and allowing dramatically smaller lots or denser developments would significantly change the character of some residential areas, so I believe most cities will take a measured approach. But twenty years from now, they will allow a wider

What Does This Fix?

Revising zoning ordinances to better promote the goal of attainable housing will address the critiques listed in chapters 2 through 4 in five ways:

- It would correct an oversimplification in the basic structure of zoning by acknowledging that the affordability of housing (not just the supply) is a zoning topic.
- It would tend to offset the inflation in housing standards (especially large minimum lot sizes and minimum dwelling unit sizes) that has occurred since 1916—and especially since 1945—as greenfield standards became the norm.
- It would allow the market to produce smaller, more efficient, and more innovative types of housing.
- By reducing the need for rezoning or obtaining special approvals or variances, it would also help reduce opportunities for NIMBYism.
- Because the economic health of most mature cities depends in part on having a good stock of attainable housing, and because the existing stock must be replaced and renovated over time, promoting attainable housing would make zoning more effective.

variety of housing types than they allow today. Smart Growth advocates, New Urbanists, and some form-based zoners have been pushing for this for a decade, and they are correct. I think the housing attainability crunch will provide an additional push toward this result. Even communities that do not embrace New Urbanism will move in this direction.

Is It Legal?

Changing use definitions and development standards to promote attainable housing fits within the legal framework discussed in chapter 5. Compliance with procedural and substantive due process and avoidance of vagueness in the drafting and adoption of those changes are no more difficult than for current housing provisions. Since these changes expand the types of uses and/or the densities of development available to property owners, it is unlikely that they would give rise to takings or vested rights claims. Objections to smaller and more affordable housing generally come from neighboring property owners, but there is no constitutional right to *not* have attainable housing near one's property.

Because adequate housing is a legitimate governmental concern, as well as very big business, many states have statutes related to residential zoning, and amendments to promote attainable housing will need to be consistent with those laws. As noted earlier, the federal Fair Housing Amendments Act of 1988 and the Americans with Disabilities Act of 1990 both have provisions that address housing and housing sites, so zoning should be drafted consistent with those requirements, or the requirements themselves should at least be cross-referenced. While the Fair Housing Amendments Act does not require zoning for attainable housing, allowing a wider variety of housing products in more locations might help keep cities in compliance with the requirements of the act addressing "handicapped persons."

Mature Areas Standards

Early zoning focused primarily on uses and only secondarily on development standards. In creating the first zoning maps, early zoners clearly took their clues from existing uses in various areas of the city. Areas with mostly residential uses were zoned residential, commercial areas were zoned commercial, and it was on the boundaries of these areas where planners earned their pay by thinking through how the land should be zoned and why. Things were easier when they drew maps for undeveloped land, because there were fewer constraints, less existing context, and more freedom to imagine what the future *should* look like.

Most development standards came later—things like requirements for off-street parking and landscaping and controls on signs and fences and lighting. When development standards were drafted carefully, they were based on careful review of what had already been built in the city. In undeveloped areas, of course, this was easier—planners could think about what the standards should be without worrying about whether existing development met the standard. But in some cases, development standards were not based on careful analysis of what had already been built, and in many cases a single new standard was adopted for both developed and undeveloped lands.

Because most planners view their role as improving the future, not just protecting the present, it is not surprising that the "should" standards were often adopted for the entire city. In some cases, owners of undeveloped lands argued that applying a higher standard for their (future) development would give a competitive advantage to older areas of the city where there was a lower standard (or no standard at all). Using a single standard avoided this complaint, created a level playing field, and allowed planners to tell the city council that "someday all of the city will look as good as our newest developments." Although the zoners acknowledged that existing properties did not meet the new standards, they assumed that this situation would correct itself as nonconformities disappeared over time. As we have seen, though, it turns out that some nonconformities do not go away very fast (see chapter 2).

Future zoning will admit that the one-size-fits-all approach to development standards was and is a mistake. Despite the rhetoric about a level playing field, the simple fact is that the playing field has never been level. Not all land was created equal, and past development patterns have a lot to do with what may be appropriate in the future. Both planners and landowners already acknowledge this in a variety of ways. Land near highways often has more intense zoning, land in wetlands or on steep slopes is zoned to restrict development, and certain uses are restricted around schools simply because there are lots of children in the area. The building patterns in developed areas should and will influence the future of the area in important ways. When large areas in mature neighborhoods are redeveloped as part of an integrated project, there is more freedom to redefine and create a unique character for that particular place—but the best redevelopments still relate the edges and the overall project to the surrounding neighborhoods in ways that they would not do on a greenfield site.

Mature neighborhoods are simply different from new growth areas, not only in how they look and feel but in how they should be regulated. In most mature neighborhoods, the goal of planning is either to protect the existing character of development (as in an area of stable older homes) or to encourage redevelopment and reinvestment (as in a declining commercial or industrial area). Regardless of which goal applies to a specific mature area, the benchmark for either preservation or reinvestment should be the established character of that area—not what is appropriate on the edge of the city. The focus should be more on managing change from that established baseline than on redesigning the neighborhood. A better way to zone will recognize this fact by having at least two different sets of development criteria, if not three (one for new areas, one for stable/mature areas, and one for redeveloping/mature areas).

Some current zoning ordinances are already dealing with this issue in a back-handed way. For example, Winnipeg's parking regulations carve out some older and denser areas and say that mandatory off-street parking requirements do not apply to some types of development in those areas. When Denver first adopted parking lot landscaping standards, they did not apply to downtown parking lots. The strongest opposition to the new standards came from owners of downtown lots who pointed out that the required landscaping would cause them to lose a fair percentage of the parking spaces in their small, physically constrained parking lots, whereas the percentage impact on larger, outlying lots would be minimal. Detroit's zoning ordinance provides three different options for screening parking lots from the street, some of which can be met in the very narrow edges available in downtown parking lots.

Arvada, Colorado, provides another good example of the need for mature area standards. Extending northwest from industrial lands near the junction of Denver's two interstate highways all the way to the foothills of the Rocky Mountains, Arvada includes older areas with mixed industrial and residential development in its southeast corner near Clear Creek, stable residential areas developed between 1950 and 2000 in the center of the city, and huge tracts of undeveloped lands annexed to the western border of the city in the 1980s and 1990s.

Beginning with a "standard" zoning ordinance designed around its stable residential neighborhoods and old main street shopping area, Arvada first realized that those rules were not workable in the older industrial areas. After intensive negotiations with landowners, the city designed a completely new set of Clear Creek districts that allowed those older areas to redevelop in different ways. At the other end of the city, when the owners of the 18,000-acre Jefferson Center property were negotiating for annexation of their very valuable land in the 1980s, they also found the standard zoning provisions out of date and overly rigid, so a third set of zoning regulations was drafted and applied to that mega-PUD. For a time, Arvada found itself operating three different zoning ordinances in three different areas of the city. Eventually, the city knit them together into a single ordinance, although the three different types of zone districts and development standards remain.

Lessons such as these demonstrate why we need to apply different development standards for mature areas of the city. Perhaps we can call them "mature area standards," because they focus on redevelopment rather than initial development of the land. For stagnant or declining mature areas, mature area standards should admit a basic fact—that one major goal of urban governance is to attract reinvestment capital into those areas. In other words, zoning ordinances need to focus less on the design and more on the management of mature areas to ensure their continued active use.

When mature areas experience continued disinvestment, they impose significant costs on city government. Tax revenues fall, crime sometimes increases, vacant buildings encourage neighboring owners to think maybe they should leave too, and housing values can fall, making it harder for existing residents to get loans to improve their properties. For all of these reasons, cities need to be encouraging the continued flow of capital into those areas. That may mean different buffering, landscaping, or parking standards. It may mean increasing maximum permitted densities or heights. It may even mean broadening the list of permitted uses to include some that are not consistent with the original functioning of the area. There are myriad examples of older "mansion" areas that have transitioned into mixed-use office/residential neighborhoods, and where the surrounding community prefers that outcome to the loss of the beautiful old homes. Regardless of what tools turn out to be needed, what is clearly not needed is to treat them just like newer areas that are not experiencing disinvestment.

Redevelopment standards need to recognize three key facts about mature areas in order to be effective at preserving character and inviting reinvestment. First, land area is often at a premium. Many mature areas were developed when lot sizes, houses, and commercial and industrial buildings were smaller. Parking on the street was also the norm because there were fewer cars. By developing more space-efficient standards for parking, landscaping, buffering, and fencing, zoning ordinances can make it cheaper for building owners to attract new users for the property when the old ones leave. Redevelopment standards should allow owners to comply with buffering, lighting, screening, landscaping, and parking standards, keeping in mind the dimensions of old lots. Space-efficient "urban" templates for each of these have already been developed in some cities.

Generally, the standard that creates the most significant barrier to reinvestment is the requirement for off-street parking and related driving aisles. The usual defense for off-street parking standards is that they are necessary to relieve traffic congestion and parking on neighborhood streets, both of which are sometimes true. But as disinvestment occurs, these hypothetical problems start to fade. Instead of worrying about the effects of too much commercial/industrial activity bothering the neighbors, planners start worrying about vacant buildings (with no traffic) bothering the neighbors. So we can reduce or waive the parking requirement. Detroit waives requirements for additional off-street parking (beyond what is already provided) for older buildings with less than 3,000 square feet of floor area, and for expansions of uses into adjacent buildings provided the combined area is less than 4,000 square feet. Yes, customers may park on the street, but so what? Better to have the buildings in use.

Second, the economics of reuse and redevelopment in mature areas is different than for new users. When raw land is developed, the owner has to find a use that will pay for not only the value of the serviced land but also the new building being built and the extension of roads and utilities to that site. Raw land development happens when those types of buyers and users exist—and there are a lot of them, as any drive down a new commercial strip will attest. Old Navy, Ruby Tuesday's, and Mervyn's can pay those types of rent. The cost of utility extensions and site improvements are then rolled into a construction loan and then a mortgage that is amortized over twenty years or more.

But once a building has been built and the mortgage paid off, the rent can be reduced to where it covers only the operating costs of the building. For older buildings in nontrendy areas, this happens frequently. Of course, the owner would like to get more rent, but building designs age, and as the economic wave moves on to other areas of the city, many owners have to lower rents (or not raise them) to keep the property in use. In many older areas, the only takers become tenants or buyers who could never cover the costs of actually building the building. The cash flow on these businesses covers rent, utilities, property taxes, salaries for employees, and not much else. When the city's greenfield development standards require that the parking be redesigned and the number of spaces reduced to accommodate suburban landscaping, that lighting be installed or lowered to meet new standards, and that the old signs be replaced, it may require a tenant with more money than the existing one. Every property owner (and every planning director) hopes that such a tenant appears, but often it does not and the building may remain vacant. At a minimum, redevelopment standards should focus on only those items that will produce the greatest community benefit at the lowest cost to the owner. Urban templates can sometimes achieve a similar result at lower cost than suburban designs.

Third, and perhaps most obviously, the intent is not to make mature areas look like the edges of the city. When you succeed in making all of the city look the same, you have already missed the point and lost the game. The point of the development standards should be to protect the neighborhoods from *increased* impacts

What Does This Fix?

Adopting mature area standards would respond to some of the failed assumptions, new drivers, and governance goals identified in chapters 2 through 4 in the following ways:

- It would correct an oversimplification in the basic structure of zoning by acknowledging that once an area has been developed, its future management should be based on that established fabric and not on standards applied elsewhere.
- It would reduce the number of exceptions required, because mature area standards could be tailored to existing built forms and site development patterns.
- It would reduce the number of nonconformities in mature areas and explicitly allow them to remain as legal developments.
- It would respond to market pressures by allowing builders to replace and redevelop properties in older areas with smaller lots and setbacks.
- By better matching the fabric of older areas—which most plans want to reinforce and retain in a healthy state—it would make zoning more effective.
- It would promote the goal of predictable flexibility by endorsing more than one set of defined development standards.

of the new user (they already agreed to live with the old impacts when they bought their properties) and to improve the appearance or functioning of the property in ways that will stimulate continued reinvestment in the area. The goal is not to create an outpost of suburban-quality development surrounded by older, urban development. That does no one any good. For this reason alone, mature area redevelopment standards need to be distinguished from greenfield standards.

What—and create an uneven playing field? Absolutely—because it was never level in the first place, and an uneven playing field will promote reuse of investments that have already been made and utility systems that have already been paid for, as well as stabilizing the surrounding neighborhoods.

The discussion above applies primarily to older neighborhoods that are not designated historic or "character" districts. Where those exist, they deserve special treatment, including perhaps detailed standards to preserve specific architectural and design feathers and the scale of the area. In fact, historic regulations and neighborhood conservation regulations are examples of how separate standards for mature areas are already used. But so far they have been primarily limited to areas where preservationists or neighborhood activists can attract the attention of the city government to the need for rules based on existing development character. This approach should be extended to most older areas, and particularly to those without the political heft to attract individualized attention from the city government.

Is It Legal?

Adopting mature area standards also matches the legal framework for zoning reviewed in chapter 5. Procedural due process requirements would be met as for all other zoning text amendments, and substantive due process can be demonstrated by the need to promote reinvestment in older areas.

Avoiding vagueness and conflicts with the First Amendment would be no harder than it is with a single set of development standards. In fact, because development standards would relate more directly to the surrounding areas, it should be possible to draft crisper language and easier to clarify what factors contribute to "appropriateness" and "compatibility" than if we had to use factors applicable across the whole city. Because they would allow investment based on the existing patterns of smaller lots in older areas, mature area standards would allow somewhat denser uses of land, and it is unlikely that they would attract vested rights or takings claims. Principles of equal protection do not require the same development standards in different zone districts, because no federally protected right is involved (see chapter 5). As in all other areas of reform, care would need to be taken to avoid conflict with areas where state or federal standards preempt local regulation.

Living with Nonconformities

One corollary of the need to develop mature area standards is the need to live with nonconformities. The Euclidean hybrid model assumes that if zoning standards are raised from level X to level Y, it doesn't matter that existing development was still at level X because eventually everything will get redeveloped at level Y. To encourage redevelopment to happen sooner, the system said that existing uses, structures, and signs cannot be expanded until they meet level Y. Legal nonconforming properties at level X are on a sort of "zoning parole," and the terms of the parole are nonexpansion, nonreplacement, and sometimes nonviolation of other property laws.

This is an example of static thinking, because cities do not just adopt zoning regulations once; rather, they amend them repeatedly over time. When the city adopts a development standard requiring one tree per 40 feet of street frontage, it makes some older parts of the city nonconforming. But twenty years later, when the city amends the standard to require one street tree per 30 feet, it makes even more of the city nonconforming. Properties developed during the preceding twenty years that met the 40-foot standard do not meet the 30-foot standard. So, while some properties redevelop and come into compliance with the then-current standards over time, other properties become new nonconformities each time the zoning ordinance is amended. At this rate, we will never be rid of nonconformities—and that is the whole point. We have to learn to live with nonconformities better than we have in the past.

Although there are four generalized types of nonconformities—uses, buildings, lots, and signs—this book will not address nonconforming signs. Arguments for and against nonconforming billboards get entangled with the National Highway Beautification Act, the First Amendment, and the passive nature of billboard investments, which do not affect the other three types of

Types of Zoning Nonconformities

Nonconforming lot. A platted lot or parcel that was legal when it was created but that no longer meets the requirements of the zoning district where it is located. Usually, this means the lot is too small or too narrow or that it does not front on a public street. Sometimes the term includes a lot that is entirely located in a flood-prone area.

Nonconforming use. A land use that was legal when it began operation but that is no longer permitted in the zone district where it is located.

Nonconforming structure. A building, fence, or other structure that was legal when it was built but that no longer meets the zoning requirements of the zoning district where it is located. Usually, this means it is too tall or is located too close to a property line.

Nonconforming sign. A sign that was legal when it was created but that no longer meets the requirements of the zoning ordinance. Usually, this is because the sign is too big or too tall or because it no longer advertises a business located on the same lot. Although signs are technically "structures" that could have been treated like nonconforming structures, many cities define them differently because they want to apply different rules for their continuation or removal.

nonconformities. So I will limit the discussion and recommendation here to nonconforming uses, buildings, and lots.

There are many examples worldwide of how cities have learned not only to live with nonconformities but to turn them into drawing cards for surrounding development. The desirable False Creek waterfront area of Vancouver, British Columbia, formerly included sawmills, foundries, and shipbuilding, metalworking, salt distribution, and warehousing facilities, some of which remain. The Darling Harbor area of Sydney, Australia, is also a showplace redeveloped industrial area, and Calgary's Quarry Park hopes to become one. Surprisingly often, it is precisely the characteristic that makes a property nonconforming that also makes it an interesting contributor to neighborhood diversity.

Almost every major city has older neighborhoods with small lots where house setbacks do not meet the requirements of their zone districts. Under Euclidean zoning theory, we are just waiting for those houses to become obsolete and torn down so that they can be replaced with new housing that meets the setbacks. But, in fact, these areas are often among the most loved older areas of the city. While the city is in theory waiting for these structures and uses to disappear, it may also be supporting historic preservation groups trying to get the same area designated as a district where new development would have to match the existing character of the area. Or the city may be thanking its stars that the older homes on smaller lots are still there to help meet the need for attainable housing.

The truth is that even where the nonconformities do not have architectural merit, the neighbors have generally gotten used to them. Of course, there are differences in the types and seriousness of existing nonconformities. Those that threaten public health and safety are the most serious, but zoning theory implicitly assumes that all nonconformities are that serious. This blanket bias in favor of conformity and against preservation of the existing structures and uses does not match our experience or our emotions about what should happen. Sometimes neighborhood residents feel strongly that the nonconformity needs to go away, but just as often they feel it should stay, and most often they don't care. This last point is the strongest. To many of the neighbors, who are the ones that zoning is supposed to be protecting, it doesn't matter.

Many cities have already realized that the "no expansion of nonconformities" rule is too strict and have tried to create some breathing room. Some allow owners to ask for variances. Others have a "tolerance" or "administrative adjustment" provision in their ordinance that, in effect, says: "Close enough. Setbacks on old buildings that are within a foot or so of where they should be are treated as perfectly legal." Most importantly, many cities use a complaint-based enforcement system to take the harshness out of these types of provisions. They say: "We won't go looking for these types of situations unless a neighbor complains about it." Because most neighbors want to get along, few complain, and most violations go unnoticed for the life of the building. Complaint-based systems are essential to the effectiveness of Euclidean hybrid zoning—because zoning SWAT teams would be expensive and unpopular—but the legality of your property should not depend on the goodwill of your neighbors. They might move out tomorrow, and who knows who will move in.

Some cities try to avoid the nonconformity problem by crafting new standards so that they don't apply to any development already existing on the date the new regulation is adopted. The regulation provides that: "This standard applies only to development built after today. It isn't even intended to apply to existing structures. They're not just grandfathered; they are not subject to it, and so they are not nonconforming." That is a legal nicety, and one I have used often, but it solves only half the problem. On the bright side, expansion or redevelopment of an existing building does not have to meet the new standards. On the downside, if the property is destroyed or significantly damaged, it must still be replaced by a conforming structure and use (i.e., the protection extends to the specific property and not to the lot or the use in the structure). The replacement structure will be built after the date of the ordinance, so it will have to comply.

Finally, some jurisdictions like Detroit have included provisions stating that expansion or reestablishment of nonconforming structures and uses are permitted subject to the approval of the board of adjustment. Under standard land use law, this would require a showing of hardship of some sort, but that criteria is sometimes weakened to a requirement that the expansion just be "nondetrimental" to the neighborhood. It all depends on how hard (or not) the city is pushing to eliminate nonconformities. Even a showing of hardship is sometimes not too difficult for property owners facing competition from newer, more efficient layouts in suburban areas.

These situations are not exceptional. They make up the very fabric of older areas of our cities. That is because it is hard to fit any zoning pattern over an area that developed without a pattern. If the development standards for older areas were really drafted based on the types of lots and houses that already existed, the zoning would fit better and those properties that did not confirm would truly be exceptions. But failures to conform are often with respect to parking, setbacks, buffering, or landscaping standards that were written later and with greenfields in mind.

Rather than inventing case-by-case methods to allow nonconformities to continue, the better way to zone will distinguish between two situations. The first is where older development will not be subject to new standards at all; they will not be nonconformities and can rebuild. The second includes cases where older development will be subject to the new standards because it creates a public health or safety risk; after a fire or accident, they will need to be replaced with structures and uses that are legal in that zone).

Zoning ordinances already distinguish between "legal nonconforming" uses and plain "nonconforming" (and, by implication, illegal) uses and structures, but this is the wrong distinction. We use the term *legal nonconforming* to mean a use or structure that does not meet the development standards but that is allowed to continue as long as it does not expand or get destroyed. In contrast, a "nonconforming" use or structure is just plain illegal—it should not be occupied or operating and is sometimes subject to being shut down. Sometimes this is because of serious environmental impacts that the city cannot condone. Sometimes it is because what used to be a legal nonconforming use ran afoul of the law (e.g., they built an addition that extended the nonconformity or they extended the nonconforming use into or onto more of the property). They violated the terms of their zoning "parole"; now they are just plain illegal and could receive a notice in the mail.

Instead of this dichotomy between "substandard but tolerated" and "substandard and not tolerated," zoning should distinguish between "preexisting and with rights to expand/replace the use or structure as others can" and "preexisting without rights to expand/replace." The difference is significant, because in the first instance preexisting development would avoid the stigma of tolerated illegality (which is important to lenders). Under this distinction, most nonconformities would not be required to meet new zoning standards either now or in the future. Only nonconformities that create risks to public health or safety would be in the second category.

This is much closer to the understanding of "grandfathering" that most city council members have in mind when they approve new zoning regulations. Some council members realize that nonconforming uses and structures will not be allowed to expand and cannot be replaced after an accident, but others don't. When they hear objections from voters whose properties will be made nonconforming by a proposed zoning change and they ask the planners "Will the existing properties be grandfathered?" they mean "Will the preexisting development be exempted from compliance with this regulation? Will they be no worse off than they are today?" Under current law, planning staff members who answer "Yes" are being a little less than truthful. To be in the same situation they are today, they would have to retain the ability to expand or replace their use and structure.

For all of these reasons, a better way to zone will distinguish between nonconformities that should go away and those that can remain and expand. Legally, the solution is simple. Instead of drafting ordinances saying that preexisting buildings that do not meet the zoning standards are "legally nonconforming," just clarify that existing buildings can be rebuilt, regardless of the amount of damage, in something like their current configuration. We can develop tools that say: "New development must meet requirement X, but we don't just tolerate older development that does not meet the requirement; we protect their rights to the same extent as if they met standard X. In new areas, the balance of public health, safety, and welfare interests requires compliance with standard X, but in older areas it does not." That is the effect of the various one-off exceptions cities are already creating, but it would be clearer to just say it.

Because building styles change over time, the city should require not that a replacement building be exactly like the old one, but shall instead require that it be no bigger, taller, or more intrusive than the one it replaces. Buildings and uses in this category might even be allowed to expand on the same basis as their neighbors, provided that any health or safety impacts are mitigated. After all, damage to old buildings by fire or accident is relatively rare, and the damage, if any, to the future image of the area if they rebuild will also be minor.

For all of the reasons outlined above, a better way to zone will abandon the myth that preexisting development must someday come into compliance with the new standards. Sometimes it should be required to, and sometimes it should not—but that choice should be up to the local elected officials. Zoning ordinances should not be drafted to reinforce the general bias (grounded in the Standard Zoning Act) that they should all come into compliance. In Home Rule jurisdictions, the zoning ordinance itself can override that assumption by stating: "In this city, we do not consider preexisting uses and structures to be nonconforming unless the ordinance changing zoning standards explicitly states that they should be treated that way." Obviously, there will be cases where the council wants to put pressure on the nonconforming use to not expand the structure or use and to relocate when it can, and council could do that simply by providing that the new change applies to preexisting structures.

This approach would have two significant impacts. First, it would support the economic health of older areas, because preexisting business would be able to expand if necessary. It would reduce a key barrier to keeping older businesses viable and older structures in use. Older houses—often a key asset of mature cities, both in terms of the character of wealthy areas and the affordability of less wealthy areas—could be routinely replaced if damaged.

Second, it would significantly reduce the administrative burdens of governance. Although staff would still have to track the dates on which individual uses and structures came into being (to know whether they predate later zoning amendments), they would not have to find some type of "out" for preexisting development when a new zoning amendment is proposed. The city would have more freedom to adopt new standards—for example, for energy and resource efficiency or for design or landscaping—knowing that, as a matter of course, it would not put burdens on preexisting development. Or, if the cause was important enough, they could decide to impose those burdens.

What Does This Fix?

The theory of Euclidean hybrid zoning is that all the old should become new over time, but the political reality is that cities don't want all that. The law should reflect this reality, and doing so would respond to the criticisms of Euclidean hybrid zoning in several important ways.

- It would reflect the reality that many nonconformities will not disappear and that neither citizens nor elected officials necessarily want them to disappear.
- Allowing existing uses and structures in older areas to continue and to be expanded on a par with those in other areas would weaken the bias toward separation of uses.
- It would explicitly recognize that in many cases greenfield standards should not be applied to existing, mature areas.
- It would reduce the need for variances and exceptions to keep older, healthy businesses in operation and to allow them to expand on a par with enterprises in other areas.
- By reducing the need for variances, exceptions, and rezonings to allow reinvestment in mature areas, it would make city government more effective and more efficient.

Is It Legal?

Legally, this change is well within the framework of the constitutional constraints discussed in chapter 5. At heart, it reflects the judgment of elected officials that after an area has been developed, the best interests of the city lie in keeping it economically healthy rather than changing it to match areas that were developed later—a judgment that easily meets the test of substantive due process. Because they liberalize development rights on older properties, text changes to remove the bias against nonconformities are not likely to lead to claims of takings or violations of due process.

First Amendment claims would be unlikely as long as the changes do not single out religious institutions for particularly strict treatment or violate general principles of sign regulations. Equal protection is not implicated because there is no federally recognized constitutional right to have nonconformities disappear from the city or from your neighborhood. There is also no federally recognized property right that requires nonconformities to be treated the same in all areas of the city. In states where zoning enabling acts closely track the Standard Zoning Enabling Act, statutory language may include a blanket statement about the elimination or nonexpansion of nonconformities, and that language may need to be amended.

Dynamic Development Standards

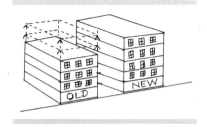

Now we come to one of the harder topics in this book. Why do zoning regulations have to be static? Why do they have to set a number (for height, setback, parking, and so forth) that can be changed only by action of the city council, even if council has amended the zoning of surrounding parcels to allow different numbers? The better way to zone will include "dynamic" standards that change over time in predictable ways, but that do not require individual council action for each change.

If this sounds strange, it should not. Governments have long realized that legislating is a slow, unruly process and that all of the details should not have to be approved by the legislative body. To take one plebian example, when city councils adopt development impact fees, they often include escalator clauses tied to inflation or the cost of doing business in that industry. Transportation impact fees may be drafted so that they are updated automatically every year or so based on some index of inflation in the cost of building roads. In this case, it is clear that council intends that the fees not "lose ground" against the facilities they are trying to fund. Everyone understands that a fixed fee would be less useful in carrying out council's intent than one that adjusted automatically with changes in the industry. The requirement is dynamic, but in a way that is understood—even if it is not completely predictable—to the parties involved. The fee changes automatically based on changes that are outside the control of either city council or the builders who pay the fees.

A second example comes from land use spacing regulations. Cities routinely require that some land uses be separated from others of the same type (e.g., adult uses from one another) or from uses of other types that are perceived as sensitive (e.g., jails from schools). But the effect of these regulations can change over time. If a new school is built, it may carry with it a "bubble" within which adult uses or jails cannot be built. That changes what nearby landowners can do on their land without any action of city council. Or, if a school closes down, that may open up new possible activities on land that would previously have been too close to the school. Some ordinances lock in the spacing bubbles on the date of enactment, but

176

others do not. The rule is understood, but its effect on individual properties is allowed to vary over time as conditions change.

A third example comes from the area of "contextual" development standards. In older areas, especially those that predate zoning, it is common to find houses with front setbacks that vary between 15 and 30, or even 40, feet depending on the size of the lots. Sometimes the front setbacks vary even between groups of homes on a single lot. Even on blocks where houses were constructed after zoning was adopted there is variation, because the city requirement for a minimum 20-foot setback did not prevent the builder from deciding to make it 25 or 30 feet. Not infrequently, older homes on smaller lots were actually built with a smaller setback than the zoning later required—they have 5 or 10 feet whereas the later (postwar) development standard assumed that there would be a car in the driveway and required 20 feet. So all of the homes in that area may be nonconforming.

When a house is replaced or a new house is built on a vacant lot, what *should* the setback be? The traditional answer is 20 feet (that's what the zone district usually says, because of the hypothetical car in the driveway), but that would result in one new house being 10 or 15 feet farther back from the street than its neighbors. This is exactly what the neighbors do not want. If the setback were 20 feet, the new house would stand out like a sore thumb and erode the existing character of the block, rather than being a new source of investment to reinforce it. Ironically, many old lots have alley garages instead of front driveways, so leaving 20 feet of space in front for a car to pull off the street really doesn't make much sense.

Surveying all of those old blocks to determine the prevailing front setback (assuming there is one) is beyond the staff resources of many cities. So several modern zoning ordinances include "contextual" zoning provisions. Instead of saying that the setback is 20 feet, it says that if most of the lots on that block have buildings constructed on them, then the required setback is the predominant front setback of those existing buildings. Others say the setback is whatever setback is used by either of the closest houses on either side, or something in between those two numbers. Sometimes the rule gives a few feet of flexibility on either side of the resulting number. In many cases, there is no one "correct" number to superimpose on an older, built-up area, but we do want the new building to fit in with what has already been built and we don't want to do a separate study each time to determine what that number should be.

Rigidly enforcing a standard 30- or 50-foot setback in an older commercial area where buildings were built closer to the street has even worse consequences. An owner may decide to tear down his or her old commercial building along the street and replace it with a building set back 30 or 50 feet, so that cars can now park in front of the new store. This is the poster child for a suburban standard that probably should not have been imposed on an older commercial area in the first place. Allowing it to operate is the zoning equivalent of "block busting." The more buildings that are built back from the street, and the more driveways that interrupt the sidewalks, the fewer people who want to walk along the street to do their shopping, and soon there will be other buildings torn down.

Allowing contextual front setbacks prevents this, because it would require that parking in front of stores be installed only on blocks where that is the norm. It avoids the bias of forcing all buildings up to the street or of forcing all buildings back from the street, and it allows the built character of the block to determine the setback. Of course, the city could decide that the street no longer has a walkable character—that it's now an auto-oriented strip that needs to be zoned that way despite the current close-to-the-street building pattern. In that case, the council could establish front setbacks to allow or require front parking. The point is that establishing an auto-oriented front setback in a previously walkable area should be the conscious choice of the council, not the result of a carried-over greenfield standard. Contextual development standards are another example of a dynamic development standard already in use.

A better way to zone will include more of these types of dynamic standards, for two reasons. The first and most important one is that cities change over time. Neighborhood character, building types, and development technologies all change, and city governments are often playing catch-up in trying to have their zoning ordinances reflect those changes. Dynamic standards can make some of those adjustments automatic.

Obviously, there are many areas of the city—particularly single-family and low-density residential zones—where property owners do not want any automatic changes at all. They want the neighborhood to stay pretty much as it is, and dynamic development standards are not appropriate for those areas. Dynamic development standards are appropriate for single-family and low-density residential zones only if there is a consensus among residents and the city council that significant change is needed to offset disinvestment in the area—in other words, in areas where the current size and scale of development do not reflect the residents' preferred future for the area, just the results of economic stagnation. In the discussion of the "mixed-use middle" earlier in this chapter, I pointed out that most single- and two-family areas, and maybe some low-density multifamily apartment/condo areas, may not want to be part of that middle. The same is true here. These stable residential areas represent the majority of most cities' land areas, and dynamic development standards are not intended for them.

However, there are many zone districts within the mixed-use middle where dynamic zoning would make sense. These include residential multifamily, mixed-use, or commercial areas that the city wants to allow to densify over time. Dynamic standards would allow development regulations in these areas to change over time in a measured way. Let's talk about some examples.

First, where an area is planned for densification, either because it is a transit-oriented development or because the land is vacant or significantly underutilized, a dynamic development standard could say that the maximum height on an individual parcel will be the height of the tallest building on an adjacent parcel plus one floor. As taller buildings are built, new opportunities would open up for the neighbors, but in a way that prevents any building from towering over its neighbors. Of course, landowners who want their projects to tower above the others could always ask city council for a rezoning, but those who would be satisfied with an additional floor of leasable area could do so without the need for a rezoning. Planning staff could approve the new, taller building through an administrative check. The City of Kalamazoo, Michigan, recently adopted this type of dynamic height control for areas surrounding its downtown core. Delhi makes maximum heights in some areas of the city a function of surrounding street widths, and St. Petersburg used to do so. If streets are widened, traffic capacities rise, perceived scale increases, and maximum heights are allowed to increase automatically.

As a second example, commercial area parking standards could be written to say that required ratios for off-street parking will vary depending on the use rates in public parking lots in the area. When city surveys of parking lots show them at or near capacity, parking ratios might automatically increase by a fixed percentage for future applications. If surveys showed lots of unused public parking capacity, the required ratio could decline by the same amount. To avoid inconsistencies from year to year, the ordinance might require that two or three years of consistent survey results are required before the automatic adjustments would be effective. My experience is that many cities adopt and maintain off-street parking ratios beyond what is needed to avoid traffic congestion but that it is relatively hard to get them reduced because of fear that the new figure might be too low. A dynamic parking standard would tie the requirement to whether there was "enough" parking in the area, which is actually what the parking standards were intended to achieve in the first place. If a new public parking structure were built (or a private one that is open to the public for a fee), parking capacity would go up, use rates in existing public parking areas would fall, and required off-street parking would also fall.

More controversially, the same principle could be applied to areas where the provision of off-street parking is capped to discourage auto commuting and reinforce public transit. Relatively few cities in the United States use parking caps, and those that do generally limit them to downtown or special focus areas. The list includes New York, Seattle, San Francisco, and Portland and Beaverton, Oregon. But there is solid evidence that the amount of parking required by national retailers and lenders is unoccupied on almost every day of the year. A dynamic development standard could provide that when public transit ridership rates fall below a given number, future developments near that transit line would be restricted to a lower cap. If public transit becomes more crowded, the parking cap could be raised for later applications.

A fourth example involves environmental standards. Where water quality in a stream or wetland has been degraded or where habitat numbers are dropping along a wildlife corridor, the city could adopt setbacks to keep development and activities away from those areas, with a proviso that if the quality indicator or numbers pass certain thresholds, then future development would have reduced setbacks.

This issue came up when the State of Colorado sponsored habitat conservation planning for the Preble's meadow jumping mouse, which was listed by the U.S. Fish and Wildlife Service as a threatened species. Most of the mouse's habitat was in or near streambeds and streambanks that many owners would not be able to build on anyway, but landowners up and down the Front Range of Colorado were still apprehensive about what the listing meant for them. Most of the discussion focused on setbacks from stream and wetland areas. In addition to questioning almost everything else about the listing and the science behind it, owners asked what would happen if significant building setbacks were put in place and then the listing was overturned on appeal or the numbers of Preble's mice increased to a point where they were no longer threatened. Well, the same city councils that adopted the setbacks could reduce them, of course, but that gave the landowners very little comfort. Their attitude was that what the government takes away it rarely gives back, and that "all those park and trail people" would then come forward and argue for the big setbacks to be kept in place. Although they still would not have been happy with the Preble's listing, the landowners would have been more comfortable with a provision that automatically repealed endangered species setbacks when the reason behind them was gone.

The second reason dynamic development standards are a good idea, in case you had not already guessed, is NIMBYism. Having development standards adjust automatically to changed circumstances can avoid some of the need for additional public hearings. This topic will be discussed again in the section on depoliticizing development approvals, but many elected officials know the value of building in adjustments without reopening the political process each time.

One common scenario is that a landowner wants a rezoning to allow more commercial development and the neighbors object because of potential traffic impacts. If is often hard to tell who is right. Neighbors tell nightmare stories of traffic problems, but the applicant waves a traffic report (approved by planning staff) saying that there is enough street capacity available to handle the proposed development. In principle, the citizens might agree that if there was more traffic capacity they would not object to the density. But if the elected officials turn down the landowner's request and ask him or her to come back when the intersection has been improved or the transit improvements have been made, the chances are good that the same objections will be raised again. Different neighbors (or even the same ones) will show up to complain that the density is still inappropriate because traffic is still bad. A dynamic development standard can avoid this scenario by enacting the initial compromise—that is, by stating that when the improvements are in place, then the additional density will be available. Some cities are already crafting these types of solutions in PUDs, of course, but it would be nice not to have to renegotiate them each time. In developing or redeveloping areas, density could be made a direct function of transportation system capacity.

The point is to avoid negative impacts on surrounding areas, and the likely negative impacts change as those areas evolve; there is no reason why zoning provisions cannot respond to those changes in predictable ways without separate city council action. It would build added flexibility into a wide range of mixed-use areas, make it easier to keep zoning ordinances in touch with actual development trends, and even defuse a bit of NIMBYism in the process.

What Does This Fix?

Including dynamic development standards in redevelopment areas would address the weaknesses of Euclidean hybrid zoning in the following ways:

- It would better correspond to market needs by allowing larger or more dense development in mixed-use areas as those areas mature.
- It could help address tax revenue shortfalls by allowing larger and more valuable development as the character of surrounding areas changes.
- If development standards are tied to available traffic capacity, it would better reflect the close interrelationship between land development and transportation systems.
- By requiring fewer rezonings and permits for proposed development that is in character with the surrounding area, it would reduce opportunities for NIMBYism.
- It would promote predictable flexibility, because development standards would flex to reflect the surrounding size and scale of development while that same character would limit the degree of flexibility.
- By reducing the need for rezonings and development approvals for proposed projects that are consistent with the changing standards over time, it would make government more efficient.

Is It Legal?

Although this would represent a fairly dramatic change from current zoning practice, I believe that dynamic development standards also pass legal muster. They reflect the judgment of the city council that adopting not only zoning standards but also rules by which those standards will change over time will result in development more consistent with the planning goals of the city as well as lowering administrative costs. If adopted with the same care for procedures applicable to other zoning changes, this should meet the requirements for both procedural and substantive due process. By allowing the possible uses and densities in mixed-use areas to scale upward over time, they would be unlikely to provoke takings or vested rights claims. Activities protected by the Fifth Amendment would not be affected unless they were singled out for specially restrictive or harsh treatments that would be unconstitutional even under static standards. Equal protection applies only when there is a constitutionally protected property right, and there is no such right to static zoning.

Dynamic development standards will have to define specifically how they will change over time (for instance, based on traffic capacities, public parking usage, or pollutant levels) and will need to ensure that the factors driving those changes cannot be manipulated; but careful drafting should survive challenges based on vagueness. As with static development standards, cities will still need to be careful to avoid conflict with standards set in state or federal law. In particular, the change allowed by a dynamic development standard cannot be something that state law requires to be adopted after a specific hearing by council unless the language of the state law is broad enough to cover a standard that changes over time.

Negotiated Large Developments

Negotiated PUD zoning is one of the four major strands that make up Euclidean hybrid zoning (see chapter 1). It was originally needed because neither standard Euclidean zoning nor performance zoning offered enough flexibility to do something really different from the norm. And there are lots of innovative ideas for great developments out there that could never get approved under standard Euclidean districts. A better way to zone will acknowledge that some types of land use issues really do require negotiated solutions, but it will minimize the administrative costs of creating and administering negotiated zoning. It will not make the mistake of assuming that negotiations need to result in a one-off PUD; sometimes the negotiations can result in better use of the more flexible zones and tools discussed elsewhere in this book.

The biggest single development in the Denver metropolitan area is Highlands Ranch, which replaced a real ranch of the same name on a large tract of land south of the core city. Highlands Ranch covers 22,000 acres of rolling land (more than triple the combined area of the three stellar mixed-use developments—Platte Valley, Lowry, and Stapleton—discussed earlier in this chapter) and is governed by a mega-PUD negotiated in the early 1980s. With a population of 88,000, Highlands Ranch has been criticized as being more-of-the-same suburbia, but few would deny that the quality of its planning, infrastructure, and open space protection exceeds many others in the western United States.

As part of the original PUD, the developer dedicated 8,200 acres (37 percent of the site) as a single, contiguous tract of open space that now forms the backbone of the Douglas County open space system. That would have been tough to achieve through application of Euclidean zoning districts, no matter how sophisticated. It required a careful look at the quality of land by *both* the developer and the government and a joint vision of how open space could benefit both the developer's property and the surrounding areas. Sometimes there is no substitute for negotiation. The need for some sort of negotiated zoning is underscored by its presence in almost all modern zoning ordinances. In more than twenty years of practice, I have worked in exactly one city that did not have a negotiated zoning tool, and I advised them to get one.

Although there are many ways to misuse negotiated PUDs (see chapter 1), they are useful for large new developments that will significantly affect the character of the city or a neighborhood. A better way to zone will encourage negotiation in that context. How large is "large" depends on the community, but general benchmarks might include any development that occupies more than 15 to 25 acres or that increases the developed land area, housing stock, or nonresidential floor area of the city by more than 5 percent. There is no magic to this formula; the key is that negotiated zoning should apply to developments so large that they will significantly affect the image, finances, or operation of the city. In big cities, the thresholds may be bigger. This recommendation is based on three facts.

First, large image-making developments are often being negotiated anyway. They seem to be negotiated even after zoning ordinances are modernized and new zoning tools are in place. I have worked for several cities that have tried to reduce reliance on PUDs by writing new zone districts reflecting what they try to negotiate in PUDs. The philosophy (which I supported) has been this: "The PUDs we have approved so far show what the city wants to get out of new development, so why not write that into a new zone district and just skip all that time-consuming negotiation? Next time we are faced with a situation like that we will cajole the applicant into accepting the new district."

The track record on this approach has been mixed. Sometimes the new districts derived from PUDs get used, and other times they sit on the shelf. After Denver drafted its seven mixed-use districts, they found many takers in different areas of the city, partly because the districts were more flexible than previous Euclidean zones and partly because the city made it clear that it would not negotiate PUDs that were just minor variations of those mixed-use districts. In contrast, when the City of Arvada, Colorado, revised its zoning ordinance, it took several design and development standards from prior PUDs and made them generally applicable to other zone districts in order to discourage use of negotiated zoning. But so many applicants still walked in the door asking for PUDs that the city largely gave up the effort to avoid them. The planning director told me: "All the big guys still wanted to do their own thing, so in the end we had to let them do PUDs anyway." Make no mistake—cities should still research and adopt standards and criteria for large new developments. But efforts to guess in advance what mix and pattern of zone districts will make the most of the opportunities available on large image-making sites is not likely to be productive. Expect and encourage negotiation based on clear criteria and benchmarks researched in advance.

It appears that applicants with smaller sites can sometimes be weaned off the use of negotiated zoning more easily than owners of large sites. Owners of smaller sites have to spread the soft costs of getting planning and zoning approvals over fewer homes and less leasable area, so the time and expense of a negotiated PUD are greater on a per-unit basis. A PUD-derived flexible zone district may be close enough to what they wanted while avoiding the time and expense of those negotiations. In addition, the more prescriptive you make the PUD-derived district, the fewer takers you will have. It is usually a mistake to take your best negotiated development—which is usually one where you sweated a lot of the design details—take a snapshot of it, and make it a new non-PUD zone district. There is a clear difference between applicants' willingness to accept very detailed design and development standards that they have drafted and their willingness to use those you drafted with someone else (or, heaven forbid, with one of their competitors).

The second reason for negotiating large developments is that it is really difficult to anticipate what will be appropriate on large sites. They just don't lend themselves to prebaked solutions. By definition, big sites offer significant opportunities to move uses and structures around in different patterns, to protect open space, to respond to site conditions, and to build in flexibility to respond to changing market conditions during the build-out period. Often there is no obvious context for development—or perhaps only along the edges of the property where previous development has taken place and impacts will be felt. Because there is no defining context to guide development, lots of good design solutions might be possible.

The fact that big sites may not have an identifiable design context does not mean that the city has no interest in the design and layout. The bigger the site, the more likely it is to include lands designated as part of the city's master transportation network, park and trail network, urban draining system, or sensitive land areas. The applicant and the city may have different views about how to respond to those areas. And the bigger the site, the more likely it is to need significant public facilities (schools, utility substations, fire stations) to serve its residents. The city may be asked to take over managing those facilities in the future, and the city and applicant may differ on where they should be located. Finally, the larger the site, the more likely it is that development will be completed in phases over time. The landowner and city may differ in their views on the order and location of those phases, with the owner wanting the flexibility to respond to market changes and the city wanting to minimize service extension costs.

All of these are legitimate issues, and ones that are hard to resolve before the city knows what the parcel's owner has in mind for the property. Depending on whether the owner wants to comply with the comprehensive plan or change it, and depending on how the owner wants to arrange the various land uses and intensities, the appropriate responses to site conditions, regional street and open space systems, and phasing may change. Negotiation is often the best way to work out these issues.

The third reason for PUD zoning on large properties is that they are some of the most obvious places to innovate—and where failure to innovate can hurt the city most. From the city's perspective, the worst-case scenario may be an owner/developer who knows how to build only one product and wants to fill up the land with that product. So, although it is likely that owners of large tracts anticipate a negotiated rezoning, there may be grounds for the city to require one anyway. Too much of even a good thing is usually a bad thing for the city, but Euclidean hybrid zoning is generally blind to this problem; sometimes it makes it easier to do a lot of the same type of development.

While working for Denver, I was approached one day by a man who introduced himself as a golf course and hotel developer from a mountain resort area. He wanted to know whether the open space bordering the highway to Denver's new airport was big enough to accommodate a golf course and two hotels. I told him it was about 800 acres, which was enough for three golf courses. "Wow", he said "I was going to ask if I could build a golf course and two hotels—but can I do three golf courses and six hotels?" While most developers need to have their niches, trying to fill up a large tract of land with your niche product can be a problem.

Big tracts of land are where the city enhances its public image for the future. Many a mature city is doing its best to manage and upgrade its older areas but is also counting on the large-scale development and redevelopment to help improve that image. Aurora, Colorado's new development corridor on the E-470 toll road, Denver's redevelopment of the Stapleton and Lowry airfields, and Orlando's redevelopment of its Naval Training Center site have all been used to do that. All have required extensive negotiations. But big image-making opportunities for mature cities are few and far between, and that alone may justify having a mandatory negotiation bias for those sites.

Having said all this, it is bad practice for cities to force property owners to negotiate by giving them no option. Cities should continue to zone lands as the U.S. Constitution requires—so that there is a reasonable economic use of the land available without negotiations. But it is usually possible to do that without zoning for the most economically beneficial uses of land; there is no requirement for zoning to authorize the "highest and best use" on any parcel of land. The city should also ensure that nonnegotiated zoning includes acceptable quality standards, varieties of products, and careful environmental protection, so that if property owners choose not to negotiate, the alternative will be acceptable to the city. But for large parcels, the preferred approach for large, image-making sites should involve negotiation, and the city can hold out incentives (more density, more flexibility, faster processing) to encourage negotiation. For the rest of the city, negotiated zoning should be available only as a second choice under narrowly defined circumstances. For large tracts, it should be the first choice, with nonnegotiated zones as a backstop.

But isn't negotiation of large development and redevelopment approvals subject to the same criticisms of PUDs outlined in chapter 1? The answer is yes—and no. Yes, it is true that they take time and effort to negotiate, but in the case of large, image-making sites, it is worth the effort. Moving away from the use of PUDs for small sites and for situations that could be handled in other ways—for example, through more flexible uses, mixed-use districts, mature area standards, acceptance of nonconformities, and dynamic development standards as discussed above—would create major savings in PUD administration. The answer to the disadvantages of PUDs is not to ban them but to limit them to truly important sites and to give other zones some of the flexibility now available only through PUDs.

The bigger question is how to deal with administration of large PUDs down the road. Even if limiting PUDs to big sites reduces the workload substantially, planning staff will still have to pull out the file to see what standards govern new development; PUDs don't lend themselves to memorization the way even flexible zone districts do. That tends to erode the gains in efficiencies from other recommendations in our better way to zone, but there are some things you can do to cut the losses.

First, the negotiations over large parcels do not necessarily have to result in a PUD. Sometimes—as in the case of the Lowry redevelopment in Denver—they could lead to an agreement to use existing districts, which are easier for staff to remember and administer. In addition, sometimes the key issues for negotiation are the phasing of development, the dedications of land, or the payment of development impact fees. If so, the resolution of those issues can sometimes be documented in a development agreement—that is, a contract between the city and the developer—that does not involve the creation of a new zoning district. Even when PUDs are used, however, they do not always have to include "one-off" text. Lots of PUDs vary some zoning parameters while simply cross-referencing standard zoning provisions on other topics. Parking standards are often handled this way, because the developer doesn't want to reinvent parking requirements or intends to impose standards higher than the city's anyway.

Finally, the administrative burdens of large PUDs can be reduced by moving toward self-certification. Some cities already allow architects to certify that buildings will meet design standards (as well as structural standards), because it is less expensive than setting up a city review system. If it turns out the building does not meet the standards, the architect (and sometimes the owner) is penalized or not allowed to self-certify in the future. The same could easily happen in zoning. Developers who want PUDs to include complex or hard-to-enforce provisions may be asked to certify compliance themselves and be subject to penalties if those terms are violated. The city would still need to inspect for compliance, but less frequently and at less cost.

Is It Legal?

Because negotiating large developments simply reflects a currently accepted practice, this recommendation does not raise new legal issues. PUDs have been used for years, and their use has been upheld against the various types of legal challenges outlined in chapter 5. Remember, however, to leave reasonable economic uses of the land available without negotiation.

What Does This Fix?

Acknowledging that large, community image–changing developments should be negotiated would respond to the critiques raised in chapters 2, 3, and 4 in the following ways.

- It would make government more efficient by reducing the number of PUDs.
- It would address the oversimplification in traditional zoning that fixed rules can anticipate the preferred patterns of development on large tracts, which has proven to be largely untrue or to result in monotonous edge development.
- It would reduce the need for variances and exceptions, which is a major reason many large developers already rely on PUDs for large developments.
- It would respond to market desires for flexibility in the design and layout of new developments, which is already a major impetus for the use of PUDs.
- It would allow better tailoring of large, new development to available and foreseeable transportation capacity and environmentally sensitive lands.
- It would allow better tailoring of new development to respond to specific neighborhood concerns and to reduce NIMBYism, which is another significant reason large landowners already choose PUDs for many large projects.
- By better reflecting the need for flexibility and the importance of incorporating new and innovative development types in large developments, it would make government more effective.
- It would acknowledge the reality that zoning for large development and redevelopment areas tends to be a political, rather than a technical, exercise.

Depoliticized Final Approvals

PLAN CHECK

NIMBYism is one of the five new forces shaping land development in the United States (see chapter 3). Of course, one person's NIMBYism is another person's spirited defense of his or her neighborhood. That is what makes the problem so intractable. Everyone agrees that NIMBYism is bad, but the same people who condemn it turn around and engage in it when the change is proposed close to their own home.

How do we distinguish between unhealthy NIMBYism and healthy interest in one's neighborhood? One answer is to focus on *when* in the development process the debate occurs. This is an area that few citizens understand and that very few cities take the trouble to explain. The development and redevelopment of cities is the outcome of a cycle of events that involves the public, the city, and private investors. In theory, it goes like this:

1. *Plan*. Adopt (or revise) a vision for the future of the city, corridor, or neighborhood.
2. *Zone*. Adjust the law to reflect the vision, or as close as politics will allow. If the plan calls for redevelopment of some areas, zoning should encourage that.
3. *Subdivide*. Create lots or parcels consistent with the zoning for sale and construction.

Note: Steps 1, 2, and 3 may need to be repeated over time before anyone files an application to actually build something on a given site. There may be more than one zone district consistent with the plan and more than one lot layout consistent with the zoning. Time may pass, and new plans or zones may be approved. The original development may become obsolete so that an entire new cycle needs to start.

4. *Review Site Plans*. When someone files an application to build something, review it for compliance with the law. Generally, that means not only for consistency with zoning and subdivision but also administrative regulations about where traffic can enter roads, whether water will drain off the site, how fire departments will access the site, and the like. If the city requires design review of the building, this is where it occurs.
5. *Review building plans*. Now review the plans for the building itself to make sure it meets building codes. This is a separate step because buildings should not be approved until the site plan (which tells you where the building will be on the site) is decided.

The key issue in NIMBYism is *when* it is appropriate for the public to get involved in commenting on a proposed development. That seems like a simple question, but it is not. The first three steps in this sequence—planning, zoning, and subdivision—are designed to look at the long-term health of the city: not only the quality of life its citizens will enjoy but the long-term effects of different types of development on the environment and on the fiscal health of the city. Decisions about what kinds of development should occur where, what kinds of uses will be allowed, how big the lots will be, and how big the buildings can be are established at these stages—and it is not only appropriate but necessary for the public to be involved.

Zoning was originally conceived as a technical exercise—knowing the plan would tell you what zoning should apply in some objective way—but that has not proved true in practice (see chapter 2). Zoning is a political act, and applicants who ask for a rezoning know that they are asking for a decision involving legislative discretion. Council may agree that the proposed rezoning is appropriate, or it may disagree. Neighbors who show up to oppose the reason may in fact be NIMBYs (they disagree with it only because it is close to their property), but zoning is the appropriate forum to have that debate, and city council is the right one to decide it.

This is especially true for PUDs. Applicants for PUDs have willingly gone into a public negotiation with city council because they want to do something that the existing zone districts do not allow—and they should expect to have a full (and possibly vigorous) public debate about that. So opposition to a rezoning can be a form of NIMBYism that is consistent with the zoning system. The only real answer to it is a city council with the skill to weigh vocal, local interests against the long-term interests of the city.

However, the last two steps—review of site plans and review of building plans—are concerned with site specifics that only come into play once someone files an application for specific development. The question at these stages is not whether building X is appropriate where it is proposed but whether it complies with the zoning ordinance, subdivision regulation, and administrative regulations of the city. If it does, it should be approved; if it does not, it should not. And it is not generally appropriate for the public to be involved at this stage unless its discussion is limited to compliance with adopted standards. In many cases, the public would like to discuss the merits of the specific proposal (not just compliance), but it has proven very difficult to structure that discussion without feeding NIMBYism.

The term *NIMBYism* has become so emotionally loaded, however, that we need to clarify what specific behavior we are talking about. For purposes of this discussion, we need to define two types of NIMBYism. Early-in-the-game NIMBYism occurs when residents organize to oppose certain types of change or development in their neighborhood during the drafting of comprehensive or neighborhood plans or zoning controls. Early-in-the-game NIMBYism also extends to the rezoning of land in anticipation of a proposed development, because that is a discretionary legislative action by the city council that is explicitly required to have a public hearing.

Next comes a gray area. Some cities provide for a public hearing on whether site plans comply with the adopted standards. If the city can ensure that testimony is limited to that topic—and not to individual preferences and opinions unrelated to the standards—then public participation in the hearing would qualify as early-in-the-game NIMBYism. History shows, however, that it is very hard to limit public testimony to compliance with zoning standards, and the safer course may be to avoid public hearings on site plans altogether. Some cities compromise by accepting letters from the public regarding whether the site plan complies with city standards. Letters that stick to that topic are considered, and those that do not are not. An emotional hearing to make the same points is avoided.

Late-in-the-game NIMBYism also includes any public involvement after this point. At this stage, the decision maker (be it city council, the planning commission, a hearing officer, or the planning director) should make a determination about compliance and mitigation of impacts and allow the applicant to respond. When that response is filed, the city can determine whether it is sufficient, which does not require another hearing. Of course, the city could decide to have a second hearing, or even a third, but these types of procedures have often been abused in order to deny projects that in fact meet all of the adopted requirements. Not holding a public hearing when it could easily be abused is as much a part of good governance as holding public hearings at the planning, zoning, and initial review stages.

Doesn't depoliticizing final approvals undermine the goal of "responsiveness" in governance that we identified in chapter 4? Yes, it does. But experience shows that we pay a high price for responsiveness at these late stages in development approvals. The need to promote the other governance goals—particularly effectiveness, efficiency, and fairness—simply outweigh the value of another round of responsiveness.

What we are worried about is late-in-the-game NIMBYism—and a better way to zone will discourage it. The way to avoid late-in-the-game NIMBYism is to depoliticize the later stages of development approvals. Some states and cities already do this in the subdivision process. When applying for a subdivision of land, many cities provide that you need to submit a preliminary plat laying out the lots, roads, drainage, fire access, utilities, and lots of other details. The documents need to show that you have complied with the law and that the lots you are creating will function as proper building sites without creating problems for the public safety, for the environment, or for service delivery. Almost invariably, the city council gets to approve preliminary plats—after all, they involve the creation of streets and other public improvements that the city will probably have to take over and maintain. Sometimes the city is required to hold a public hearing (in those states where they can exercise discretion in the approval process), and sometimes not. Often the city council's review will also include their judgment of whether the proposal is consistent with the comprehensive plan—and subdivisions are sometimes denied on that ground alone, even if the surveying and engineering are perfect. If changes to the subdivision are recommended during staff review or the hearing, someone lists them and the city council approves the preliminary plat subject to the applicant making the listed changes.

The applicant then goes back, makes those changes, and takes any other steps required to finalize the plat. For example, if the city requires dedications of land areas for park or school sites, it may not be possible to calculate those dedications until the pattern of lot sizes, park sites, and school sites has been established—that is, they can be calculated only after city council has approved the preliminary plat. So the applicant may have to draft deeds to the dedicated lands or pay fees in lieu of any lands that are not being dedicated and then deliver them to the city along with the final plat. But often the final plat does not go back to city council; it goes to the planning director instead. The only question at this point is whether the applicant has done everything city council and the land dedication ordinances required. Why would you hold another public hearing on the plat when compliance with technical conditions and regulations is the only topic left. Of course, some cities do require the final plat to come back to council for a second hearing, but the fact that many cities do not shows that is a workable option.

So we already use some depoliticized final approvals that involve the exercise of judgment, and we are comfortable with it. Finalizing plats may require only compliance with laws and conditions, but that does not mean it is a "turn the crank" exercise. The planning director can usually refuse to accept a pattern of parks or school sites that is unacceptable to the city based on adopted criteria. We often allow back-and-forth discussions between the subdivider and the planning director about how to comply with the city council's direction, without requiring another trip back to city council. The gains in efficiency are obvious—one less public hearing and a less crowded agenda for city council—but I think there is something more important at stake. The more important gain is in not reopening for debate a matter that has already been debated with notice to the public.

This approach should be extended further into zoning. Although local politics will differ, a better way to zone will depoliticize final approvals by making site planning a staff review function. That does not mean that the public will lose its say in how big or tall buildings should be or where they are located on the site, but those matters will be addressed in zoning and subdivision regulations so that the applicant can design to meet them. They will not be subject to "beauty contests without rules," as sometimes happens now.

In most cases, opening final approvals up to public debate is just asking for bad decisions. The real damage is in creating a public perception that it is fair to change the rules during the last inning of the game if the voices are loud enough. Unfortunately for applicants, the further you get toward a final approval, the easier it is to rally troops against change. Individuals who stayed home before will come and help pack the room. This puts elected officials in a very bad position. They can either disappoint the applicant, whom they know has designed the project to comply with the regulations city council itself adopted, or they can disappoint a roomful of voters and friends. Or, they can "split the baby" and find some last-minute change that will create the appearance of having sided with the neighbors without denying the project. Often they choose the last option, but that puts the applicant in a bad situation. Having designed the economics of the project based on predictable costs and revenues, he now finds the costs increased (e.g., more buffering) or the revenues decreased (e.g., less leasable area) when it is too late to make up the losses somewhere else.

Some elected officials see this for what it is: a setup. City council members with less experience will occasionally say: "I want to see all the details of every development—that's what my voters elected me to do." But those with more experience often say the opposite: "Don't put me in the situation of publicly approving an unpopular project that has met all the rules. Give it to staff." In a small town, everyone knows their elected officials and expects personal involvement to the very end, so the first position may be justified. But large cities cannot function with individualized political approval of each stage or each project; they need systems based on objective standards. My experience is that as smaller cities grow into big cities, the change from relational governance to systems governance is one of the harder ones they face. Depoliticizing final approvals is a key step in moving toward systems governance and more predictable results.

What Does This Fix?

Depoliticizing final approvals would address the weaknesses of Euclidean hybrid zoning in several ways.

- Most obviously, it would reduce opportunities for NIMBYism by directing concern about surrounding development to earlier stages in the planning, zoning, and subdivision approval process.
- By avoiding last-minute derailments of developments that have already been reviewed and determined to be consistent with the zoning, it would make the government more effective in achieving the city's planning goals.
- By avoiding late-in-the-game hearings or rehearings on controversial projects, it would promote the goal of procedural equity—sending similar types of applications through similar review and approval processes.
- By avoiding an additional round of review hearings and by reducing the number of last-minute revisions of projects that already meet zoning standards, it would improve the efficiency of both the government and the development process.

Is It Legal?

Removing late-in-the-game public hearings for developments that already meet substantive zoning requirements is a procedural change, so the major legal questions will concern due process. Most state enabling acts require public hearings on zoning text or map changes (including PUDs), many require hearings on changes to comprehensive plans, and some require public hearings on variances. Beyond that, state laws vary widely as to when public hearings are required. State law seldom requires public hearings for things like conditional uses or site plans. Where they exist, those requirements were often created by city governments as new procedures not required by state law.

There is almost never a requirement for a second public hearing at any given stage, and those hearings should clearly be eliminated. In general, as long as there has been one substantive hearing on the application of law to the specific proposal, the fundamental requirement of due process has been met. Of course, if the applicant changes the project so dramatically that it is really a new proposal, then a second hearing should be required, but that is seldom the case.

Removing additional hearings is generally an advantage to the applicant and does not raise questions of takings. Because of the specific language of state law, however, it may create questions about vested rights (i.e., if the state law requires a public hearing before the creation of a statutory vested right, it may be necessary to clarify when the hearing occurs). Although it may affect the timing of when vested rights are created, the removal of additional hearings will not result in the denial of vested rights that would otherwise exist. First Amendment issues should not arise unless protected activities are singled out for special procedures, since the proposed changes are procedural and not substantive. As with all other changes, the city should take care to avoid removing any final hearings that are required by detailed statutes that preempt local powers.

Better Webbing

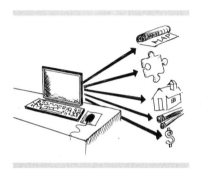

Most readers find zoning ordinances to be daunting documents—usually bulky, sometimes poorly organized and indexed, and often the obvious result of numerous uncoordinated amendments. I frequently leave a zoning text encounter with a nagging doubt that maybe I still don't know the answer—that there may be some little section hidden somewhere else that would qualify (or reverse) what I thought I learned.

All of that can be improved upon, of course. Written ordinances can be reorganized, illustrated, clarified, and indexed so that information is easier to find and less onerous to read. When you do that, you get the pleasure of hearing: "Wow, it's so much easier to find information in the new ordinance." But you still wouldn't call the zoning ordinance a good read. And there is a trade-off. To minimize the chances of missing something when amending the ordinance, drafters like to state each substantive requirement one time and then cross-reference it. But that means readers have to flip back and forth between sections to find answers. Still, zoning professionals generally lean that way because the alternative—an ordinance that actually repeated each substantive requirement every time it might apply—would be a massive tome indeed.

Part of the problem is that we are used to thinking of zoning ordinances as books. City attorneys, zoning administrators, developers, and sometimes planners need to "have it all in one place" on their bookshelf, because for them it is a reference book they may need to look at for several different reasons. It's a user's guide to land in the city—maybe the equivalent of what the *Physician's Desk Reference* is (or was) to doctors. But most citizens don't need a reference book; they need the answer to a specific question about their property. The same is true for many investors: they want to buy land where they can build X, but they don't need to know everything about where and how to build Y and Z.

Twenty years ago, publishers spent a lot of time thinking about how to organize massive amounts of information in books so they could serve as both a reference for an entire field and a quick way to answer discrete questions within that field. For years, encyclopedia publishers alphabetized everything by topic, so you just had to know the name of the topic. Then Encyclopedia Britannica came up with a completely different organization: several volumes of *Micropedia* (which had articles of about three hundred words giving an overview of many key topics) and about twice as many volumes of *Macropedia* (which contained more lengthy, detailed discussions of major themes and topics, often integrating entire subfields of knowledge). It was a sensation (and controversial) when it first came out, because it challenged the idea that there was one right way to organize an encyclopedia.

So why don't we all follow the Encyclopedia Britannica approach today? Because of the even newer approach provided by the World Wide Web—a change in how we organize and access information so dramatic as to make the previous debate irrelevant. Using Web searchability, we could delve into a topic just as deeply (or as shallowly) as we wanted, because somewhere out there somebody had probably addressed the topic at the level we needed. We just had to find it, and the Web allowed us to do that.

Fortunately, the Web has the potential to revolutionize the use of zoning ordinances just as it did encyclopedias. Zoning ordinances will use the Web to become much more user-friendly in the future; the only question is which cities will get there faster and which will lag. Many cities already have their zoning ordinances in digital form on the Web, accessible through their city Web site or through the Municipal Code Corporation's Web site. Municipal Code Corporation, based in Tallahassee, Florida, was the first major firm to devote itself to the business of updating zoning ordinances for cities. Instead of entering every amendment yourself after the Monday city council meeting, you could hire them to do it and they would mail you the new pages to insert in your ordinance.

When the Web came along, the Municipal Code Corporation climbed on board, and they have already made many zoning ordinances searchable. Other cities choose to have their zoning ordinances published online through American Legal Publishing Corporation or other legal publishing services. The Visual Interactive Code, developed by faculty at the University of Pennsylvania, is another approach to publishing zoning ordinances on the Web. It has a more user-friendly approach, but fewer cities use it. Perhaps most encouragingly, many cities have developed very user-friendly zoning Web sites on their own. Lots of people are working on this issue, and they have already developed several alternative ways to structure and access zoning information, but this is only the beginning.

A better way to zone will pursue these improvements in four ways. First, future zoning ordinances will develop Web portals that link planning, zoning, subdivision, and utility information. Much of that information is already available but not linked. For example, the owner of 850 Walnut Street generally cannot find out what the comprehensive or neighborhood plans say about his property or his area of the city, what zoning designation applies to the property, whether there are any overlay districts, where the lot boundaries are, and where the utilities are, all from a single Web portal. Since it is easier to draw and digitize maps than it is to interpret how written policies affect different parcels of land, the piece that is usually not linked up is the information on comprehensive or neighborhood plans. But understanding what the neighborhood plan calls for in a specific neighborhood is one of the best ways of involving the public in land use decision making early on, so they don't have to resort to late-in-the-game NIMBYism.

Second, a good planning and zoning Web portal will make clear to owners of property the difference between the plan designation and the zoning. Is the plan binding or isn't it? Can the plan designation be used to turn down an application that is consistent with zoning, or can it not? The answers to both those questions vary among states and cities. If your property is really two legal lots but they are too small to comply with the minimum size for lots in your zone district (usually because they predate zoning), are you going to be allowed to build a house on each one of them or only on one? A good Web portal could clarify that, removing significant confusion in the process. The more the public knows, the better they can participate at the policy- and rule-making level.

The third significant improvement will be in zoning procedures. Right now, only neighborhood activists know how zoning and subdivision procedures work when an application is filed. Anyone can read the printed procedures (if they can find them), but neighborhood activists know how the system works when more than one approval will be needed for a complex or multistage development, or how the city will treat apparently inconsistent processing requirements. Those people are invaluable. For years, one of the best-known living rooms in Denver's Capitol Hill area belonged to Mike Henry, the chairman of Capitol Hill United Neighborhoods' zoning committee. Why? Because he knew how the zoning ordinance worked, and in particular he knew how and at what points in the process neighborhoods would have a chance to influence the process. To get that information efficiently, you had to show up in Mike's living room on a zoning committee meeting night.

Remember that the initial zoning ordinances had only two procedures: how to amend the text or map and how to ask for a variance. But there are now myriad types of approvals in many cities. We have conditional use permits, floodplain permits, floodplain variances, sign permits, sign variances, site plan approvals, fence permits, lighting permits, design approvals, certificates of (historic) appropriateness, and on and on. And despite periodic attempts to herd the cats into a few categories (such as "minor land use approval" and "major land use approval"), the cats tend to get out again. Some new conflict will come up to which the political solution is a new procedure "kind of like what we do for X-type applications . . . but a little different." Even when cities get their procedures simplified, the ordinances generally do a poor job of communicating those to the public.

Future Web-based zoning ordinances will be able to identify not only what permits may be required for a proposed development but the types of notice required, a map of who must be notified and how, what the steps in the approval are, who makes the decision, what the criteria for decision will be, whether or not a public hearing will be held, who can appeal and on what grounds, and who will hear the appeal. When an application has been filed, it may allow neighbors to see where the proposed development would fit on the site and where access points would be. You will no longer have to know the chairman of the local community group to understand what will happen to the proposal you heard about down at the coffee shop.

This leads us to the fourth and biggest improvement through Web-based zoning ordinances: the ability to tailor complete answers for specific addresses. With a zoning ordinance book, you may have to flip between pages and triangulate what they mean when read together, but the Web can do that for you. Today, you can use the Internet to search your zoning ordinance for "fence" and the software will list out for you each time the ordinance uses that word. If you have an old-style ordinance, it will find the word in zone district R1, again in R2, again in R3, maybe in the landscaping regulations, maybe in the design regulations, and maybe in a section on fence permits. Reading those together, you can (hopefully) figure out what kind of a fence you might build and what kind of a permit you need.

But if you visited the zoning office, experienced planning staff would not answer the question that way. They would say: "In the R zones, you can build a fence up to 4 feet tall in your front yard; it cannot be solid—it has to be chain link or something transparent. You can build one up to 6 feet tall in the side and rear yards, and they can be solid. If your lot is on the creek or river, you cannot put a fence in the floodplain. If you have a corner lot, you cannot block drivers' views within 30 feet of the corner. You cannot build fences out of trash materials, and you cannot hang a commercial sign on your fence. You need a fence permit, and we can issue one if you show us a drawing of where on the property the fence will go, what type of fence it is, and how tall it will be."

A better way to zone will lead to Web-based structures that do something similar to the staff answer. They will be designed to answer discrete questions for specific addresses or for a specific type of proposed development. The address-based architecture will know what zone district you are in, whether you are in the floodplain, and whether you are on a corner lot. It will also know whether any of your neighbors have obtained a variance to build a fence taller or closer to your property than you thought they should. These responses are well within the capabilities of Web-based tools today; the advances will come in making them responsive to the questions that people really ask, and staff already know what those are. The key will be linking address-based data structures with more sophisticated query-based searchability.

This fourth change will also include another big step forward in user-friendly organization of information. Web-based tools can tailor answers to the date your lot was platted and the date your building (or addition) was built. So when city council approves a new ordinance changing maximum building heights or setbacks in your zone district, the Web portal will be able to answer your question based on which parts of the zone district language preexisted your home and which came later. This is something that staff usually cannot answer quickly, because building permit data is often in a different system than zoning information. This improvement alone will save many hours for building officials and city attorneys. The picture of "what is legal" in the zone district is in fact not a snapshot but a moving picture, and placing your lot and building into the timeline of that moving picture can be a big help in understanding how the law affects you.

Incidentally, when it's possible to find a discrete answer to a discrete question, most readers really won't care how long the printed zoning ordinance is. They're not going to take it along as light reading. Just as Web research has largely replaced paper encyclopedia research, Web-based zoning research will replace use of the book even among city attorneys and staff. After all, they are using the book to find the same answers as the public—just more often.

Finally, the graphic capabilities of the Web will help communicate all this information to users. Lots of zoning ordinances already use drawings and illustrations to visually demonstrate key dimensions and how they are measured. But the Web can do much more. Today, you can visit a carmaker's Web site, choose the type of car you like, and get a picture of the car that you can rotate 360 degrees. Want to see it from the back? Just use your mouse to turn the drawing that way. Zoning ordinances will soon have the same capability. Want to see the restrictions on backyards in the R3 zone district? Click on R3, and turn the drawing that way. Want to see all the setbacks from overhead plan view? Move the drawing that way. Want to know what the biggest garage you could fit on your lot would look like, given your current house? Click to get a computer visualization of that type of structure.

The technology for each of these tasks is already there, but few cities have committed themselves to making the most of it. Instead of organizing a zoning ordinance like an old book encyclopedia, we can create Web-based codes with hyperlinks that save a lot of flipping back and forth. More importantly, we can design user-driven interfaces that lead citizens through a series of linked sections depending on the question they ask. Of course, these will not be truly usable until the specifics of approved PUDs are in there too, which could take a real effort, because they are typically organized into terms and categories that do not appear in the rest of the ordinance. When interpretations of the ordinance are made by the director, or when staff determines how they will resolve apparent inconsistencies, those can be posted on the Web with hyperlinks so that more people are aware of the practice.

Although this is a rapidly changing field, there are already some good examples. At the time of this writing, the Henderson, Nevada, VIC code is notable for its user-friendly graphics and searchability, and the Chicago zoning ordinance is known not only for its multiple search options but also its linkages to maps and other GIS information. Many cities are making progress with interactive mapping, but relatively few have made the leap to user-friendly linkages between the zoning ordinance and those maps.

What Does This Fix?

Using more sophisticated tools to communicate zoning regulations and to link zoning, planning, and other geographic information would address the shortcomings of Euclidean hybrid zoning in three key ways.

- By making it easier to obtain accurate information about zoning on specific sites and by clarifying how the various aspects of zoning relate to one another, it would facilitate market reinvestment decisions by both developers and homeowners.

- It would dramatically improve the understandability of zoning to citizens, both by answering specific queries based on site-specific constraints and by communicating key provisions through drawings and visualizations.

- It would reduce the demands for staff time to answer case-by-case questions in person and would free up that time for other planning activities, making government more efficient.

Is It Legal?

Better webbing just improves how various types of public information are made public, so it does not overlap the legal framework of zoning discussed in chapter 5, with one exception. In some states, zoning enabling acts may refer to the zoning ordinance as a physical book, or to the official zoning map as a physical map that exists in one and only one place, so those laws would need to be changed.

But there may be a need to change the attitudes and expectations of those who administer zoning law. Some city attorneys continue to resist the move toward drawings in zoning ordinances because they raise the question of which is "the law"—the text or the drawing. Most cities resolve this by simply saying that, in case of a conflict, the text governs (form-based zoners would want it the other way), but this is another area where problems are more theoretical than real. I have never seen a reported lawsuit caused by unintentional differences between zoning text and illustrations. If they are out there, they are very rare.

Other city attorneys resist the idea that the "official" version of the zoning ordinance is an electronic version, not a paper book, but this will soon pass. It is so much easier to update the Web version in real time (or the morning after the council meeting) that books will soon be seen as "unofficial" paper versions of an "official" document that actually lives on the Web. Incidentally, a Web-based ordinance also makes it much easier to keep track of what the ordinance said on August 3, 2001, or on any given date on which a dispute arose. Right now, city attorneys have to keep archive copies of multiple books and ordinances and then try to manually piece together what parts of the ordinance had been adopted on the date in question.

Scheduled Maintenance

One failed assumption underlying Euclidean zoning is that the rules need to be "static"—that once the rules line up with our preferred snapshot of the future, we are done (see chapter 2). But zoning rules change all the time. By the late 1980s, Denver's 1957 zoning ordinance had been amended more than a thousand times. That number must be far higher now, and a comprehensive rewrite is now under way. In most cities, some amendments reflect thoughtful, consultative solutions to well-defined concerns, but others are less thoughtful reactions to poorly understood situations. Adopting more flexible uses, the mixed-use middle, mature area standards, dynamic development standards, and more tolerance for nonconformities should reduce the need to amend zoning frequently, though changes will still be needed. But a constantly changing zoning ordinance fuels complaints that "Every time I think I understand it, they change it again." How can we keep the zoning ordinance up-to-date without sending ever-changing signals to the very citizens and developers that we need to invest in the community?

The answer is scheduled maintenance, which fits in with the need for predictable flexibility (see chapter 4). This is hard to achieve because it is seldom a high priority. Building political support for a full redraft of the zoning ordinance can be very difficult, and carrying the effort through to adoption is even more difficult. After the new rules have been adopted, there is seldom political support to go back and do periodic scheduled maintenance.

But thinking of scheduled maintenance as an "extra" that can be dispensed with is another example of the static thinking that makes zoning changes so hard in the first place. Redrafting zoning ordinances is hardest in those cities that have put it off the longest. They are the ones whose regulations are most out of touch with current development types and procedures but in which the business community may be so used to the "spit and baling wire" fixes that they oppose a comprehensive rewrite. When consultants arrive in large cities to begin a long-awaited zoning redraft, there is an almost palpable fear that starting to unravel the jerry-rigged system may cause the whole house of cards to come down. Only repeated examples of other cities that have successfully completed major zoning revisions keeps some stakeholders at the table.

Generally, when cities put the time and energy into fixing a broken zoning provision, they think through the major ways this new regulation will interact with the existing law, which helps avoid unpleasant surprises. The worst amendments are the knee-jerk responses to political emergencies where the first plausible solution is the one adopted. The answer to knee-jerk change is predictable change. Instead of entertaining amendments to the zoning text on demand, cities should adopt a predictable schedule for considered changes, for at least two reasons.

First, zoning is a set of interrelated rules, and amending one rule can reinforce or undermine others. Amending the buffering ordinance this week can undermine the effect of the xeriscaping ordinance you adopted last month. Amending the sign ordinance this week can either support or erode the gains you made when you adopted the mountain view protection ordinance last week. Bringing zoning amendments forward in a package gives both citizens and staff a better chance to think through how different changes will affect one another. It also allows elected officials to focus on the *system* of zoning instead of reacting to a single amendment that everyone in the audience seems to like (or hate). Again, experience tells. Council members with years of experience are much more likely to say: "No one ever thinks about how all these amendments relate to one another. Let's take it slow and think it through."

Second, bringing amendments forward on a predictable schedule avoids the problem of "ramrod" amendments, which can favor either citizens or builders or some other group. Being faced with an "It's gotta be done tonight or the neighborhood will be ruined" or an "It's gotta be done tonight or the developer will walk away" amendment should send up a red flag to any reasonable council member. But with a roomful of earnest supporters or angry opponents, ramrod amendments often get adopted. I think most elected officials know this is wrong. Not only does the fate of a neighborhood or a development rarely turn on immediate action, but it is not good practice to force quick decisions on complex problems. Adopting a schedule for amendments avoids this kind of setup and defuses some of the adversarial quality of the debate. It allows staff to consult with other interested parties before the amendment moves forward. Those who know they cannot rush through an amendment are much more likely to talk to potential opponents anyway.

Bringing forward a package of amendments periodically is also more efficient governance. It allows for a single notification to business and neighborhood groups about the proposed package of changes and increases the chances of their paying attention. When amendments are proposed every week or month (as they really are in some large cities), both business and neighborhood groups find it hard to track them and to sort out which ones they have time to get involved in. It is particularly hard on volunteer associations without paid staff. Reading the weekly zoning announcements from the city and deciding whether to call yet another meeting of volunteers gets old after a while. By knowing that zoning text amendments arrive on a six-month basis, these organizations can review them all at one time and decide where to invest their time and energy.

Following a comprehensive redraft of the zoning ordinance, there are always unintentional gaps, mistakes, and unintended consequences that need to be addressed. It is rare to find a thoroughly revised zoning ordinance that does not need to have minor oversights corrected soon after adoption. Zoning drafters are human, and mistakes happen, so plan for them. Schedule a periodic review for six months or one year after adoption, and have staff present a comprehensive package of clean-up amendments at that time. In cities with Home Rule powers, the council could even grant the board of adjustment additional powers to grant variances to avoid unanticipated hardship during the first months of operation. In other words, they could say: "In addition to granting variances for hardships, for the next six months you can also grant variances to property owners who seem to have gotten caught in some application of the new ordinance that was not discussed or expected." That gives staff time to work out a thoughtful fix for the problem while protecting property owners from unforeseen outcomes. Some elected officials cannot bring themselves to adopt a whole new set of rules without knowing that there is this kind of safety net in place.

After a new zoning ordinance has been adopted and the dust has settled—that is, the unforeseen oversights have been addressed—the city should still pursue a regular schedule for presenting and debating zoning text amendments. Packages could be scheduled every six or twelve months. There is always a trade-off between the time that passes between amendments and how big the next package of amendments will be. In general, I think shorter is better. Telling a proponent that their proposed amendment will be included in a package to be considered within six months is easier than asking them to wait a year. But even scheduling an annual amendment process is better than amending the text on demand.

So a better way to zone will include periodic maintenance of the zoning text in lieu of amendments on request. But zoning map changes will still be available through application. Although those opposed to change in general might like a system in which the zoning map stood still, that is simply not realistic. Promoting investment and reinvestment in mature cities means allowing zoning map amendments to go forward for city council action when needed. Council can continue to sort out whether the proposed change in the application of the zoning rules is wise. After all, zoning map changes are case-by-case decisions on specific sites; they don't make rules for the rest of the city.

PUDs combine map changes and text changes, so they represent a hybrid situation. Like other map changes, they should also be allowed to move forward as needed rather than restricted to a six-month schedule. But remember that the better way to zone will also limit PUDs to large, image-changing developments and

What Does This Fix?

Scheduled maintenance of zoning regulations would respond to critiques of current zoning practices in the following ways:

- It addresses the failed assumption that static rules will be effective. Although some development standards can be made dynamic, others require discussion and debate as to how the city intends to respond to changed conditions. Doing this on a regular schedule would minimize gaps between written zoning rules and the realities of neighborhoods and the development industry.

- By addressing emerging topics where exceptions and variances are being requested, it could ensure that the zoning text is adjusted to reduce the need for variances.

- It would allow the zoning ordinance to respond to new uses and new types of development to avoid creating unintended barriers to the market.

- It would allow development standards, especially densities and potential traffic generation, to keep aligned with available transportation capacity and changes in transportation management.

- By better reflecting the dynamic nature of city development and changes in the way development and redevelopment are organized, phased, and financed, it would make city government more effective.

- By avoiding the need for on-demand changes on an unpredictable schedule, and by avoiding situations where the zoning ordinance is far out of step with the realities of market and development, it would make city government more efficient.

that the other changes recommended in this chapter should reduce the need for PUDs. More flexible uses, mixed-use zoning, mature area standards, and more tolerant regulation of nonconformities will all mean that PUDs will not be needed as often as they currently are in many cities.

Still, staff should have the ability to recommend denial of a PUD if they conclude that it is being proposed only to avoid the six-month text amendment schedule. In other words, if staff conclude that the only point of the PUD is to get the benefit of a text change that staff is proposing for the next round of amendments, staff could recommend denial on the ground that this is a misuse of the PUD tool. In many cities, staff have an analogous power: if they conclude a PUD is being filed only to obtain a package of variances with no added value to the city, they can recommend denial.

Is It Legal?

Some state zoning enabling acts already require periodic updates to plans or zoning ordinances, and any proposed schedule of periodic updates needs to be consistent with those requirements. Similarly, if state law grants property owners or citizens the right to petition for zoning change, any schedule adopted will need to be consistent with that requirement. Finally, if state law requires that applications for text amendments be acted on within a fixed time, the schedule will need to be made consistent (or the state law changed). In many states, though, the enabling act requires simply that there be hearings before the zoning text is amended; it remains silent on the frequency of those changes. In states without a legal mandate, the frequency (or not) of updates to the zoning ordinance is left completely to the discretion of the city government.

What About the Other Good Ideas?

The ten principles discussed above are not the only ways to make zoning more effective and understandable. Any list of ten is bound to disappoint planners and citizens interested in promoting other values and patterns of urban development. The fact that other possible changes did not make the list does not mean that they are not important; it simply reflects a decision to focus more on how zoning

207

works as a *system* to regulate land in mature cities rather than on the promotion of specific values.

Three of the most important substantive values that I would like to see included in zoning ordinances are environmental sustainability, Smart Growth, and form-based controls. All three continue to emerge as important and popular trends in land use, and compelling books have been written on each topic.[9] All three could have been included in this book but were not for the following reasons.

First and most importantly, the ten principles that make up a better way to zone would improve the effectiveness and understandability of zoning *regardless* of the specific urban design and environmental values endorsed by the city council. Both environmental advocates and environmental timids will find that zoning is more effective, efficient, and understandable using the ten directions in this chapter. The same is true for council members who believe that the city should actively promote specific building forms and for those who disagree.

Second, all three of these missing topics have substantial constituencies and vocal advocates who are already pushing to integrate them into zoning. They represent three healthy examples of ways that zoning will continue to evolve to reflect the preferences of city voters. In contrast, the ten directions listed above address shortcomings in the basic zoning tool itself, a topic with fewer and less vocal advocates. Ironically, the fact that environmental sustainability, Smart Growth, and form-based controls have already caught the ears of city policy makers made them less important to include in this book.

Finally, the ten changes outlined above would unclutter Euclidean hybrid zoning and make room for more detailed development standards where the city council feels they are appropriate. Most cities have significant neighborhoods, corridors, or transportation nodes where form-based tools would more effectively preserve or achieve the intended character than do current zoning tools. And in most mature cities, applying Smart Growth regulations would pay rich dividends in quality of life, resource conservation, and cost savings. By getting rid of overregulation and misregulation in other areas, a better way to zone can make room for these specialized controls where they are appropriate and can reduce complaints that new regulations are always layered on top of existing zoning controls.

Similarly, environmental sustainability needs to be designed into new development and redevelopment, and zoning ordinances are a good way to help that happen. We are rapidly moving up the learning curve on how to integrate resource conservation and pollution prevention in ways that are cost effective, market supportive, and understandable to citizens. But this is a topic that many cities address in legislation other than the zoning ordinance, including building codes, stormwater drainage regulations, and road and utility engineering standards. Zoning needs to be an important part of these solutions, but it will not be the only part. A better way to zone will also make room for appropriate environmental land use regulations by simplifying other zoning topics. The result will be a better balance of regulations that emphasizes development form, scale, and environmental impacts while deemphasizing the specific land use activities inside the buildings.

CHAPTER 8

The Way Forward

THERE IS NO SHORTAGE OF GOOD IDEAS about how to improve our zoning and our cities. But there is a pressing shortage of citizens and planners who can see the path toward change and a shortage of leaders with the political will to build a system based on the long-term interests of the city. This book cannot address the creation of political will—that comes only from the convictions and courage grounded deep inside those we elect. But it can address the path forward for those who have that will. In the United States, we usually end meetings with an agenda item called "next steps," but I prefer the phrase used in Uganda: "the way forward." It conveys a better sense of direction. So how do we find the way forward from good ideas to better zoning?

To begin with, it is important to think about zoning change as a *process*, not a destination. There is no "model code" that embodies the ten changes listed in chapter 7. The larger the city, the more difficult it is to achieve sustainable change (as opposed to radical reform that gets overturned with the next election) and the more important it is to start from the zoning ordinance you already have. Most cities understand this intuitively, but sometimes frustration with the current ordinance is so high that we are tempted to chuck it all and start over. Telling cities to throw away their zoning ordinances is a great way to get press coverage and personal notoriety, but it is remarkably poor public policy. Three times in my career, I have had a new client city say: "It's so broken it cannot be fixed. Just take the best ordinance you've written for a city about our size, substitute our name for theirs, and let's start with that."

And each time I have refused, because it won't work. The very first time the stakeholders come across a proposed change they don't understand or don't agree with, someone is bound to say: "Why don't we handle it like we did in the old ordinance? People seemed to accept that, and everyone understood it." If we have just pitched the old zoning ordinance, we will rapidly find ourselves rooting around in the wastebasket to get parts of it back.

So a first rule of the journey is to start from where you are. Start with the zoning ordinance you have. Despite the venting about "starting all over" from those who know the ordinance best, most citizens feel more comfortable fixing what is broken and keeping the rest. Starting all over makes most citizens who are not zoning junkies nervous about how the brave new world will treat their house and their neighborhood.

The way forward is not a blank sheet of paper, and it is not a model of what the perfect ordinance looks like. It is a set of tools to be used carefully to work on specific problems. In theory, it would be nice if we could work on the most serious problems first, but, in fact, it sometimes works better to start on the easiest problems first because initial success can build confidence. In fact, however, we usually end up working on neither the hardest nor the easiest problems, but on the ones that are politically ripe for action. Mature cities take the steps along the road to change as it is politically feasible to do—not according to an outside schedule. Zoning is a political act, but the tools listed in this chapter can help ensure that the political acts move forward rather than stalling in the discussion stage—or moving backward.

The next step is to keep the citizens informed about the process and involve them in the solutions. It is their city, after all. Zoning was invented to protect the quality of life in their neighborhoods and their property values. Anyone who attempts to craft a zoning solution without good public discussion deserves to have their motives questioned. The most dysfunctional zoning reform efforts I have watched are those where the city set out to negotiate with handpicked interest groups about a technical solution to a specialized problem and intended to inform the public about the outcome when those discussions were over. The best reform efforts have had citizens at the table—the same table with other stakeholders—throughout the process. Involving citizens has a leavening impact on "technical" discussions, preventing them from becoming narrow, polarized discussions where defensive thinking becomes the norm. Incidentally, it turns out that citizens regularly have good ideas about possible solutions, even on technical topics. Not only is ignoring them unethical, but it wastes one of your good problem-solving resources.

Finally, you almost always need citizen involvement to get anything controversial passed through city council. Zoning redraft efforts tend to focus on drafting the right language to get the key stakeholders on board (particularly the loudest ones). But that ignores two important constituencies: citizens who are not at the table and those who administer the ordinance in the city government. You need a strategy to bring along even those citizens who are not involved in stakeholder discussions. No matter how carefully you craft the solution, or how long the task force has worked, there will probably be at least one elected official who will ask: "Do my neighborhoods like this solution?" A few confident voices in support can make a world of difference. On the other hand, admitting that there was no early public outreach, or that you can't get even a single citizen group to voice support, can give elected officials serious qualms about going forward. Thoughtful technical solutions to zoning problems can get tabled quickly, and in spite of strong stakeholder support, if council members learn that no one has been consulted except the industries or businesses most directly concerned.

Beyond these two baselines—starting from what you have and seriously involving citizens from the start—the five steps on the way forward are to (1) audit for specifics, (2) prioritize for political will, (3) draft for integration, (4) illustrate how, and (5) adopt the possible. Each of these steps is reviewed in more detail below.

Audit for Specifics

The first step is to get beyond general frustration with the current zoning ordinance to identify in detail what is wrong. That requires the city to compare the zoning ordinance against the ten principles in chapter 7 and to identify—specifically—the areas where it is most out of line. Statements like "Our uses are too inflexible" don't help much. Which ones, and how do you know? What adverse impacts (e.g., constant amendments, too many variances, frustrated business community) are you trying to address?

Similarly, the statement "We have too many zone districts" does not help. What types of districts do you think you have too many of, and why? What specific impacts need to be addressed (e.g., staff frustration at having to administer similar things as if they were different; citizen frustration with the sheer number of districts; the time required to create a new district for each new idea that comes along; developers regularly asking for specific new types of districts)? Just like a financial audit, a true zoning audit identifies specific shortcomings that can be addressed. The inability to identify specific failings is the first clue that the city is not ready to start reforming its zoning ordinance. If you can articulate specific problems in only three of the ten areas identified in chapter 7, start with those three areas. On the other hand, if the city has made a policy decision to implement Smart Growth policies or green building policies, the audit should also look for specific shortcomings in those areas. The topics discussed in chapter 7 are not intended to be an exclusive list of what is important, but they do represent "big picture" issues that often get overlooked.

Prioritize for Political Will

The ten good ideas discussed in chapter 7 are too many to act on at once, so it is important to prioritize. Personally, I have a hard time thinking about a complex problem from more than about three perspectives at a time. If I am reviewing an ordinance to look at its efficiency, clarity, and procedural due process, it is hard to also think about it in terms of consistency with the plan and predictable flexibility. I need to make more than one pass through the document to think about it from multiple perspectives. I suspect the same is true for the planning commission, city attorneys, and elected officials. It is sometimes unrealistic to ask them to focus on a long list of "fixes" at the same time, and it would be even more difficult to keep the citizens informed—citizens who don't speak zoning for a living and would rather spend evenings with their families. If you want to talk about protecting neighborhood open space, they're with you. But if you want to talk about redrafting the zoning ordinance to achieve ten goals simultaneously . . . where did they go?

So, for the sake of effective public participation if nothing else, it is wise to prioritize the topics that need to be addressed first. As with the audit for specifics, prioritization will probably have a strong dose of politics in it. Political priorities may reflect the latest round of embarrassing headlines that city council wishes it could have avoided. Or the latest broadside from a business or environmental group. Or the latest corporation or institution that decided to leave the city. Or the theme of the latest planning conference that a key council member attended. Again, zoning is political, and the problems that can be solved are those the elected officials are willing to solve.

Having said that, each round of reforms should try to tackle at least one of the ten topics that falls into the "serious-but-not-yet-on-fire" category. Those are the types of problems that usually get ignored year after year. If the problem is on fire (i.e., recent bad headlines or controversy), then it is not too hard to find some political will to take it on, because that looks like responsible government and pleases the voters. It is also not too hard to find the courage to handle "cleanup" changes— things that need to get done but that only staff and those who use the ordinance regularly will even notice were improved. These are usually introduced with a comment like this: "We didn't change what people can do with their property— we just cleaned up the language."

The hard changes to address are those that are more than housekeeping but not yet on fire. Solving this middle range of problems requires rethinking detailed topics like permitted uses, zone districts, rights and responsibilities, and the costs of development. But they are generally topics on which the media is not demanding action. This is one of those areas where democracy can lead to poor governance unless there is good leadership willing to bridge the gap. Poor governance says you act on a problem only when it can no longer be ignored—that way you get credit for working on "real problems." But working on solutions when the problem is front-page news—when it is on fire—is often the worst time to work on it. Tempers are high, sound bites steer the debate, and political pressure may push for quick, popular solutions rather than thoughtful ones.

Zoning problems are often complex, and the best solutions usually come from having all of the affected parties at the table, where they can articulate their interests without much risk of being quoted in the press or being accused of taking sides in a front-page debate. That doesn't mean the meeting should be secret— they should be open and noticed—but if the problem is not front-page news, then public and stakeholder discussions to resolve it will not be front-page news either. It takes strong municipal and elected leadership to realize that the right time to tackle some of the thornier issues is when they are not news.

Draft for Integration

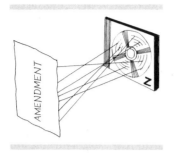

Now that the city has agreed on a prioritized list of what it is trying to fix, the drafting can begin. This can be done by zoning or planning staff, by the city attorneys, or by consultants. There is no magic involved, but four key steps are to put specific text on the table for discussion, to make sure the new provisions fit into the structure of the existing regulations, to provide illustrations as you go along, and to avoid "legalese." The first two of these steps are discussed here, and the last two are discussed in the next section.

As long as stakeholders are discussing broad concepts like predictability, flexibility, mixed use, and pedestrian-friendly approaches, there will always be wide latitude for them to misunderstand one another (or to think they agree when they really don't). It is common for stakeholders with diametrically opposed views of what is wrong with zoning to endorse the need for both predictability and flexibility (see chapter 4). The problem is that one wants predictability in exactly the areas where the other wants flexibility, and vice versa. I want predictability that the areas of the ordinance that are favorable to my project will not change and flexibility in areas where I don't quite meet the adopted standards—and you want exactly the opposite. Talking past each other can be avoided only by having everyone look at the same proposed text (even a very preliminary draft) fairly early in the process.

After the specific text changes have been debated and refined, they need to be integrated into the existing ordinance—that's "integrated into," *not* "stapled onto." Many cumbersome zoning ordinances got that way because past amendments did not respect the structure of the document. For example, a new ordinance on cell towers is just stapled onto the end of the ordinance. If we had seventeen zoning chapters, then this one is chapter eighteen. The cell tower ordinance includes provisions on the height of these structures, but those are not reflected in the zoning chapter dealing with structure heights (and, in most cases, the two are not even cross-referenced). The new chapter creates new procedures on how to get a cell tower permit, but they are not inserted into or cross-referenced with other provisions on permits and procedures. "Don't lose any sleep over it," the city attorney tells you. "The later one trumps inconsistent earlier acts as a matter of law, and more specific rules trump more general ones as a matter of law anyway—so it's clear to me." But it is often not clear to the public, who wonder whether the general provisions on public notice apply to the new procedures for cell tower permits, which don't mention public notice.

In short, amendments are usually structured as if they are freestanding books and the only people who need to read them are the stakeholders who sat around the table to draft them. Of course, the telecommunications industry would like to have all the cell tower provisions in one chapter so that they do not have to read all the rest of the ordinance, but doing so is a disservice to everyone else who is trying to understand what might be built on the corner lot—including but not limited to a cell tower.

For paper ordinances, integration may mean that new pages have to be slipped into the general section on heights (to reference the new provision) and procedures (to reflect the new permits and public notice requirements). That takes a little more time than just stapling a chapter onto the end of the ordinance, but it is more sustainable in the long run. Fortunately, Web-based ordinances will handle this easily. Web pages on heights, permits, and a variety of other regulations can be updated in real time so that the new answers show up seamlessly and where they are supposed to. The Web doesn't really care whether the provisions are in one chapter or two, because it simply links together related provisions electronically.

Illustrate How

Illustrations are important, and they should not be left until the end of the reform process. In modern zoning ordinances, almost everyone (except perhaps a few city attorneys) wants drawings and charts and pictures (and if it is Web-based, even movies) to illustrate what is required or desired. Form-based zoning communicates desired building forms visually rather than trying to describe shapes in words. But in the press of refining draft language to make everyone happy, it is all too common to say: "We'll do the drawings at the end. It will save time if we only have to do them once." I hear myself saying those words.

But the very reason we want illustrations is why they should not wait until the end of the zoning text discussions. Some people (mostly lawyers, it seems) understand development regulations through words written on a page, but many others (especially architects but also a surprising number of citizens and elected officials) understand rules from pictures much better than they do from words. Producing the illustrations early—even if they are just draft sketches—can help citizens and stakeholders better understand the draft language and can hasten agreement on what it should say. We want visual learners to say: "I thought I agreed with the proposal, but if this picture shows how it works, I want something different," or "I don't understand all those words, but if this picture shows how it will work, I'm comfortable with that." Illustrations help that level of understanding to emerge sooner rather than later.

Finally, avoiding legal terms helps include the public more meaningfully. Even if some citizens understand what those legal terms mean, the need for specialized words suggests that zoning is a technical matter where citizens are out of their depth. But that is not true. Citizens can easily grasp all of the important principles of zoning and the trade-offs involved among different types of regulations. So why use language that suggests otherwise? Almost all legal concepts express ideas that could also be expressed in other words, and using "or part thereof" instead of "or part of the building" is a poor way to save trees.

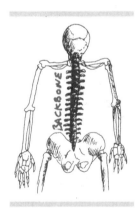

Adopt the Possible

Benjamin Franklin once wrote: "Energy and persistence conquer all." Getting zoning reforms through the finish line (i.e., getting them adopted) is sometimes hard. In fact, it is usually hard. Expectations have been set and investments made based on the current zoning rules, and there are always some who benefit from the status quo. Many property owners really believe in their hearts that fundamental changes to the zoning rules cannot be made, while others are confident that "politics as usual" will ensure that only minor changes are made.

Regardless of how well the city publicizes its intention to reform the zoning ordinance, no matter how many public meetings it convenes, and no matter how well it uses cable TV, Web sites, press coverage, and elementary school contests to build awareness, as the amendments move toward final adoption, it is very likely that someone (often someone important) will claim to have known nothing of the entire effort. Further, he or she will claim that if the city is really serious about changing zoning it needs to start the process all over in a more inclusive way. Sometimes what that really means is: "If I ever thought it would get this far I would have participated earlier, but I really don't like the decisions that were made without me. Since I really can't admit that I voluntarily sat out the discussions, I have no choice but to discredit the process itself." Whether the proposed zoning improvements survive this last-ditch tactic depends on three factors.

First, the city must have done a good job conducting business in the open and giving plenty of opportunity for stakeholder and public comment, and it must have documented that effort. An extensive list of outreach events and copies of Web pages, newspaper advertisements, and invitations almost speaks for itself. It is easy to say that you couldn't make it to a public meeting or two, but say that you missed all ten meetings and you can expect city council to take your comments with more than a grain of salt.

Second, the city needs to have created an atmosphere of compromise. Many efforts to reform zoning are dominated by small groups of citizens who are highly vocal about a few discrete interests—a magic density number, or group homes, or the environment, or property rights in general. The city needs to conduct a process that does not allow niche groups to drive the agenda or to hold the long-term interests of the city hostage to the personal goals of the loudest people in the room. Narrow interest groups that try and fail to dominate zoning reform do one of two things—they become more moderate (which is fine), or they leave the process (which is also fine). Staff noted their concerns before they left. Just as importantly, city council knows exactly what it means when angry people walk away from an well-run public involvement process, and they don't conclude that the process was flawed.

However, assuming that the process is not being dominated by narrow interests, the city still needs to be willing to compromise—right up to the last minute. In many reform efforts, a lot of good work that everyone can support gets held up at the end over a "hot button issue" debate. When that happens, my experience is that it is not worth forcing that last ounce of reform. Not insisting on the final yard allows everyone to take credit for the reforms that are adopted and preserves the most contentious debate for another day. Remember, the better way to zone described in this book is a *process*—not a product—that involves periodic maintenance of the ordinance. Forcing the last bit of zoning change often destroys goodwill, makes it harder to reconvene stakeholders in the future, and risks having the losers run single-issue candidates in the next election. And successful single-issue candidates sometimes try to reverse not just the final unpopular change but the whole reform effort. It happens—regularly.

Finally, getting important zoning reforms adopted takes backbone. It takes political will, and it takes elected officials who recognize that they were elected to represent the long-term interests of the city (or their district) even if it makes some people unhappy. Usually, elected officials want to be presented with a deal—something that all the key stakeholders agree with, so the hard work of getting there has already been done. But sometimes there is no deal. The stakeholders made effective compromises, but there is still vocal opposition. Or the stakeholders just couldn't agree on the last few issues and refused to compromise any further. That is when it takes backbone. Council needs to resolve the last issues or carve them out for additional work and then approve the remaining reforms. Ordinance reforms are not like a site-specific rezoning, where city council's "no" just means "your land will not be changed to another zoning district." Zoning text reforms concern the long-term operation of the city's zoning system, and a city council "no" vote on the reform package leaves all the systemic weaknesses in place. It's far better to solve some of them than none of them.

The city should also create an expectation that it will pursue zoning ordinance improvements to completion. Failure to carry at least some of the reforms through the finish line creates an impression that zoning is too complicated to reform or that a few loud voices can derail the process, which is much more damaging. Who can blame stakeholders and citizens for not showing up to participate if the city's past behavior shows that their time may be wasted? This is particularly important because of the need for periodic maintenance of the zoning ordinance. The city will be asking for regular involvement in zoning text reforms, and stakeholders need to know that the city will complete what it starts. Over time, that will produce a better way to zone.

Euclidean zoning is now ninety years old, and it has proven itself to be useful, durable, popular, and changeable. As it has changed to meet our needs over the years, it has become more complex, less understandable, and less well matched to the needs of America's large mature cities. But it does not have to be that way. The soil of Euclidean hybrid zoning has already proven to be fertile ground for innovation, and it will continue to produce new ideas in the future. By following the guidance in this book, American zoning practice can turn a corner, and future zoning can be simpler, more effective, and easier to understand. If that happens, not only will we have learned from the mistakes of the past, but we will be creating more livable cities for the future. Our children will thank us.

SUGGESTED READING LIST

CHAPTER 1. A Brief History of Zoning

Bosselman, Fred, and David Callies. *The Quiet Revolution in Land Use*. Washington, DC: Council on Environmental Quality, 1971.

Burchell, Robert. *Planned Unit Development: New Communities American Style*. Trenton, NJ: MacCrellish & Quigley, 1972.

Duany, Andres, Elizabeth Plater-Zyberk, and Jeff Speck. *Suburban Nation: The Rise of Sprawl and the Decline of the American Dream*. New York: North Point Press, 2001.

Mumford, Lewis. *The City in History: Its Origins, Its Transformations, and Its Prospects*. Orlando, FL: Harcourt, Inc., 1961.

Smith, Herbert. *The Citizen's Guide to Zoning*. Chicago: APA Planners Press, 1983.

CHAPTER 2. Failed Assumptions

Kelbaugh, Douglas. *Common Place: Toward Neighborhood and Regional Design*. Seattle: University of Washington Press, 1997.

Kunstler, James Howard. *The Geography of Nowhere: The Rise and Decline of America's Man-made Landscape*. New York: Touchstone, 1993.

CHAPTER 3. Evolving Land Use Drivers

Inhaber, Herbert. *Slaying the NIMBY Dragon*. Edison, NJ: Transaction Publishers, 1997.

Rusk, David. *Cities without Suburbs*. Washington, DC: Woodrow Wilson Center Press, 1993.

Schwieterman, Joseph, Dana Caspall, and Jane Heron. *The Politics of Place: A History of Zoning in Chicago, Illinois*. Chicago: Lake Claremont Press, 2006.

CHAPTER 4. Governing Well

Hackworth, Jason. *The NeoLiberal City: Governance, Ideology, and Development in American Urbanism*. Ithaca, NY: Cornell University Press, 2006.

Hoch, Charles, Linda Dalton, and Frank So, eds. *The Practice of Local Government Planning*. 3rd ed. Washington, DC: ICMA Press, 2000.

Hopkins, Lewis. *Urban Development: The Logic of Making Plans*. Washington, DC: Island Press, 2001.

CHAPTER 5. The Legal Framework for Change

Blaesser, Brian, and Alan Weinstein. *Land Use and the Constitution: Principles for Planning Practice*. Chicago: Planners Press, 1989

Nivola, Pietro. *Laws of the Landscape*. Washington, DC: Brookings Institution Press, 1999.

CHAPTER 7. A Better Way to Zone

Barnett, Jonathan, F. Kaid Benfield, Paul Farmer, Shelley Poticha, Robert Yaro, and Armando Carbonell. *Smart Growth in a Changing World*. Chicago: American Planning Association, 2007.

Betsill, Michele. *Cities and Climate Change: Urban Sustainability and Global Environmental Governance*. Routledge Studies in Physical Geography and the Environment. New York: Routledge, 2005.

Hawken, Paul, Amory Lovins, and L. Hunter Lovins. *Natural Capitalism: Creating the Next Industrial Revolution*. New York: Little, Brown, 1999.

Leitmann, Josef. *Sustaining Cities: Environmental Planning and Management in Urban Design*. New York: McGraw-Hill, 1999.

Porter, Douglas, Robert Dunphy, and David Salvesen. *Making Smart Growth Work*. Washington, DC: Urban Land Institute, 2002.

Shoup, Donald. *The High Cost of Free Parking*. Chicago: APA Planners Press, 2005.

Steuteville, Robert, Philip Langdon, et al. *New Urbanism: Comprehensive Report and Best Practices Guide*. 3rd ed. Ithaca, NY: New Urban Publications, 2006.

Szold, Terry, and Armando Carbonell, eds. *Smart Growth: Form and Consequences*. Cambridge, MA: Lincoln Institute of Land Policy, 2002.

Talen, Emily. *New Urbanism and American Planning: The Conflict of Cultures*. New York: Routledge, 2005.

CHAPTER 8. The Way Forward

Flanagan, Richard. *Mayors and the Challenge of Urban Leadership*. Lanham, MD: University Press of America, 2004.

Morgan, David, Robert England, and John Pellisaro. *Managing Urban America*. Washington, DC: CQ Press, 2006.

Popper, Frank. *The Politics of Land-use Reform*. Madison: University of Wisconsin Press, 1981.

NOTES

CHAPTER 1. A Brief History of Zoning

1. See the Suggested Reading List in the back of this book.

2. Although Los Angeles adopted an ordinance defining residential zones as early as 1909 (see http://www.cr.nps.gov/nr/publications/bulletins/suburbs/text1.htm), the New York City ordinance is generally considered to be the first full zoning ordinance.

3. City and County of Denver, *Building Zone Ordinance and Amendment to City Charter* (adopted May 15, 1923); and *Zoning Ordinance of the City and County of Denver* (adopted April 15, 1957).

4. Ruth Knack, Stuart Meck, and Israel Stollman, "The Real Story behind the Standard Planning and Zoning Acts of the 1920s," *Land Use Law and Zoning Digest* (February 1996): 3–9, at page 4.

5. Knack et al., "The Real Story," 4–6.

6. Knack et al., "The Real Story," 6.

7. Robert Burchell, *Planned Unit Development: New Communities American Style* (Trenton, NJ: MacCrellish & Quigley, 1972).

8. Jane Jacobs, *The Death and Life of Great American Cities* (New York: Random House, 1961), 35.

9. Readers who are interested in pursuing readings on New Urbanism can refer to the Suggested Reading List in the back of this book.

10. Christopher Alexander, Sara Ishikawa, and Murray Silverstein, *A Pattern Language* (New York: Oxford University Press, 1977).

11. Anton C. Nelessen, *Visions of a New American Dream: Process, Principles, and an Ordinance to Plan and Design Small Communities* (Chicago: APA Planners Press, 1994).

12. As of June 2007, the SmartCode Web site (http://www.smartcodecomplete.com/learn/links) reported that a total of twelve cities had adopted a SmartCode. The list included Abbeville, Louisiana; Conway, Arkansas; Flowood, Mississippi; Fort Myers, Florida; Gulfport, Mississippi; Leander, Texas; Liberty, Missouri; Montgomery, Alabama; Pass Christian, Mississippi; Petaluma, California; Pike Road Alabama; and Sarasota, Florida. However, in about half of these cities, use of the SmartCode was optional (i.e., property owners could still choose to follow the Euclidean rules if they wished). In most of the larger cities (including Fort Myers, Gulfport, Montgomery, and Petaluma), use of the SmartCode was mandatory in only a specific downtown or special development area.

13. Placemakers, Information Clearinghouse, http://www.placemakers.com/info/infoClear.html (visited March 21, 2007).

CHAPTER 2. Failed Assumptions

1. *Denver Post*, April 22, 2003.

2. *Nashville Zoning Ordinance*, sec. 17.20.040.E.

3. MIT Zoning Variance Database, http://web.mit.edu/11.521/www/labs/lab3/lab3.html (visited February 10, 2007).

4. Tom Wilemon, "Small Lot Waivers Considered," *Biloxi Sun Herald*, November 8, 2006; "Rebuilding-Automatic Variance Vote Is Today," *Biloxi Sun Herald*, November 14, 2006; "Biloxi Puts Off Vote on Zoning Variances," *Biloxi Sun Herald*, November 15, 2006; "Blanket Variance Waiver Hearing Not until January," *Biloxi Sun Herald*, December 4, 2006.

5. Ruth Knack, Stuart Meck, and Israel Stollman, "The Real Story behind the Standard Planning and Zoning Acts of the 1920s," *Land Use Law and Zoning Digest* (February 1996): 3–9, at page 9.

6. See, for example, Delhi Development Authority, *Master Plan of Delhi 2021* (Delhi: Delhi Development Authority, 2007).

7. Richard Babcock, *The Zoning Game* (Cambridge, MA: Lincoln Institute of Land Policy, 1966); *The Zoning Game Revisited* (Cambridge, MA: Lincoln Institute of Land Policy, 1990); Roger Waldon, *Planners and Politics* (Chicago: APA Planners Press, 2006).

CHAPTER 3. Evolving Land Use Drivers

1. Mongabay.com, "Population Estimates for Delhi, India, 1950–2015," http://books.mongabay.com/population_estimates/full/Delhi-India.html (visited January 12, 2007).

2. U.S. Census Bureau, Census of Housing, "Historical Census of Housing Tables," http://www.census.gov/hhes/www/housing/census/historic/owner.html (visited January 12, 2007).

3. U.S. Census Bureau, Census of Housing, "Historical Census of Housing Tables," http://www.census.gov/hhes/www/housing/census/historic/owner.html (visited January 13, 2007).

4. U.S. Census Bureau, "1997 Economic Census: Summary Statistics for United States, 1997 NAICS Basis," http://www.census.gov/epcd/ec97/us/US000.HTM; U.S. Census Bureau, "2002 Economic Census: Summary Statistics by 2002 NAICS, United States," http://www.census.gov/econ/census02/data/us/US000.HTM; Answers.com, "Real Estate Industry," http://www.answers.com/topic/real-estate-industry (all visited January 18–20, 2007).

5. Realtor.org, "Field Guide to the History of the National Association of Realtors," http://www.realtor.org/libweb.nsf/pages/fg002 (visited January 15, 2007).

6. National Association of Home Builders, "Our Organization," http://www.nahb.org/page.aspx/generic/sectionID=89 (visited February 12, 2007).

7. Dapeng Hu and Anthony Pendington-Cross, "The Evolution of Real Estate in the Economy," *Journal of Real Estate Portfolio Management* (April–June, 2001): 169–76.

8. Andy Serwer, "The Malling of America: Unabated—and Frenzied—Growth in Retail Space Is a Trend That Might End Badly," *Fortune,* October 13, 2003, available at http://money.cnn.com/magazines/fortune/fortune_archive/2003/10/13/350907/index.htm (visited February 6, 2007).

9. Neil Irwin, "Is Reliance on Real Estate a Crack in the Foundation?" *Washington Post*, April 5, 2006.

10. Mahendra Kumar Singh, "GoM Expands SOHO List, Okays Master Plan," *Times of India*, January 24, 2007.

11. Thomas Friedman, *The World Is Flat* (New York: Penguin Books, 2005), 12.

12. Enterprise Nation, "Home Based Business Makes Chart History," January 24, 2007, http://www.enterprisenation.com/content/currentaffairs/TopStories/article_46_699.aspx (visited March 2, 2007).

13. Nathan Anderson, "Property Tax Limitations: An Interpretive Review," *National Tax Journal* 59 (September 2006): 685–94.

14. For an early analysis of this changing relationship, see, for example, R. Mitchell and C. Rapkin, *Urban Traffic: A Function of Land Use* (New York: Columbia University Press, 1954).

15. See, for example, Yan Song and Gerrit Knapp, "Is Portland Winning the War on Sprawl?" *Journal of the American Planning Association* 70, no. 2 (2004): 210–25.

16. Paul Waddell, "UrbanSim: Modeling Urban Development for Land use, Transportation, and Environmental Planning," *Journal of the American Planning Association* 68, no. 3 (2002): 297–314.

17. Jean-Paul Fitoussi, "Local Systems, Europe, and Globalization: How to Get It Right?," citing data from Banque Mondial and OCDE, presentation at European Colloquia on Culture and Knowledge: Local Systems and Globalization, Prague, November 30, 2006.

18. U.S. Department of Labor, Bureau of Labor Statistics, "Employment Status of the Civilian Noninstitutional Population, 1940 to Date," http://www.bls.gov/cps/cpsaat1.pdf (visited January 30, 2007).

19. Ruth Simon, "Housing Affordability Hits 14-year Low," Wall Street Journal On-line, December 23, 2005. http://www.realestatejournal.com/buysell/markettrends/20051223-simon.html.

20. Keith Wardrip and Danilo Pelletiere, "Recent Data Shows Continuation, Acceleration of Housing Affordability Crisis," *National Low-Income Housing Coalition Research Note* 06-06 (December 11, 2006), 3–6; J. M. Quigley and S. Raphael, "Is Housing Unaffordable? Why Isn't It More Affordable?" *Journal of Economic Perspectives* 18 (Winter 2004): 198–214.

21. Wardrip and Pelletiere, "Recent Data," 6–8.

22. Morris A. Davis and Michael G. Palumbo, "The Price of Residential Land in Large U.S. Cities," *U.S. Federal Reserve Board Finance and Economics Discussion Series* 2006-25 (May 2006): 1–37.

CHAPTER 4. Governing Well

1. See, for example, *Portsmouth Advocates, Inc., v. City of Portsmouth*, 133 N.H. 876, 587 A.2d 600 (N.H. 1991); and *In re: Appeal of Realen Valley Forge Greenes Associates*, 838 A.2d 718 (Penn. 2003).

2. *Gas Mart v. Loudon County*, 611 S.E.2d 340 (Va. 2005).

3. Chris Steins, "E-government: The Top 10 Technologies," Planning Magazine, September 2002.

CHAPTER 5. The Legal Framework for Change

1. For good coverage of this complex field of law, see, for example, Edward Zeigler, ed., *Rathkopf's The Law of Zoning and Planning* (St. Paul, MN: Clark Boardman Callaghan, 1975); Christopher Duerksen and Richard Roddewig, *Takings Law in Plain English* (Washington, DC: National Trust for Historic Preservation, 2002); Dwight Merriam, *The Complete Guide to Zoning* (New York: McGraw-Hill, 2004); Bradford White, Paul Edmonson and Julia Miller, *Due Process in Plain English* (Washington, DC: National Trust for Historic Preservation, 2004); and Daniel Mandelker, *Land Use Law* (Charlottesville, VA: LEXIS Law Publishing, 1997).

2. Community Environmental Legal Defense Fund, "Home Rule Status by State," http://www.celdf.org/HomeRule/DoesmyStatehaveHomeRule/tabid/115. (visited December 6, 2007).

3. White, Edmonson, and Miller, *Due Process in Plain English*.

4. *Morristown Road Associates v. Borough of Bernardsville*, 394 A.2d 157 (N.J. Super 1978).

5. See, for example, *Dodd v. Hood River County*, 136 F.3d 1219, 1230 (9th Cir. 1998).

6. *Nollan v. California Coastal Commission*, 423 U.S. 825 (1987).

7. An excellent review of the takings law can be found in Duerksen and Roddewig, *Takings Law in Plain English*. It is important to realize at the start, however, that the field of regulatory takings is not at stake in the recent spate of litigation over Urban Renewal powers. Those cases involve eminent domain, or the power of the government to compel property owners to sell their land. They do not arise from the police power under discussion here. See, for example, *Kelo v. New London*, 545 U.S. 469 (2005).

8. For an example of a "per se" takings case, see *Lucas v. South Carolina Coastal Council*, 505 U.S. 1003 (1992). For a good example of the "nuisance" exception to the "per se" rule, see *Colorado Dept. of Health v. The Mill*, 809 P.2d 434 (Colo. 1991); reversed, 887 P.2d 993 (Colo. 1994).

9. For a more detailed discussion of this topic, see Duerksen and Roddewig, *Takings Law in Plain English*.

10. See, for example, *Palazzolo v. Rhode Island*, 533 U.S. 606 (2001).

11. See, for example, *Keystone Bituminous Coal Association v. DeBenedictis*, 480 U.S. 470 (1987).

12. See, for example, *First English Evangelical Church v. Los Angeles County*, 482 U.S. 304 (1987).

13. See, for example, *Dolan v. City of Tigard*, 512 U.S. 374 (1994).

14. See, for example, *Tahoe-Sierra Preservation Council v. Tahoe Regional Planning Agency*, 535 U.S. 302 (2002).

15. See, for example, *Palazzolo v. Rhode Island*, 533 U.S. 606 (2001).

16. See, for example, *City of Monterey v. Del Monte Dunes at Monterey, Ltd.*, 95 F.3d 1422 (9th Cir. 1996); affirmed, 526 U.S. 687 (1999).

17. *Palazzolo v. Rhode Island*, 533 U.S. 606 (2001).

18. The Religious Freedom Restoration Act, 42 U.S.C. sec. 2000bb, was ruled unconstitutional in *City of Boerne v. Flores*, 521 U.S. 507 (1997).

19. See, for example, *Young v. American Mini-Theatres*, 427 U.S. 50 (1976).

20. *Euclid v. Ambler Realty*, 272 U.S. 365 (1926).

21. See, for example, *Whaley v. Dorchester County*, 524 SE.2d 404 (S.C. 1999).

22. See, for example, *Rodgers v. Tarrytown*, 96 N.E.2d 731 (NY 1951).

23. *Carron v. Ouray County*, 976 P.2d 444 (Colo. App. 1987).

24. See, for example, *Crider v. Boulder County*, 246 F3d.1285 (10th Cir. 2001).

25. See, for example, *Village of Willowbrook v. Olech*, 528 U.S. 562 (2000).

26. See, for example, *Unity Ventures v. Lake County*, 841 F.2d 770 (7th Cir. 1998); *Lisa's Party City, Inc. v. Town of Henrietta*, 185 F.3d 12 (2nd Cir. 1999).

27. See, for example, *Village of Belle Terre v. Boraas*, 416 U.S. 1 (1974); *Moore v. City of East Cleveland*, 431 U.S. 494 (1977); *City of Cleburne v. Cleburne Living Center*, 473 U.S. 432 (1985).

28. See, for example, *Village of Willowbrook v. Olech*, 528 U.S. 562 (2000); *Osborne v. Grussing*, No. 06-2021 (8th Cir. Feb. 26, 2007).

29. See, for example, *Forseth v. Village of Sussex*, 199 F.3d 363 (7th Cir. 2000).

30. See, for example, *Metropolitan Development Commission of Marion County v. Pinnacle Media LLC*, 836 NE.2d 422 (Ind. 2006).

31. See, for example, *Cline v. City of Boulder*, 450 P.2d 335 (1969).

32. For discussion of this standard in federal law, see, for example, *City of Chicago v. Morales*, 527 U.S. 41 (1999).

33. For an example of a successful zoning challenge on vagueness grounds, see *Anderson v. City of Issaquah*, 851 P.2d 744 (Wash. Sup. Ct. 1993).

34. For a discussion of this topic, see Transit Cooperative Research Program, "The Zoning and Real Estate Implications of Transit-oriented Development," *TCRP Legal Research Digest*, Monograph 12 (January 1999).

35. See, for example, *South of Second Associates v. Town of Georgetown*, 580 P.2d 807 (Colo. 1978).

36. 47 U.S.C.A. sec. 151 et. seq.

37. 42 U.S.C.A. 2000cc-2000cc-5.

38. *Midrash Sephardi, et al. v. Town of Surfside*, 366 F.3d 1214 (11th Cir. 2004).

39. *Cutter v. Wilkinson*, 544 U.S. 709 (2005).

40. 42 U.S.C.A. sec. 5401 et. seq.

41. 42 U.S.C.A. sec. 12101 et. seq.

42. 42 U.S.C.A. sec. 3601 et. seq.

43. 23 U.S.C.A. sec. 131.

44. 42 U.S.C.A. sec. 7401 et. seq.

45. 33 U.S.C.A. sec. 1251 et. seq.

CHAPTER 7. A Better Way to Zone

1. American Planning Association, "Land-based Classification Standards," http://www.planning.org/lbcs (visited February 10, 2007).

2. American Planning Association, "FAQs and Quick Answers," http://www.planning.org/lbcs/standards/FAQ.html#ZoningMaps (visited February 10, 2007).

3. Data from Denver Regional Council of Governments' estimates of Denver metro region housing growth 2000–2004 and projections to 2006; http://198.173.149.138/website/housingtract2004/viewer.htm (visited March 7, 2007).

4. Matthew Goebel, *Reducing Housing Costs through Regulatory Reform* (Denver: Colorado Department of Local Affairs, 1998).

5. The Santa Cruz program is described at http://www.ci.santa-cruz.ca.us/pl/hcd/ADU/adu.html (visited February 25, 2007).

6. See, for example, Thomas Fetters and Vincent Kohler, *The Lustron Homes: The History of a Postwar Prefabricated Housing Experiment* (Jefferson, NC: McFarland Publishing, 2001).

7. See, for example, *Colo. Manufactured Housing Ass'n v. Pueblo County*, 946 F. Supp. 1539 (D.Colo. 1996).

8. For a good discussion of this topic, see Eric Weitz, "Manufactured Housing: Trends and Issues in the 'Wheel Estate' Industry," *Practicing Planner* (Winter 2004).

9. See the Suggested Reading List at the end of this book.

BIBLIOGRAPHY

Alexander, Christopher, Sara Ishikawa, and Murray Silverstein. *A Pattern Language*. New York: Oxford University Press, 1977.

Babcock, Richard. *The Zoning Game*. Cambridge, MA: Lincoln Institute of Land Policy, 1966.

———. *The Zoning Game Revisited*. Cambridge, MA: Lincoln Institute of Land Policy, 1990.

Blaesser, Brian, and Alan Weinstein. *Land Use and the Constitution: Principles for Planning Practice*. Chicago: APA Planners Press, 1989.

Calthorpe, Peter. *The Next American Metropolis: Ecology, Community, and the American Dream*. Princeton, NJ: Princeton Architectural Press, 1997.

Congress for the New Urbanism. *Charter of the New Urbanism*. San Francisco: Congress for the New Urbanism, 2001.

Duany Plater-Zyberk and Company. *SmartCode*. Miami: Duany Plater-Zyberk and Company, 2003.

Duerksen, Christopher, and Richard Roddewig. *Takings Law in Plain English*. Washington, DC: National Trust for Historic Preservation, 2002.

Friedman, Thomas. *The World Is Flat*. New York: Penguin Books, 2005.

Garreau, Joel. *Edge City: Life on the New Frontier*. New York: Doubleday, 1991.

Jacobs, Jane. *The Death and Life of Great American Cities*. New York: Random House, 1961.

Katz, Peter. *The New Urbanism: Toward an Architecture of Community*. New York: McGraw-Hill, 1993.

Kelbaugh, Doug and Peter Calthorpe, eds.. *The Pedestrian Pocket Book*. Princeton, NJ: Princeton Architectural Press, 1996.

Lynch, Kevin. *The Image of the City*. Boston: MIT Press, 1960.

Mandelker, Daniel. *Land Use Law*. Charlottesville, VA: LEXIS Law Publishing, 1997.

Merriam, Dwight. *The Complete Guide to Zoning*. New York: McGraw-Hill, 2004.

Nelessen, Anton C. *Visions of a New American Dream: Process, Principles, and an Ordinance to Plan and Design Small Communities*. Chicago: APA Planners Press, 1994.

Ohm, Brian, James LaVro Jr., and Chuck Strawser. *Model Traditional Neighborhood Development Ordinance*. Madison: University of Wisconsin Press, 2001.

Sobel, David. *Longitude: The True Story of a Lone Genius Who Solved the Greatest Scientific Problem of His Time*. New York: Walker Publishing Company, 1996.

Waldon, Roger. *Planners and Politics*. Chicago: APA Planners Press, 2006.

White, Bradford, Paul Edmonson, and Julia Miller. *Due Process in Plain English*. Washington, DC: National Trust for Historic Preservation, 2004.

Whyte, William. *The Social Life of Small Urban Spaces*. New York: Project for Public Spaces, 2001.

Zeigler, Edward, ed. *Rathkopf's The Law of Planning and Zoning*. St. Paul, MN: Clark Boardman Callaghan, 1975 and updates.

INDEX

Oregon, land use and
transportation planning
in, 76
Overlay zoning, 13, 152

P

Palazzolo v. Rhode Island,
113–14
Parking caps, 180
Parking requirements. *See
also* Transportation
dynamic development
standards and,
179–80
in Winnipeg, 164
redevelopment and,
166
variances and, 49
zoning and, 144–45
Pattern Language (Alexander), 30
Pedestrian Pocket Book
(Kelbaugh and
Calthorpe), 29
People's Initiative to Limit
Property Taxation, 72
Performance zoning,
23–26, 102
Permitted use, identification of, 140–41
Per se takings, 112
Pipeline problems, vested
rights and, 121
Planned unit developments
(PUD)
flexibility and, 102
history of, 18–23
negotiated PUD zon-
ing and, 183–89
NIMBYism and, 82–85
overreliance on, 130
state constitutions and,
106–7
uniqueness and,
119–20
Planners and Politics (Waldon), 59
Plater-Zyberk, Elizabeth,
29, 31

Platte River Valley, 148,
183–84
Police power, 17, 107–8
Policy plans, 56
Politics
administrative zoning
decisions and, 95
Euclidean hybrid zon-
ing and, 43–45
pressures exerted on
zoning by, 59,
131–32
removal of from final
approvals, 189–96
understandability of
zoning and, 101
Pollution, 69–70, 126–27
Preble's meadow jumping
mice, 180–81
Predictable flexibility
drafting and, 216–17
governance and,
102–4, 130–31
maintenance of zoning
plans and, 203–7
Preemptions, state and
local law and, 125–27
Prioritization, 214–15
Procedural due process,
94–97, 108–9, 132
Process of zoning change,
133–36, 211–14
Prohibited use, identification of, 140–41
Property rights, Standard
Zoning Act and, 17
Property values, takings of
private property and, 112
Proposition 13, 72
Public land use zones, 69
Public participation,
NIMBY and, 190–91
Pyramid zoning, 28

R

Rational relationship test,
25, 30
Real estate industry, land
use drivers and, 64–71

Real estate taxes, sales taxes
vs., 71–72
Redevelopment standards,
165–66. *See also* Mature
area standards
Religion, freedom of,
114–15
Religious Land Use and
Institutionalized Persons
Act of 2000, 115,
125–26, 145
Replacement structures,
50–51
Residential zones, land use
drivers and, 67–69
Responsiveness, 91–92,
192–93
Results similarity, 93,
118–19
Retailing, classification of,
142
Revenge, takings of private
property and, 113
RLUIPA. *See* Religious
Land Use and Institu-
tionalized Persons Act
of 2000
Russia, 73–74, 134–35

S

Safe, Accountable, Flexible,
Efficient Transportation
Act: A Legacy for Users
(SAFETEA-LU), 77
Safety, mixed-use development and, 27
Sales taxes, real estate taxes
vs., 71–72
Santa Cruz, CA, 157
Scale
Euclidean hybrid
zoning and, 42
form-based zoning
and, 141, 145–46
mixed-use zoning and,
151
zoning and, 143
Secondary and incidental
use, 43, 116–17

Trusses, 160
Tyranny of the
   intermediate, 88

U
Understandability,
   governance and, 99–101
Unified Development
   Ordinances, 132–33
Uniqueness, 54, 118–19
UrbanSim model, 76
U.S. Constitution. *See also*
   Specific amendments
   equal protection and,
      117–18
   negotiated PUD
      zoning and, 187
   zoning laws and, 105–6
Uses, separation of,
   41–45

V
Vagueness, 123–24
Variances
   Canadian zoning and,
      62–63
   Euclidean hybrid zon-
      ing and, 48–49
   history of zoning and,
      11, 15
   nonconformities and,
      54, 171
   planned unit develop-
      ments as, 21
   Standard Zoning Act
      and, 16
Vested rights, 99, 121–23
Vision plans, 56
*Visions of a New American
   Dream* (Nelessen), 30
Visual Interactive Code, 198
Visual preference surveys, 30

W
Waldon, Roger, 59
Water quality, dynamic
   development standards
   and, 180–81
Websites. *See* Internet
Whyte, William, 27
The World is Flat
   (Friedman), 68

Y
Yards, desire for,
   149–50

Z
Zero discretion, 42
Z-lots, 157–58
Zoning by variance, 63
Zoning Game (Babcock), 59
Zoning plans, master plans
   vs., 17